THE
ULTIMATE
SPY
BOOK

PIPE WITH CONCEALMENTS

SMERSH CREDENTIALS

SHOULDER HOLSTER

COIN WITH BLADE

SURREPTITIOUS ENTRY KIT

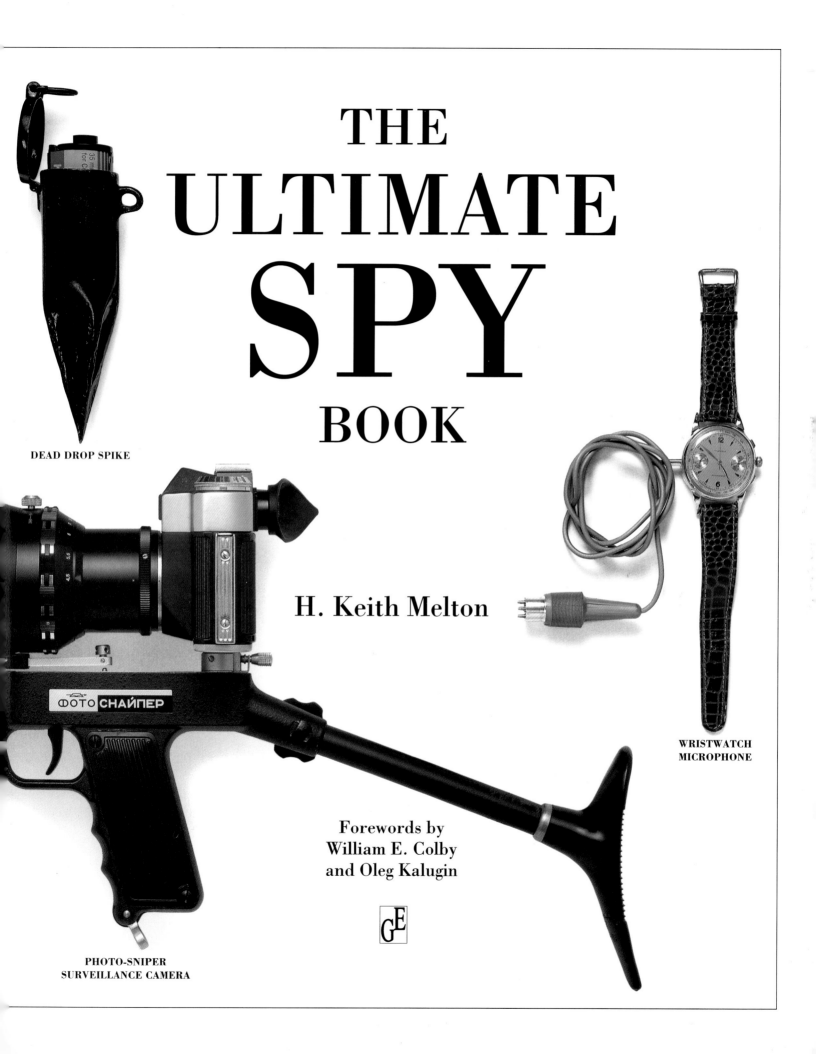

DEAD DROP SPIKE

THE
ULTIMATE
SPY
BOOK

H. Keith Melton

**WRISTWATCH
MICROPHONE**

Forewords by
William E. Colby
and Oleg Kalugin

GE

**PHOTO-SNIPER
SURVEILLANCE CAMERA**

Project Editor Louise Tucker
Editor Nicholas Turpin
Consultant Editors Paul Cornish, Hayden B. Peake
Senior Editor Edward Bunting

Project Art Editor Clare Shedden
Designer Christina Betts

Managing Editor
Martyn Page
Managing Art Editors
Philip Gilderdale, Bryn Walls

Senior Managing Editors
Ruth Midgley, Josie Buchanan, Krystyna Mayer
Senior Managing Art Editor
Lynne Brown

Production Alison Jones
Picture Researcher Anna Lord

First published in Great Britain in 1996
by Dorling Kindersley Limited,
9 Henrietta Street, London WC2E 8PS
4 6 8 10 9 7 5 3
Copyright © 1996 Dorling Kindersley Limited, London

This edition published in 2000 for Greenwich Editions

A member of the Chrysalis Group plc

A CIP catalogue record for this book is available from the British Library
ISBN 0 8628 8395 4

Reproduced by Bright Arts, Hong Kong
Printed and bound in China by L.Rex Printing Co., Ltd.

CONTENTS

FOREWORDS 6
WHO SPIES? 8
WHAT DO SPIES DO? 10
SPIES OF THE FUTURE 14

**FAMOUS SPYING
OPERATIONS 16**

EARLY ESPIONAGE 18
Court intrigues 20
American Civil War 22
World War I 24
Revolutionary Russia 26

WORLD WAR II 28
Special Operations Executive 30
Office of Strategic Services 32
German secret services 34
Code-breaking 36
Soviet spy networks 38
Japanese intelligence 40

COLD WAR 42
Berlin: spy city 44
US security agencies 46
Codename Anna 48
House of spies 50
U-2 spy aircraft 52
Walker spy ring 54
Spying from space 56

EQUIPMENT AND TECHNIQUES 58

CAMERAS 60
Concealed cameras 62
Robot camera 64
F21 concealed camera 66
Subminiature cameras 68
Minox camera 70
Copy cameras 72

SECRET OPERATIONS 76
Visual surveillance 78
Listening devices 82
Receivers 86
Surreptitious entry 90
Lockpicks 92
Escape and evasion 94
Sabotage 96
Amphibious sabotage 98

COUNTERINTELLIGENCE 100
Detectors 102
Anti-bugging devices 104
Countersurveillance 106
Letter interception 108

CLANDESTINE COMMUNICATIONS 110
Suitcase radios 112
Agents' radios 116
Specialized communications 118
Cipher devices 120
Enigma machine 122
Ciphers and secret writing 124
Microdots 126
Concealments 128
Dead drops 132

WEAPONS 134
Special issue weapons 136
Silenced weapons 138
Crossbows and darts 142
Close-combat weapons 144
Concealed weapons 148
Assassination devices 152

HOW TO BE A SPY 156

Training and recruitment 158
Covers and legends 162
Spy networks 164
Fate of a spy 166

GLOSSARY 168
INDEX 171
ACKNOWLEDGMENTS 176

KEITH MELTON has performed many fine services for the
intelligence profession, and this book stands high in that
tradition. Mr Melton is perhaps the world's most outstanding
collector of, and expert in, intelligence equipment, and his superb
collection has been put on display in many intelligence centres
and agencies. *The Ultimate Spy Book* sums up his great experience
and study to give a comprehensive and accurate account of the
profession, and the technology and techniques it has developed
in order to carry out its secret missions. Some of these have
only come to light as a result of the end of the Cold War, during
which they were always held in the deepest secrecy. Today's reader
can thus now see the results of the inventiveness, ingenuity, and
imagination that worked to conceal the secret transmission of
information and to maintain the secret contacts which are essential
to espionage and intelligence.

Many of the items covered in this book evoke fond memories
in one like myself who first encountered them on missions behind
enemy lines during World War II or during secret contacts with
agents and clandestine allies during the Cold War. Some of the
items also appear in the KGB Museum in Moscow, and some
certainly lie in the deep recesses and files of the CIA in Langley,
Virginia. Oleg Kalugin used some of them, as I did, when we
both worked for our countries on opposite sides – thankfully the
end of the Cold War allows us to cooperate on common projects,
rather than confront each other as in the past. Readers of this fine
book can now get a sense of how those struggles were carried out,
and how those struggles are still carried out against our common
enemies: terrorists, purveyors of ethnic and religious hatred,
nuclear proliferators, and crime and drug lords.
We owe Mr. Melton much gratitude in so
comprehensively presenting our profession.

William E. Colby
Former Director of the CIA

S PYING HAS BEEN with the human race from time immemorial; it has often been called "the second oldest profession", and was used by ruling elites as a major tool to protect their power from real or imaginary threats and rivals, both domestic and external. Though espionage never played a decisive role in the history of mankind – it can neither replace responsible policy-making, nor significantly alter political and military imperatives – its impact on international relations increased dramatically in the second half of this century when two world superpowers and their respective allies, guided by irreconcilable ideologies, clashed in a deadly struggle for human minds and ultimately world domination.

That was the essence of the Cold War. After the classic Cold War crises of the 1950s and 1960s, espionage evolved into a far more sophisticated and diverse trade, in which psychological warfare, conspiracies, and assassinations featured more prominently than mere clandestine collection of information. Intelligence-gathering was transformed by satellites, lasers, computers, and other gadgetry capable of ferreting out secrets from every corner of the globe.

Methods of spying may have changed considerably through the ages, but even in this modern age of high technology the role of the human spy is as important as it has ever been. As a member of the KGB, I spent most of my career attempting to gain the secrets of those Western nations that were seen as potential enemies of the Soviet Union. Often I succeeded. The spies and agents that I handled, such as the American John Walker, had to be trained in techniques that this book describes – gaining information, passing it on, and remaining undetected.

Throughout the Cold War the CIA was one of my main adversaries. Now that the United States and Russia are no longer enemies, I am glad of the opportunity to share this foreword with William Colby.

Oleg Kalugin
Major-General (retired), First Chief Directorate, KGB

WHO SPIES?

Hidden listening device
This demonstration model shows a "bug" hidden inside a plug.

T HE SPECIFIC ACT of gathering information from an enemy is rarely carried out by an intelligence officer in person. To accomplish this task, intelligence officers recruit agents who, perhaps by virtue of their position, have access to the information required. Officers who recruit and handle agents are known as case officers. Most work from an embassy under some form of official cover (see p. 162) and are protected legally by diplomatic immunity. Others may operate without diplomatic immunity, perhaps living under an assumed identity. When recruiting agents, case officers are guided by the factors most likely to motivate people to become spies. These can be summed up by the acronym MICE – money, ideology, compromise, and ego.

Aldrich "Rick" Ames
Ames (b.1941) voluntarily became a KGB mole and revealed CIA secrets to the Soviets in exchange for $2.7m. By his own account, he offered his services to pay off his debts and to finance his wife's heavy spending habits.

M = MONEY

Financial problems such as deep debt, or greed for material possessions, are very fertile ground for those attempting to recruit agents. This has certainly proved to be true in both capitalist and communist countries. Many Soviet agents were initially lured into spying for the West by the offer of a solution to money problems. The CIA (see p. 46) sometimes succeeded in targeting officers of the KGB (see p. 50) who were unable to pay back operational funds that they had used personally. Once a potential agent has accepted money, it becomes increasingly difficult to escape recruitment.

The major KGB successes that have come to light in recent years were also achieved by exploiting greed. The most significant American agents in the history of the KGB, Aldrich Ames (see p. 158) and John Walker, Jr. (see p. 54), both offered their services in return for financial reward.

I = IDEOLOGY

A person may alternatively be led into becoming an agent because of a belief in the ultimate superiority of the social and political institutions of a foreign country. During the 1930s in particular, the Soviet

George Blake
Inspired by communism, Blake (b.1922) served the KGB as a mole within Britain's MI6.

Union was able to recruit agents by exploiting the attraction that communism held for many in the West at that time. These included five idealistic students who were to become the Soviet Union's chief spies in Britain – Kim Philby, Anthony Blunt, Guy Burgess, Donald Maclean, and John Cairncross. Despite the decline of communism, ideology remains a factor in the recruitment of agents. Jonathan Pollard was an American who worked as an analyst for the US Naval Investigative Service. He agreed to spy for Israel because of his ideological commitment to Zionism. Like many others, his motivation for spying was mixed – he was later to accept money from the Israelis.

Glove pistol
During World War II, the US Navy's Office of Naval Intelligence conceived this self-defence weapon for possible use by intelligence support and other administrative personnel who were stationed close to the front line.

John Vassall
While working as a clerk at the UK embassy in Moscow, Vassall (b.1924) was compromised and recruited by the KGB.

C = COMPROMISE

A first step in recruitment by compromise is to identify an element in a potential agent's lifestyle that he or she would not wish others to know about. Homosexuals, for instance, at least in postwar times, often risked ruin if their private lives were revealed. This made it possible for the KGB to recruit John Vassall when he was an embassy clerk in Moscow (see p. 160). In 1955 the Soviets carried out an intricate operation in which they set him up in an embarrassing situation, took photographs, and used these to blackmail and entrap him. Seven years later the West was shocked when Vassall was convicted of passing secrets to the Soviets between 1956 and 1962.

The KGB kept special hotel rooms in Moscow that were used for photographing visiting Westerners in compromising circumstances – with prostitutes, for instance. With pictures in hand, the KGB could usually blackmail its chosen target individuals into becoming agents. Today, homosexuality and, of course, many heterosexual relationships, are no longer such effective means of coercion. On the other hand, financial and marital difficulties are still exploited with success.

E = EGO

Case officers are often trained to appeal to the egos of candidates vulnerable to intellectual flattery in order to entrap them. Typically, a case officer might commission a candidate to write articles for publication. Initially they may be on safe, unclassified subjects. If asked, later, to write on subjects of a more sensitive nature, the writer may already be ensnared by the praise, money, and possibly the sense of adventure gained through previous efforts.

Hugh Hambleton was lured to the KGB by flattery and a sense of adventure (see p. 160). Despite an awareness of the risks involved, some subjects continue in the belief that they can outwit intelligence professionals.

Hugh Hambleton
The KGB used flattery to recruit Hambleton (b.1922), an academic who later rose to the rank of professor.

WHAT DO SPIES DO?

THE PEOPLE WHO APPEAR IN THIS BOOK have all been active within the general field of intelligence, covert action, or special military operations. In a broad sense, these individuals can be conveniently brought together under the term "spies", but this is not a precise term. Depending on one's point of view, the word may carry dishonourable overtones, and be taken by some people as an insult. There are cases where this is appropriate. And yet there are other people working in this field –

Wristwatch microphone
This fake watch contained a microphone that was connected to a tape recorder hidden beneath the user's clothing.

equally spies – on whose skills and strengths their country relies for its survival. Secondly, the fictional world of spying is one of action and excitement, but the reality is infinitely more discreet, professional, and subtle.

Maria Knuth
Knuth began her spy career in 1948 as a courier for Polish intelligence in West Berlin.

VARIETY OF ROLES

Those entering a career in special military operations must face the unglamorous aspects of military life, as in the other armed forces. The physical training is hard, as is the competition with others aiming to be selected for special duties. For those who are chosen, training will become much more diverse, as there are many different roles in today's special military forces, each requiring a course of specialized training.

There are many different roles, too, in the intelligence agencies. Similar roles, and similar structures, occur in each country. Typically, there is one agency for intelligence – the gathering of sensitive information – and one for counterintelligence – defence against enemy spies. An important distinction exists between officers, most of whom are career members of their agency, and agents, whose status varies with the country and the individual, and whether they are operating in war or in peacetime. A case officer is one

who recruits and runs agents, and may try to encourage case officers of hostile nations to defect or act as moles. An agent is assigned tasks in intelligence or various other covert activities but is not an agency employee.

Some officers deal with administration, which generally accounts for around 10 per cent of all agency staff. The other 90 per cent are usually divided evenly between analysis and operations, and what follows is a brief overview of some of their roles.

THE COURIER

Couriers are the links between the agents and their controllers. They sometimes also serve as cut-outs – intermediaries who enable the system to work with no contact between sender and receiver. If neither of these two parties knows the other, they will be unable to betray one another. Some couriers work in embassies, collecting information from local agents. The Israeli agency, Mossad, makes use of couriers called *bodlim* to do this. Other couriers transport intelligence across international borders, sometimes in the guise of diplomatic couriers, as in the case of Alfred Frenzel (see p. 48).

Concealments
Intelligence agencies often use ingenious adaptations of everyday objects as hiding places for secret information or equipment.

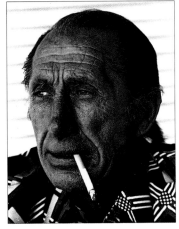

Dusan Popov
Popov was already reporting to British intelligence when German military intelligence (the Abwehr) approached him in 1940. He did join the Abwehr but passed secrets to the British.

A courier's task is often a dangerous one, as his or her fate is far less important than the information he or she carries. Some agencies have developed concealments that will self-destruct if anyone tampers with them. Although the destruction of the information will not save the courier from being incriminated, it may protect the identity of the agent who gathered it. Some agents begin their careers as couriers, before moving on to other tasks. An example is the Polish agent Maria Knuth, who started in 1948 as a courier in West Berlin, carrying secrets on microfilm.

THE DOUBLE AGENT

These are agents who turn against the intelligence service that originally recruited them and work for another agency, while at the same time making the original agency believe their loyalty has not changed. They may do this for ideological reasons, for personal gain, or to save their lives after being captured. Double agents are a dangerous threat to intelligence operations, as they can be used by their new controllers to feed misleading information to their original employers.

During World War II, Britain's MI5 (see p. 164) set up an organization known as the Twenty, the XX, or the Double Cross Committee. This body clandestinely controlled much of Germany's intelligence-gathering effort in Britain. It went so far as to set up a series of notional German intelligence networks that reported to the Germans without arousing suspicion, but were in reality under the control of MI5.

Two of the most successful double agents actually volunteered their services to British intelligence during World War II. Dusan Popov (see p. 41) was a Yugoslav who ran a network of three double agents for MI5. He passed misleading intelligence to the German Abwehr.

The other example was also a British agent in World War II – the Spaniard Juan Pujol, codenamed Garbo, who was so successful in deceiving the Germans on behalf of the Allies that he was decorated by both sides!

THE DEFECTOR

A defector is an intelligence officer who abandons his or her original agency and betrays it by giving information to a foreign intelligence service. Some defectors are motivated by ideology, while others act out of fear for their own safety. The latter was the case with Vladimir Petrov, a KGB officer in Australia. In 1954, facing allegations that he had been involved in a plot, he evaded recall to Moscow and turned himself over to the Australian authorities. As soon as they had

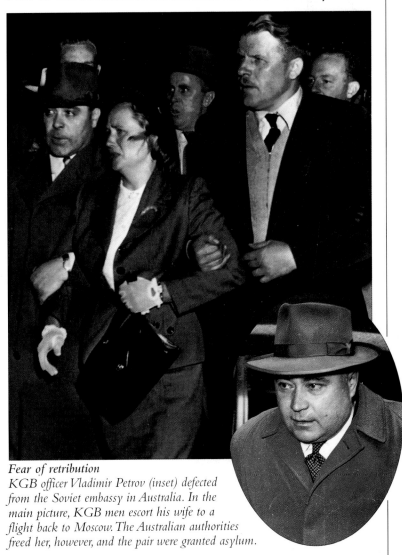

Fear of retribution
KGB officer Vladimir Petrov (inset) defected from the Soviet embassy in Australia. In the main picture, KGB men escort his wife to a flight back to Moscow. The Australian authorities freed her, however, and the pair were granted asylum.

Supporting role
Odette Sansom served as a
courier for an SOE circuit
organizing sabotage in France.

abandoned the KGB, Vladimir Petrov and his wife were granted asylum in Australia, and in return gave valuable information on Soviet espionage activities in Australia. A more recent and dramatic defection was the escape from Moscow of Oleg Gordievsky, a KGB officer who was working for British intelligence. He realized that he was under suspicion, but evaded KGB surveillance. Gordievsky was smuggled out of the Soviet Union by MI6.

If they are not under suspicion, however, would-be defectors are often encouraged to remain within their intelligence service to work clandestinely as moles.

KGB defector Peter Deriaban was an example of a defector whose knowledge of his old agency proved useful long after he escaped. He served for years as an advisor to the CIA. In particular, he followed the organization and structure of the KGB and its officers, and lectured on the subject inside the agency.

THE SABOTEUR

The word "sabotage" is French in origin, and refers to the action of a disgruntled workman who destroys machinery by throwing a wooden clog (*sabot*) into it. The destruction of enemy equipment is a frequent objective of sabotage. But there are also more sophisticated forms of sabotage, such as the ingenious but largely ineffective attempt by the Germans in World War II to sabotage the British economy by flooding world markets with counterfeit English banknotes (see p. 34).

Tyre ripper and sheath
Saboteurs and special operations personnel
used tyre rippers to sabotage enemy vehicles.

It was in World War II that saboteurs were most regularly and effectively employed, especially by the British SOE (see p. 30) and American OSS (see p. 32). Both organizations sent teams of officers to assist local resistance groups in campaigns of sabotage. Some of these personnel were trained in the various sabotage methods, others were needed for support roles. The latter was the case with Odette Sansom, who was sent to France by the SOE in 1942 as a courier. She was unwittingly revealed to the Gestapo by a captured member of the resistance and was arrested in 1943.

THE MOLE

Moles are ostensibly employees of one intelligence service who are actively working on behalf of a hostile agency. As such, they can be extremely valuable to the intelligence agency that runs them. Provided they have sufficiently high-level access, they will be able to

Long-term undercover informer
CIA officer Larry Wu Tai Chin worked as a mole for Chinese intelligence,
supplying secret information from the early 1950s until his suicide in 1985.

provide information on many aspects of the work of their employers. People have a variety of motives for becoming moles. Some may do so for ideological reasons, others because of the lure of money. Whatever the case, the double life that they lead is one of extreme stress, often causing such personal problems as alcoholism or irresponsibility with money.

Ring concealment
This World War II ring concealed microdots and signals' plans.

The CIA has suffered at least two major penetrations by moles. In one instance, Larry Wu Tai Chin joined the CIA in 1948 and, from early in the 1950s until his death by suicide in 1985, he secretly worked for Chinese intelligence. A recent and well-publicized example of a mole was CIA officer Aldrich Ames (see p. 8 and 162), who offered his services to the KGB in return for money. From 1985 until he was arrested in 1994 he sold a vast number of secrets to the Soviet Union.

THE ANALYST

The information gathered by espionage and technical means forms only a small part of the material that needs to be evaluated by intelligence services. Much of the vast quantity of information that passes through their hands is acquired from publicly available sources. Analysts have the task of combining these diverse elements of intelligence into their written reports and digests. Their output is a potentially valuable aid for military and political decision-makers.

The role of the analyst is unglamorous compared to that of spies who take part in operations, and analysts seldom come to the notice of the public. Without them to provide a usable end-product, however, espionage would be much less effective than it actually is. With the current rapid development of information technology (see p. 15), the analysts' role is likely to become still more important.

Walther PPK
Being easy to conceal, this reliable weapon is commonly adopted for self-protection by personnel in a number of intelligence agencies.

THE ASSASSIN

Assassins take their name from a medieval Muslim sect who exerted their power by murdering the leaders of those who opposed them. The role of the intelligence service assassin is essentially the same. Contrary to common belief, assassinations are not frequently carried out by spies. US Senate hearings in 1976 established that the CIA had never actually participated in the murder of a foreign leader, despite some abortive plans to that end. The CIA is now prohibited by executive order from taking part in assassinations.

By contrast, the intelligence services of the Soviet Union made effective use of assassination to liquidate political enemies. As early as the 1930s they created a special laboratory, the *kamera*, to develop poisons and other assassination tools. Their most prominent victim was Leon Trotsky, one of the founders of the communist state, who was killed in 1940 on the orders of his rival, Stalin.

Later killings included those of two Ukrainian nationalist exiles in Munich by the KGB. These were carried out in 1957 and 1959 by a KGB officer named Bogdan Stashinsky. The device he used was hidden in a newspaper and sprayed poison gas in the victim's face, causing death within seconds. In the 1957 incident there was no suspicion of foul play, and even after autopsy the death was not attributed to assassination. Stashinsky revealed all when he defected to West Germany in 1961.

Assignment in Munich
While serving as a KGB officer, Bogdan Stashinsky assassinated two Ukrainian nationalists.

SPIES OF THE FUTURE

T HE FUTURE OF ESPIONAGE will inevitably be affected by changes resulting from the end of the Cold War and the demise of communism in Eastern Europe. In place of the old certainties of superpower rivalry, there is a much more unpredictable world order, made additionally unstable by the forces of nationalism and religious fundamentalism. Spies have a role to play, both in advancing these causes and in countering the new threats that they present. Future spies will also, more often than the spies of today, turn their attention to industrial espionage, crime, terrorism, and the exploitation of new technology.

Fighting the drugs trade
This bullet contains a homing device which, when fired into a consignment of drugs, facilitates electronic tracking.

INDUSTRIAL ESPIONAGE

The commercial rivalries between developed nations in the post-Cold War world are likely to increase. In the mercantile wars and technological battles of the future, economic spies will be the foot soldiers. There is nothing new about industrial espionage: the Hebern machine (see p. 120) was invented to protect business communications in the early 20th century.

Industrial espionage is particularly prevalent in the field of computer technology. The cost of research and design work means that any company that can steal a fully designed concept can make vast financial savings. In the United States in 1981, Kenji Hayashi, a senior engineer for the Japanese company Hitachi, attempted to acquire the details of a new computer disk drive being developed by the American IBM corporation.

Hayashi's downfall came when an intermediary, whom he approached with a view to acquiring the secrets, informed IBM. The matter was investigated by the FBI. Hayashi was arrested after arranging to pay $525,000 for a batch of IBM secrets. He was given a five-year suspended jail sentence and fined $10,000. It was reported that, in settlement of a civil suit brought by IBM, Hitachi paid $300 million in compensation.

Industrial espionage can also be carried out by state agencies. The national intelligence services in some countries, notably France and Britain, have engaged in espionage to help companies in their own countries to compete with foreign companies.

Kenji Hayashi
Hayashi was arrested while attempting to ship stolen IBM computer secrets to his employers in Japan, in a large-scale industrial espionage operation.

COMBATING CRIME

The fall of communism has created a more unstable world, but has also allowed intelligence services more time to devote to countering the new threats that are emerging. Organized crime is already being targeted. American intelligence agencies are involved in the war against the drug cartels of Central and South America. The agencies in Europe, meanwhile, are alert to the menace of criminals from the former communist bloc seeking to establish themselves in the West.

Intelligence agencies may also be employed to combat new types of technologically based crime. Modern computer ciphers enable criminals to hide their profits as they move them around the global electronic banking system. Computer microchips have become the world's most valuable black market commodity.

More alarmingly, substances that are required for making nuclear weapons have already been illegally sold from the former Soviet Union. Espionage will certainly play a part in preventing such material from falling into the hands of terrorist groups or being acquired by states that currently lack nuclear weapons.

Christopher Boyce: satellite traitor
While employed by an American satellite communications company, Boyce conspired to sell satellite secrets to the Soviet Union. He received a long jail sentence (see p. 57).

Digital listening devices are already available, too. These have a solid state memory – they record the sound on a silicon memory chip, transmitting it afterwards in a burst (see p. 118).

Another improvement in audio surveillance is the use of fibre-optic cables instead of wires to carry signals from microphones. Developments such as these make audio surveillance much harder to detect.

Satellite technology has reached the stage already where it can provide constant, real-time surveillance of a target area, both in pictures and in intercepted radio communications.

SYSTEMS ESPIONAGE

Perhaps the most important influence on the spies of the future will be new developments in computing. Future voice recognition systems will enable automated electronic surveillance to become more sophisticated. New electronic ciphers will enhance the security of communications, although they will, conversely, make code-breaking a harder task. "Software robots" may cruise the Internet public access network, programmed to detect such items as an illicit message between an agent and his controller. And there may be yet more sophisticated "viruses" – destructive programs which, once in the computer operating systems of an enemy, remain dormant until activated in time of war or crisis. While human spies will still be needed, computers will be increasingly important in the gathering and processing of information. And it may be that those who control access to the information will decide who the superpowers of the future will be.

SURVEILLANCE

A number of technological advances are likely to have an influence on the work of the future spy. Video cameras are bound to play a growing part in surveillance. They can already be made smaller than a postage stamp, and images can be enhanced by means of digital manipulation.

Satellite launch
Modern satellites provide immensely detailed intelligence, sending back high-resolution images and intercepting telecommunications worldwide.

Micro-video camera
This tiny camera is easy to conceal and can even record pictures through the weave of the user's clothing.

FAMOUS
SPYING
OPERATIONS

◆

Spying has been part of human activity since time immemorial. Many of the techniques of spying that are used today were developed in the courts of Renaissance Italy and Elizabethan England. Successive generations of spies and spy agencies have distilled the experiences of the past, learning more sophisticated methods of acquiring and passing information while undermining the ability of the enemy to do the same. The 20th century has been the golden age of spying. Both the World Wars and the ideological struggle known as the Cold War created an insatiable demand for information. World War II was responsible for the enormous Soviet spy networks and the rapid development of cryptography. The Cold War created the great intelligence agencies – the KGB and the CIA – and also led to the application of new technologies, such as computers and spy satellites, to espionage. In this section some of the most famous and important spying operations in the history of espionage are explained.

EARLY ESPIONAGE

R ULERS AND MILITARY LEADERS have always needed to know the strengths, weaknesses, and intentions of their enemies. Consequently, the trade of spying is as old as civilization itself. Around 500 BC, the ancient Chinese strategist Sun Tzu wrote about the importance of intelligence and espionage networks in his classic book, *The Art of War*. The Bible contains more than a hundred references to spies and intelligence-gathering. Most of the elements of modern espionage, however, originate in 15th- and 16th-century Europe.

SPIES AT COURT

The political, philosophical, and cultural changes of this period fostered the development of intelligence-gathering. During the 15th century, the principles of polyalphabetic ciphers were laid down; these principles were still in use in the early 20th century. During the 16th and 17th centuries, the European courts became centres of intrigue as rulers strove to maintain and increase their power. The ambassadorial system of diplomacy was established, and ambassadors were expected to combine official duties with espionage and subversion. Intelligence services were created and were used to great effect by such men as Cardinal Richelieu in France (1585–1642) and Sir Francis Walsingham in England (1537–90).

Cardinal Richelieu
Richelieu, chief minister to King Louis XIII of France, created the Cabinet Noir intelligence service.

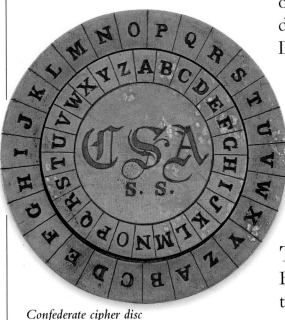

Emblem of the Pinkerton Agency
Allan Pinkerton, founder of Pinkerton's National Detective Agency, headed "Pinkerton's Secret Service", which was active on the northern side during the American Civil War (1861–65).

Confederate cipher disc
This brass substitution disc, a type of cipher wheel (see p. 120), was used by the Signal Service of the Confederate States for secret communications in the American Civil War.

THE AMERICAN CIVIL WAR

By the time of the American Civil War (1861–65), a number of technological advances had occurred that changed the methods used to gather and communicate intelligence. Photography was used for this purpose for the first time. The Confederate States even made use of an early form of the microdot. Telegraphy was

Ring revolver
This tiny five-shot weapon, shown with its case and ammunition, was sold under the brand name Le Petit Guardian. It was made in late-19th-century France.

used for the first time in a major war in military communications, but messages were often intercepted and deciphered. Aerial photography was also devised, using hot air balloons.

WORLD WAR I

Early in World War I (1914–18), human spies were seen as the main threat by the public on both sides of the conflict. But it was signals intelligence that was to prove far more decisive, and indeed it attained a greater importance than in any previous war. For instance, British Admiralty cipher experts deciphered a top-secret German government telegram offering Mexico an offensive alliance against the United States. By subtle use of this discovery, Britain helped to bring America into the war on the Allied side (see p. 24). In America, a cryptology section for military intelligence had been created under Herbert Yardley (see p. 24).

Silver dollar concealment
This 19th-century silver dollar could be used to conceal secret messages. The side with the eagle was hinged, and opened when pressed at a point near the rim.

CHANGES IN RUSSIA

Russia's participation in World War I led to the seizing of power by the Bolshevik Party in Russia after the 1917 revolution. The party created its own secret police, the Cheka, which conducted a ruthless offensive, called the Red Terror, against opponents of bolshevism. Once bolshevik power was firmly established, the Cheka extended its activities to foreign countries. After the formation of the Soviet Union in 1923, the Cheka was replaced by the OGPU, the direct predecessor of the NKVD and KGB (see p. 26).

Cheka badge
The Cheka replaced the Okhrana, the old security service of the Tsarist regime.

Cheka credentials
The Cheka was founded in 1917. Its name is the Russian-language abbreviation for "Extraordinary Commission for the Struggle against Counter-revolution, Espionage, Speculation, and Sabotage".

Court intrigues

SEVERAL IMPORTANT FEATURES of modern espionage had their origins in the Renaissance, the cultural movement of rebirth and modernization that spread through Europe in the 15th and 16th centuries. In the arts and sciences a new, enlightened age began. But in public life dynamic changes were taking place, and bitter struggles for power and religious authority gave new scope for intrigue and treachery. This was the world observed by writer Niccolo Machiavelli (1469–1527) and dominated by a new class of politicians such as Cesare Borgia (1475–1507).

By a combination of deceit, charm, and aggression, Cesare Borgia carved out a kingdom for himself in central Italy. Other rulers of the period were just as much in tune with the new political spirit of the age. In the prevailing climate of mistrust, the growing craft of espionage could hardly fail to flourish.

CESARE BORGIA

The tools of the trade were already being developed. Impressively complex polyalphabetic ciphers were devised in the 15th century by two scholars, Leon Battista Alberti (1404–72) and Johannes Trithemius, his contemporary. Others, such as Giovanni Soro (d.1544) in Venice, contributed to the science of cryptography (the study of codes and ciphers).

The Renaissance also saw the emergence of the modern nation-state, and it was at the courts of such states that the most important developments in espionage took place. By the second half of the 16th century, states such as France, England, and Spain had set up official structures for the gathering of political and military intelligence at home and abroad. Ministers of state

and diplomats were made responsible for gathering intelligence, and ambassadors abroad were expected to combine their official duties with espionage.

ELIZABETHAN INTRIGUES

An effective intelligence service was maintained in England during the reign of Queen Elizabeth I (1533–1603). As a Protestant nation with a weak army, England was constantly threatened by the Catholic powers, France and Spain. War with either could have proved a disaster for England, so intelligence about their intentions was vital.

Elizabeth herself was unmarried and childless, and there were several foreign princes who wanted to marry her and so gain the throne. Within England, too, she had Catholic opponents who wished to overthrow her and replace her with a Catholic monarch. The security of the Protestant state depended on protecting

Christopher Marlowe

```
The English poet and playwright
Christopher Marlowe (1564-93)
was recruited into the secret
service while studying at
Cambridge University. In 1587,
posing as a Catholic student,
he entered a seminary at Rheims
in France. Gaining the trust of
the Jesuit students, Marlowe
learned details of Jesuit plots
in England. Marlowe's death in
a tavern brawl is believed by
many to have been linked to his
secret service work.
```

NICCOLO MACHIAVELLI

Machiavelli (1469–1527) was a scholar and writer with an interest in political philosophy. While serving as a diplomat for the Republic of Florence, Machiavelli met Cesare Borgia, whose political subtlety and cunning he later held up as an example to other rulers, in his book *Il Príncipe* (The Prince). Machiavelli also wrote a book about the art of warfare, in which he emphasized the usefulness of military intelligence.

the Queen from such dangers. In 1573, Sir Francis Walsingham (1537–90) was appointed secretary of state. By skilful use of espionage and counterespionage, he was able to defeat a number of plots aimed at the overthrow of Elizabeth and the restoration of Roman Catholicism.

One possible heir to the English throne was Elizabeth's cousin Mary, Queen of Scots (1542–87). A Catholic, she featured in many political intrigues of the reign, such as the Babbington Plot of 1586. This aimed to release Mary, who had been imprisoned in England after being forced to flee Scotland. The principal elements of the plot were an

Queen Elizabeth I
The motifs decorating the Queen's dress in this portrait are emblematic of various aspects of her power. The eyes and ears (inset) symbolize the activities of her secret service.

uprising by the Catholics of England, invasion by an army financed by Spain and the Pope, and the assassination of Queen Elizabeth herself.

At the centre of the conspiracy was John Ballard. A priest of a militant Catholic order, the Jesuits, he was well known to Walsingham's staff. Ballard recruited Anthony Babbington, who had formerly acted as a messenger for Mary. Walsingham meanwhile employed a double agent who gained the trust of the conspirators and soon learned how they communicated with Mary.

This correspondence was intercepted and deciphered by Thomas Phelippes, Walsingham's master cryptographer. It contained enough evidence to ensure the arrest and execution of the various plotters and even, on 8 February 1587, of Mary, Queen of Scots.

There were also threats from overseas to the security of the English state. King Philip II of Spain (1527–98) believed that it was his duty to restore England to the Catholic faith. Walsingham sent Anthony Standen to gather intelligence in Spain. Standen gained the help of the Florentine ambassador at Philip's court,

and secured the help, too, of a Flemish courtier whose brother was a servant to the Grand Admiral of the Spanish fleet. In 1587 information from these sources alerted Walsingham to the great fleet, or Armada, that was being prepared for the invasion of England. Using his influence abroad, Walsingham secretly contrived to delay the bank loans Philip needed to finance his expedition. This gave the English time to prepare for the arrival of the Armada, which was duly defeated.

RICHELIEU AND THE CABINET NOIR

During the 17th century, the French court became a centre of espionage activity. In the early years of the century, France suffered from an over-powerful nobility and from internal religious divisions. It was threatened externally by the power of the Hapsburg family – the rulers of Spain, Austria, parts of Italy, and the Low Countries.

These difficulties were triumphantly overcome by Louis XIII's chief minister, Cardinal Richelieu (1585–1642). Louis himself was an ineffective ruler, with the result that from 1624 to 1642 France was virtually run by Richelieu. One of Richelieu's first acts after being appointed was to set up an intelligence service, known as the Cabinet Noir. This service monitored the activities of the French nobility by intercepting their correspondence.

Using the information gained in this way, Richelieu thwarted plots against the King and strove to establish the absolute power of the monarchy. His greatest successes were in frustrating plots to seize the throne devised by the King's brother, Gaston of Orleans, and the Duke of Cinq Mars.

Cardinal Richelieu
Cardinal Armand Duplessis, Duke of Richelieu, instituted and used a national intelligence service to establish royal absolutism in France.

Richelieu also used agents abroad in support of his policy of weakening the Hapsburgs without involving France in costly wars. They subverted Spain, for example, by encouraging Portugal and Catalonia to rebel against Spanish rule.

The cardinal's machinations helped to bring Sweden into the Thirty Years' War (1618–48) against the Holy Roman Empire. With Germany paralysed by this conflict, Richelieu was able to seize Alsace for France. By means such as this, his secret service helped to make France a powerful, absolutist nation-state.

American Civil War

THE AMERICAN CIVIL WAR (1861–65) was a conflict between the northern states (the Union), which wanted all the American states to remain united in one country, and the states in the south (the Confederacy), which fought unsuccessfully for independence. The ability of both sides to obtain information from each other was enhanced by the new technologies of the time. Photography, for instance, was exploited for espionage purposes, and gave rise to an early form of microdot (see p. 126).

Allan Pinkerton
Detective agency chief Allan Pinkerton (left), head of the Union secret service, with Abraham Lincoln (centre) and General John McClernand.

SECRET SERVICES

At the outbreak of the war in 1861, neither side had an established intelligence organization. Both the Union and the Confederate forces initially relied upon patriotic volunteers such as Rose Greenhow for intelligence.

Union army commander General George McClellan established a secret service early in the war, selecting a detective, Allan Pinkerton, to be its head. Before the war Pinkerton had owned a detective agency, which had provided security for the railroads. Pinkerton's detectives had limited success as spies, but they established a process of debriefing escaped slaves for information. Conflict arose when another Union commander, General Winfield Scott, started his own secret service, led by Lafayette Baker. Baker proved to be even less effective than Pinkerton, despite personally spying in the South, disguised as a roving photographer. Both Pinkerton's and Baker's men actively sought out Confederate spies operating in the Union capital of Washington, sometimes arresting each other by mistake.

More efficient regional military intelligence operations were set up by

Belle Boyd, "The Rebel Joan of Arc"
A flamboyant Southern patriot, Belle Boyd (1843–1900) achieved limited success as a spy and courier. After the war she romanticized her activities in a book and enjoyed a long career enacting her espionage work on the stage.

SPY PROFILE — Rose Greenhow

Rose O'Neal Greenhow was an accomplished Confederate spy. A society hostess in Washington, she set up a spy network just before the war began; using her charms she gathered information from Union politicians and the military. The first battle of the war — at Bull Run — was won by the Confederates aided by information supplied by Greenhow. Even when under house arrest, she continued to gather and pass on information.

Confederate cipher disc
Used to provide a substitution cipher for secret communications, this disc was adopted by the Confederate Signal Service Bureau in 1862.

Union commanders in the field, notably that run by Colonel George H. Sharpe for General Ulysses S. Grant.

In the South, Colonel Thomas Jordan and later Major William Norris ran an intelligence-gathering operation that obtained daily information by courier from the North. It was only towards the end of the war, in 1865, that an official Confederate secret service was set up.

NEW TECHNOLOGY

Several new methods of intelligence-gathering were used during the war. Photography was so new that few commanders saw it as a threat. Photographers were allowed to take pictures of military defences and camps, and both sides obtained information in this way. Confederate couriers photographically reduced messages so they could be hidden inside hollow metal buttons. Telegraphy was used for quick communication and both sides devised ciphers for secrecy. Aerial reconnaissance from tethered hot air balloons was developed during the war, but it was of limited use because the balloons could be shot down easily.

Doll with secret compartment
There was a great shortage of medicine in the South. Women and children carried medicine in the body of this doll through enemy lines.

THE PLOT TO ASSASSINATE PRESIDENT LINCOLN

In 1865, as the American Civil War neared its end, the Confederate secret service devised several plots against Union leaders. Although these plots failed, some key conspirators continued to plot after the official Confederate surrender on 9 April 1865. The most ambitious of these plots was one to assassinate the Union President, Abraham Lincoln, the Vice President, and the Secretary of War.

John Wilkes Booth, a famous actor, was selected to kill Lincoln, and he shot him as he watched a play at the Ford Theatre in Washington on 14 April 1865; the President died later. Booth escaped from the theatre, but was later found and shot. A search of his possessions revealed a Confederate cipher device. In popular history Booth is generally considered to have acted alone in his assassination of Lincoln. But he definitely had connections with the Confederate secret service, and questions remain about the group's role.

Abraham Lincoln
This picture shows President Lincoln (1809–65) being shot by Booth, as he sits in a box at the Ford Theatre.

John Wilkes Booth
President Lincoln's assassin, actor John Wilkes Booth (1838–65), had also been involved in an earlier attempt to kidnap the President.

World War I

WORLD WAR I (1914–18) began as a struggle between the great European powers: the Triple Entente of France, Britain, and Russia against the Central Powers of Germany and Austria-Hungary. As the war progressed, more nations were drawn into the struggle. It was during this war that code-breaking (cryptography) began to take on the great importance that it has in intelligence-gathering today.

Count Johann Heinrich von Bernstorff
Germany's ambassador in Washington, DC during World War I, von Bernstorff relayed the famous Zimmermann telegram to Mexico.

During the early 20th century, technology for sending long-distance messages made great advances. Telegraph and radio messages, in Morse code, were soon vital to the conduct of war. The intelligence-gathering work of the "agent on the ground", known in the trade as human intelligence, or HUMINT, was joined by a new craft, signals intelligence – later known as SIGINT. As well as sending and receiving messages, it was now necessary to break the ciphers of enemy nations. Early in World War I, Russia had not learned the importance of this: the first German victory against Russia was the result of German signals intelligence intercepting Russian army signals that had been transmitted in unenciphered Morse code. Some other countries did establish special centres for deciphering messages.

Concealments for invisible ink
This talcum powder tin and dentifrice bottle, full of invisible ink, were seized from German spies captured by the British security service.

For example, the British set up Room 40 of naval intelligence, which was renowned for its deciphering skills.

THE ZIMMERMANN TELEGRAM

In 1917, Germany planned a campaign of unrestricted submarine warfare on all ships that visited British ports, including those of neutral countries. Realizing that this could antagonize the United States (still neutral then), the Germans made a plan for this eventuality.

From Berlin, Foreign Minister Arthur Zimmermann sent a telegram in a high-security cipher to Count von Bernstorff, Germany's ambassador in Washington, DC. The same text was to be relayed in a lower-grade cipher to the embassy in Mexico. The message was that Mexico was to be offered a war alliance with Germany against the United States.

British intelligence intercepted the second telegram (to Mexico). Having deciphered it, they were able to break the cipher used for the first telegram, which had been intercepted but not

HERBERT OSBORNE YARDLEY

As a young man, the American Herbert Yardley (1889–1958) gained a reputation for his ability to break codes used by the US State Department, where he worked as an ordinary clerk. After the outbreak of World War I he was commissioned into the US Army and put in charge of the newly formed cryptography section of Military Intelligence (MI8). He devised new codes for use by the US Army, and helped to convict a German spy, whose secret message had been decoded by MI8.

After the war, Yardley established a permanent office, the American Black Chamber, to assist the State Department and US Military Intelligence with code and cipher investigation work. (For the difference between a code and a cipher, see the Glossary, p. 168.) Yardley's greatest success came when his office's ability to

break Japanese codes and ciphers gained significant advantages over Japan for the United States at the international naval disarmament conference, held in 1921.

AMERICAN COMMISSION TO NEGOTIATE PEACE
PASS No. 92
Permit Bearer YARDLEY, H.O., Capt.
To enter HOTEL CRILLON,
PLACE DE LA CONCORDE
R. H. VAN DEMAN
Colonel, General Staff,
U.S.A.

Peace conference credentials
Herbert Yardley led the cryptographic bureau of the US delegation at the 1919 Paris Peace Conference, after the end of World War I.

Suspect cigars
These cigars, sent to two Dutch spies who posed as cigar importers in Portsmouth, were slit open by the British in search of hidden messages.

deciphered. The British hoped to bring the United States into the war on the Allied side, while keeping secret the fact that Germany's high-priority cipher had been broken. They sent a transcript of the telegram to American intelligence.

The Americans obtained a copy of the second telegram for themselves and released the text to the press. They claimed to have intercepted it without any help from the British. This gave the Germans the impression that their high-priority cipher was still secure. At the same time, a wave of public anger at the German telegram led to the entry of the United States into the war.

GERMAN SPIES

A fear of German spies spread through Britain and France at the outbreak of World War I. Although some spies were present in both countries, there were actually far fewer than imagined, and most were captured at the beginning of hostilities. One spy who succeeded in evading capture was Jules Silber. He operated in Britain, taking a job in the Office of Postal Censorship and passing censored information to the Germans.

Two Dutch agents who were sent to Portsmouth to spy for the Germans were not so successful. They pretended to be cigar importers and used their orders for cigars as codes for the ships they saw in Portsmouth harbour. These bogus orders were intercepted by the British postal censors, who became suspicious about the quantity of cigars ordered. The spies were captured and executed in 1915.

MATA HARI

Dutch-born Margaretha Zelle (1876–1918) became famous throughout Europe as a dancer under the stage name Mata Hari. She performed a dance which was, by her account, an authentic Hindu temple ritual. Her fame brought her many influential lovers.

Mata Hari took up espionage in 1914 when the German consul in Amsterdam persuaded her to use her lovers to gain information for Germany. He gave her inks with which to send secret messages. It was not long before Mata Hari's amateurish attempts at spying aroused the suspicions of both French and British intelligence. In spite of this, the French accepted her offer to spy for them. She seduced the German military attaché in Madrid, hoping he would give her information that she could pass on to France.

Mata Hari's end came when she was mentioned in a German secret service telegram from Madrid to Germany. Although referred to as "agent H-21" she was identifiable, and the message was intercepted by the French – it was in a code that they had already broken.

Mata Hari was arrested as a German spy on her return to Paris. She was tried in a French military court, found guilty, and executed by firing squad in 1918.

**MATA HARI IN PRISON
IN FRANCE**

**MATA HARI AS A DANCER BEFORE
WORLD WAR I**

Revolutionary Russia

THE RUSSIAN REVOLUTION of 1917 replaced the feudal government of the Tsars with the communist government of the Bolsheviks (the Communist Party). The revolution took place as a result of hardships during World War I and of political pressures for a change in government. The Tsarist government had an intelligence and security service called the Okhrana. One of the key tasks of the Okhrana had been to spy on revolutionaries such as the Bolsheviks. After they came to power, the Bolsheviks copied the Okhrana's techniques for gathering information.

Felix Dzershinsky
The Russian secret police was founded by Felix Dzershinsky (seated in centre). The huge and powerful organization that he established was to survive for longer than the Soviet Union itself.

EARLY CHEKA BADGE

The Tsarist intelligence services had a history of mixed achievement. In 1913, military intelligence achieved a major success against the Austro-Hungarian Empire. Important military secrets were acquired from an Austrian army officer, Colonel Alfred Redl. The colonel was homosexual, and the Russians were able to blackmail him into passing Austro-Hungarian war plans to them.

In 1914, on the other hand, it was an intelligence failure that caused the first great Russian disaster of World War I, the defeat at the battle of Tannenberg. Radio signals relating to the deployment of the Russian forces were broadcast in plain Morse code (without the use of a cipher to ensure secrecy). This gave a crucial advantage to the Germans, who were monitoring the broadcasts.

THE OKHRANA

The Okhrana was more aware of the possibilities of signals intelligence than the military, and it employed spies to assist in code-breaking activities. The organization also had some success in bribing foreign journalists to present a favourable picture of Russia. This helped the Tsar to secure war loans from countries allied to

Cheka credentials
This is the earliest known example of a Russian secret police identification credential. It belonged to a member of the Bolshevik Cheka.

Russia. The most effective work of the Okhrana took place in Europe. A system of informers and agents was developed to penetrate revolutionary groups. The information gathered was so good that Okhrana files are a major source of information on the early history of the Bolsheviks. When the Bolsheviks gained power, they were quick to see the value of the Okhrana's spying techniques and records.

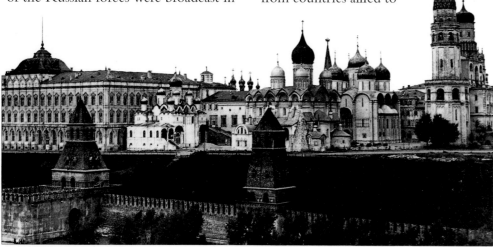

Moscow: the Kremlin
The Kremlin, a walled fortress in the centre of Moscow, became the seat of Bolshevik power in 1918; today, it houses Russia's government.

THE CHEKA

After gaining power in late 1917, the Bolsheviks created their own secret police, the Cheka. Under the command of Felix Dzershinsky (1877–1926), the Cheka immediately set about securing the Bolshevik hold on power. Political opponents of the regime were arrested, imprisoned, or executed. In the face of growing threats to the regime, these actions reached their peak in late 1918. Hostages were taken, concentration camps set up, and torture by Cheka interrogaters officially approved as a tool for extracting information. Combining this extreme ruthlessness with the interrogation techniques of the Okhrana and the pre-revolutionary Bolshevik Party's expertise in clandestine activities, the Cheka was able to establish itself as the primary agency for espionage abroad and for counterintelligence at home.

THE OGPU

In 1922, with the Bolsheviks firmly in power, the Cheka was converted into the GPU (State Political Administration), still under Dzershinsky. When the Soviet Union was created in the following year, the GPU became the OGPU (United State Political Administration). The constitution of the Soviet Union charged the OGPU with the mission to "struggle with political and economic counter-revolution, espionage, and banditry". The OGPU, with its headquarters at Lubyanka in Moscow, had power over virtually all aspects of Soviet life, and also conducted intelligence operations abroad. It was particularly active against anti-Bolshevik émigrés. Eventually, the organization had 800,000 members. The OGPU remained, under a number of names, a central part of the government of the Soviet Union until 1991.

Silenced OGPU revolver
The 7.62 mm Nagant Model 1897 revolver was a standard weapon of both the Imperial Russian and Soviet armies. This special example was used by the OGPU. It had a silencer, here shown removed.

OGPU credentials
In 1923, Felix Dzershinsky's intelligence and secret police organization became known as the OGPU. It was the direct forerunner of the later NKVD, MGB, and KGB. *After the demise of the communist state in 1991, the KGB was dissolved and its directorates were renamed.*

THE "TRUST" AND SIDNEY REILLY

The "Trust" was a deception operation, devised by the secret police chief Felix Dzershinsky (see above). Its purpose was to entice émigré counter-revolutionaries back to the Soviet Union so that they could be killed or imprisoned by the secret police.

Officially called the Moscow Municipal Credit Association, the organization was based in Paris. Its ostensible purpose was to offer support to anti-Bolshevik groups. To gain the trust of the émigré community, Dzershinsky allowed the Trust to engineer the escape of a famous anti-Bolshevik general from Russia. Then, in 1924, the Trust persuaded an émigré leader, Boris Savinkov, to return to Moscow, supposedly to lead a counter-revolution. Once in Moscow, Savinkov was arrested and tortured. Subsequently, he was killed by being pushed down a stairwell in the OGPU headquarters at Lubyanka in Moscow.

In 1925, a British intelligence operative named Sidney Reilly was lured to a meeting with Trust members in Moscow, where he was arrested and forced to write a confession revealing all his Moscow contacts. He was then executed. His body was photographed in the Lubyanka morgue, as proof for OGPU records that he had been captured and killed.

Sidney Reilly
Reilly was targeted by the OGPU because of his work for the British intelligence and his wide range of important Russian contacts.

WORLD WAR II

Tyre ripper
Designed by the SOE (see opposite), this device was worn around the neck and used for slashing tyres of enemy vehicles.

T HE MAJOR COMBATANTS of World War II deployed their intelligence services with varying degrees of success. At the start of war in Europe in 1939, the Soviet Union, Germany, Japan, and Britain had well-established foreign intelligence networks, although America did not.

The most extensive networks operated were the Soviet ones, including the west European network under Leopold Trepper. Among other things, Trepper warned of the German invasion of the Soviet Union in 1941. Warnings were sent, too, by Richard Sorge, a Soviet spy in Japan. Unfortunately, Premier Stalin did not trust his own intelligence sources. But there was one message from Sorge that did help significantly, prompting Stalin to move Soviet troops from the east to halt the German advance in the west and prevent the fall of Moscow.

AXIS INTELLIGENCE

German espionage efforts were less successful. The intelligence community was split into two rival camps, the Army-controlled Abwehr and the Nazi Party SD. Towards the end of the war, the SD became the dominant force. Germany's intelligence services seriously underestimated the military power of the Soviet Union, and they were completely taken in by Allied deception plans that masked the 1944 D-Day landings. German attempts to establish agents in Britain and the United States, too, were a failure. Furthermore, when good information was acquired by the German intelligence agencies, for example through the agent known as Cicero (see p. 34), it was badly mishandled. In contrast, Japan used its intelligence sources well, having gathered intelligence to good effect prior to its successful attacks on Pearl Harbor and on a number of countries in southeast

Lapel badge
In 1945 the OSS (see opposite) issued this badge to its veterans.

Counterfeit matchboxes
Special operations personnel operating in occupied countries had to have belongings that seemed to be locally made. These matchbox labels and colour printing blocks were made for the SOE (see opposite).

Walter Schellenberg
Following the assassination in 1942 of SD head Reinhard Heydrich (see p. 35), Schellenberg (1910–52) took over SD foreign intelligence operations.

Asia that were dependencies of European powers. The Japanese also maintained a spy ring in America, controlled from neutral Spain.

THE WESTERN ALLIES

The British and Americans had to invent intelligence strategies to cope with war against an enemy who seized vast areas of territory. In 1940, European stations of Britain's senior intelligence service, MI6, were all overrun by the Germans. The British created a new service, the Special Operations Executive (SOE). This was the first service that combined intelligence-gathering with clandestine warfare (including support for resistance groups). In 1942, the United States created the Office of Strategic Services (OSS) to play a similar role but with a stronger intelligence-gathering component. Together, and in concert with local resistance groups, the SOE and OSS caused chaos behind enemy lines, in both Europe and Asia.

NEW SKILLS

In terms of influencing the outcome of the war, the intelligence operations that proved to be most effective were those of the Allied code-breakers. British cryptographers broke the ciphers of the German Enigma and its derivatives, while the Americans broke the Japanese Purple cipher. Information thus gathered gave the Allies insight into enemy intentions. This did not guarantee them victory, but it had far-reaching effects on their conduct of the war. For instance, in 1943 it helped to defeat the German submarine fleet, which otherwise would have blocked essential Allied shipping lanes in the North Atlantic.

Cipher machine
Japan produced its own innovations in intelligence codes and ciphers. This is a Japanese rotor-type cipher machine.

Shoulder holster
Holsters of this type were used by SOE officers who chose to carry a pistol for personal protection. This example contains a Colt .32 pistol.

Special Operations Executive

THE BRITISH SPECIAL OPERATIONS EXECUTIVE (SOE) was founded during World War II in the summer of 1940, after Germany had invaded much of continental Europe. Its task was to equip, train, and help lead resistance groups in areas occupied by the German forces, as well as to take part in aggressive sabotage operations. SOE officers and operatives worked with local resistance groups, coordinating their activities with one another and with the campaigns of the anti-German Allied armies for the liberation of Europe.

SPECIAL FORCES' WINGS

All the SOE's recruits were volunteers, and were often dismissed by the more established intelligence services as amateurs, meddling in "cloak-and-dagger" warfare.

ORGANIZATION

The SOE was controlled by the Ministry of Economic Warfare, and for most of the war was led by Major General Sir Colin Gubbins. The SOE was divided into separate sections, or "desks", for each country in which operations were planned. Each desk recruited, trained, and operated its own personnel. In action the SOE operated in groups of between two and thirty members. From 1943, the SOE cooperated with the American Office of Strategic Services, the OSS (see p. 32).

SOE jumpsuit
Designed for use by covert-action personnel parachuting into occupied territory, the suit provided camouflage, protected the clothing from damage, and had pockets to hold vital equipment.

Celluloid goggles

Padded helmet

Lanyard for knife used to cut parachute

Retaining strap for helmet

Opening where spine-protection pad is inserted into pouch

Inner padded pocket for spade used to bury jumpsuit on landing

Integral holster

Full-length zip for ease of stepping out of jumpsuit

SPY PROFILE

Odette Sansom

French-born SOE agent Odette Sansom (1912–95) was sent to southern France in 1942. Her codename was Lise. She served as a courier with an SOE unit led by Captain Peter Churchill. In 1943 they were unwittingly betrayed by a member of the French resistance. Sansom and Churchill were captured and interrogated by the Germans, and sent to concentration camps. Both of them survived and married after the war.

OPERATIONS

SOE operatives and officers were sent into enemy territory clandestinely, some landing in aircraft in fields or dropping by parachute, others using submarines and small boats. The SOE's approach was always to cooperate closely with local resistance groups. Together they made sabotage attacks on communications, factories, and power lines to disrupt the enemy. Back in Britain, the SOE set up laboratories to develop equipment for its operatives and officers. Special forms of explosives were created, as were original ways of concealing them, camouflaging them, and controlling their detonation. The SOE laboratories also made special concealable and silenceable weapons. They devised advanced radio equipment that operatives could use to receive messages from headquarters as well as passing back information, for example, on enemy troop movements.

.32 calibre revolver
This weapon was carried by the SOE operative Violette Szabo, who was an excellent shot.

SPY PROFILE — Violette Szabo

British-born Violette Szabo (1921–45) joined the SOE after her husband, an officer in the Free French army, was killed fighting the Germans. Szabo's last mission to France was on 6 June 1944 (D-Day), when she was sent to assist a resistance group. Within days she was captured but, although tortured by the Gestapo (see p.34), she refused to talk. Szabo was sent to a concentration camp, and executed on 26 January 1945.

THE RISKS

Since their work involved resistance and sabotage, SOE operatives were relentlessly hunted by enemy forces. If captured, the operatives risked torture and death. From 1940 until 1944, 393 SOE operatives were sent to work in France – 17 were captured and survived, 104 were killed. Despite such sacrifices, the SOE was never fully accepted by the established intelligence services. Officers of its British rival, the Secret Intelligence Service (MI6), disliked the SOE's policy of combining guerrilla warfare, sabotage, and subversion with more conventional forms of intelligence-gathering.

The SOE nonetheless played a vitally important role in organizing resistance forces and coordinating their operations in support of the Allied invasion of Europe, which finally came in 1944.

THE FRENCH RESISTANCE

The French resistance was made up of groups within France that actively opposed the German occupation. The resistance provided a ready-made network of spies and saboteurs for the nations allied against Germany. Particularly valuable intelligence was provided by resistance members and sympathizers who were employed in German military bases and other establishments. The resistance often supported the escape lines set up by the British and American intelligence services, through which many airmen and escaped prisoners of war were helped to reach safety. A sabotage campaign was mounted, in which the resistance was aided by the SOE and OSS. This gave rise, in June 1944, to widespread attacks on German transport and communications in support of the Allied invasion of Europe, the D-Day landings. On 10 August 1944, a series of work stoppages began in Paris that led to a full-scale public revolt against the German occupiers. By 24 August the Allied forces, including elements of Free French armoured units, entered Paris. The German garrison surrendered the following day.

The Maquis preparing their weapons
The first Maquis units were made up of people evading a German forced labour scheme. Later, the whole French resistance was called the Maquis.

Lapel blade, sheath, and armband
The sheath shows the Cross of Lorraine, symbol of the Free French army, which fought against the Germans from outside France.

Office of Strategic Services

THE OFFICE of Strategic Services (OSS) was created in June 1942, six months after the United States entered World War II. Its director, William J. "Wild Bill" Donovan, had previously held the key intelligence post of Coordinator of Information, reporting directly to the President. He formed a new service that was truly worldwide in scope. The OSS did not restrict itself to intelligence-gathering; it also waged clandestine warfare, using tactics that were similar to those of the British SOE (see p. 30).

.45 calibre Liberator pistol
This simple, cheap weapon was intended to be supplied in large numbers to resistance fighters. Its role was to capture a better weapon from an enemy soldier.

OSS COLLAR INSIGNIA **OSS LAPEL PIN**

To carry out this dual role, Donovan divided the OSS into a series of separate branches with different responsibilities. The Research and Analysis Branch employed academics to plan the strategy for invasions. The Morale Operations Branch produced propaganda, using the skills of advertising copywriters and screenwriters. The Labor Division encouraged subversive activity within trades unions in enemy-occupied Europe, in order to disrupt production and communications systems. Three of the main functional branches of the OSS were: Special Operations (SO), Secret Intelligence (SI), and Counterintelligence (X-2).

CLANDESTINE WARFARE

The SO branch, modelled on Britain's SOE, supported resistance movements in parts of Europe and Asia. Usually working in groups of between two and thirty people, members of the SO branch operated behind enemy lines. Lines of communications and supply, factories, and airfields were sabotaged.

SECRET INTELLIGENCE

The SI branch of the OSS established a comprehensive system for the gathering of intelligence. To ensure worldwide coverage, the SI branch was divided into four geographical "desks", dealing with parts of Europe, Africa, the Middle East,

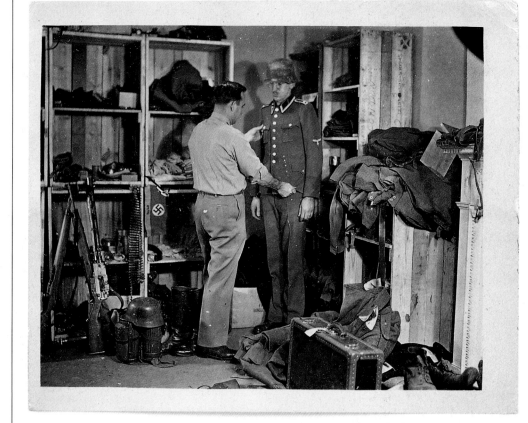

OSS clothing warehouse in London
Clothing such as this German army uniform was taken from prisoners and used by OSS operatives on secret missions in German-occupied territory.

OSS DETACHMENT 101

The first OSS unit created to carry out secret operations was called Detachment 101. Its personnel were trained at an SOE base, Camp X, in Canada. Captain (later Colonel) Carl Eiffler was the commander of Detachment 101 from April 1942 until December 1943. The detachment's mission was to conduct a campaign of sabotage and guerrilla warfare in Burma behind Japanese lines. In the autumn of 1942, the detachment entered the Burmese jungle and made contact with local Kachin people, who, having suffered badly at Japanese hands, were willing to help the United States. The Kachins were provided with equipment and training by the Americans, and also possessed tribal ambush techniques of their own. Detachment 101 eventually reached a strength of 500, assisted by more than 10,000 Kachins. This combined force caused over 15,000 Japanese casualties.

101 DETACHMENT CAMPAIGN BAR

COLONEL CARL EIFFLER

and Asia. A number of other sections assisted the SI branch in its operations. A Reporting Board analysed the agents' reports and distributed them. The Ship Observer Unit gathered information on the enemy from seamen's organizations and shipping operators. The Technical Section reviewed technical reports and provided information for Britain, as well as America, about matters such as the development of V1 and V2 rockets.

SPECIAL EQUIPMENT

The OSS was supplied with a range of specialized equipment by the Research and Development Division, which was led by Stanley Lovell (see p. 149). Many innovative weapons and devices were produced specially for the OSS. The Liberator pistol was a cheaply-made weapon intended for distribution to resistance groups in occupied countries. Special explosives were invented, along with devices for camouflaging them and delaying their detonation. Advanced radio equipment was made for contact between OSS headquarters and operatives in the field. Secret cameras were developed for taking clandestine photographs.

DONOVAN'S ACHIEVEMENT

During World War II, the OSS achieved notable successes in both clandestine warfare and intelligence-gathering, and demonstrated the benefits of combining these two major roles in one organization. Nevertheless, its mode of operations was new to America and had not yet been wholly accepted. Not only this, but Harry S. Truman, who became US President in 1945, saw Donovan as a political rival and had no reason to keep him on in a top government post. The OSS was abolished in 1945 and its intelligence-gathering role was

False German identification card
Produced for OSS chief William Donovan, these credentials demonstrate the ability of OSS forgers to create realistic German documents.

taken over by the US State Department, while responsibility for field operations went to the War Department. Donovan had hoped that he would be able to set up a post-war intelligence service, but the plan he put forward was reviewed unfavourably by President Truman.

Although Donovan never attained his goal of creating a single, centralized US intelligence service, a variation of his plan did come into being two years after the OSS had been disbanded. This was the Central Intelligence Agency (CIA) (see p. 46). Donovan also left another legacy to US intelligence in the form of several highly experienced OSS veterans who joined the CIA, including William Colby and Richard Helms.

William Egan Colby

During World War II, William Colby (b.1920) served with the OSS in both France and Norway, carrying out sabotage with local resistance groups (see p.141. After the war, Colby held posts around the world with the Central Intelligence Agency (CIA). Later, in Vietnam, on leave from the CIA, he headed a key military-intelligence programme with the rank of ambassador. He was Director of the CIA from 1973 until 1976.

German secret services

DURING WORLD WAR II (1939–45), Germany had two intelligence agencies – the Abwehr and the Sicherheitsdienst or SD. The Abwehr was the intelligence and clandestine warfare section of the armed forces. The SD was controlled by the Schutzstaffel (the SS), an arm of the National Socialist Party (Hitler's Nazi Party), which ruled Germany from 1933 until the end of the war. The role of the SD was to spy on the other Nazi Party members for the SS.

ADMIRAL WILHELM FRANZ CANARIS (1883–1945)

Gestapo warrant disc
Numbered warrant discs were carried by members of the Gestapo as proof of authority for use only when carrying out arrests and house searches.

From 1935, the head of the Abwehr was Admiral Wilhelm Canaris. As a naval officer, Canaris had been involved in undercover work during World War I. When appointed head of the Abwehr, his first task was to establish a working relationship with the SD, as previously there had been very little cooperation between the two agencies. Reinhard Heydrich was the chief of the SD. In 1938, the Geheime Staatspolizei (the Gestapo, the secret state police) and the Kripo (criminal police) came under control of the SD. Heydrich had served as a cadet under Canaris in the navy, and they agreed on a compromise that made the Abwehr responsible for military espionage and all counterespionage, while the SD took responsibility for political intelligence and police work.

Cooperation between the Abwehr and the SD did not last, and Canaris soon expanded the Abwehr in an attempt to become more important than the SD and free himself from Nazi Party control. But he failed to gain the authority he wanted for the Abwehr and, despite some successes, the Abwehr's foreign intelligence operations produced few significant results.

CICERO AND OPERATION BERNHARD

Cicero was the codename for Elyesa Bazna (1905–71), the Albanian valet of the British ambassador to Turkey, Sir Hugh Knatchbull-Hugessen. Bazna worked as an agent for the SD between 1943 and 1944. Having stolen the keys to the ambassador's safe, Bazna photographed documents about conferences in Moscow, Cairo, and Teheran and information relating to the impending D-Day invasion of German-occupied Europe. The Germans did not gain much advantage from this information, however, because it was mishandled by the German intelligence services. The SD paid Bazna £300,000 in counterfeit notes. These notes had been made as part of a plan – Operation Bernhard – to destabilize the British economy by distributing large amounts of forged currency. The SD used Jewish master forgers from concentration camps to forge the currency, which they did to such a high standard that the forgeries were not discovered until after the war. Bazna's post-war retirement plans collapsed when the forgeries were detected; he sued the German government, without success.

Elyesa Bazna
Years after the discovery of his spying activities, Bazna demonstrated how he had photographed secret documents with a Leica camera.

Counterfeit ten-pound note
Jewish master forgers in concentration camps were coerced into forging British banknotes, causing the recall of an entire series of currency.

THE SD

From 1935 onwards, the SD expanded greatly in size and power. Reinhard Heydrich enjoyed the support and patronage of the chief of all German police, Reichsführer SS Heinrich Himmler. Under Heydrich

OPERATION ANTHROPOID

On 27 May 1942, Reinhard Heydrich (1904–42), acting Reichsprotektor of Bohemia and Moravia (now the Czech Republic) and head of the SD, was fatally injured in an attack known as Operation Anthropoid. A Czech team, trained by the British SOE (see p. 30), threw a grenade at Heydrich's car as he drove through Prague, inflicting wounds from which he later died. The attackers died a few weeks later, after a gun battle with German forces.

REINHARD HEYDRICH

the SD gradually extended its activities into areas that were supposed to be the preserve of the Abwehr. In 1939 his power was increased when he was appointed head of the Reich Central Security Department (the RHSA). Heydrich gathered intelligence from all sectors of society, even opening an exclusive brothel, known as Salon Kitty, equipped for electronic eavesdropping on its clients. During the war the SD mounted a wide range of operations, some of which – such as Operation Bernhard (see opposite) – were too ambitious to be successful.

THE FALL OF ADMIRAL CANARIS

Following the death of Heydrich on 4 June 1942, Canaris became the most important person in the German intelligence services. But he did not have the support of Himmler, who in February 1944 persuaded Hitler to dismiss him. The Abwehr was merged with other intelligence agencies under the RHSA. Canaris was arrested after a failed assassination attempt on Hitler in July 1944, and was executed in April

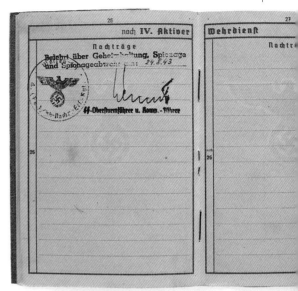

Page from an SD credential
This credential was issued to a member of the SD who had attended a training course on secret work, espionage, and counterespionage.

1945. Himmler was probably right not to trust Canaris – since 1938 Canaris had been expressing increasingly hostile views towards Hitler and his political and military policies, and the Abwehr ultimately suffered because of its leader's uncertainty about the regime he served.

Tuning dial   Crystal socket

Power switch

Morse key

Power dial

Front cover of radio

SE 109-3 Abwehr radio
This small battery-powered radio set allowed Abwehr agents in the field to transmit and receive Morse code messages to listening stations. So as not to be incriminating if the set was discovered, any labels on the cover were in English.

Code-breaking

SPIES, DIPLOMATS, military personnel, and others often relied on cipher machines to protect the secrecy of their messages during World War II. Messages enciphered by means of the German Enigma cipher machine (see p. 122) and the Japanese Alphabetic Typewriter 97 were deciphered by code-breakers working in special establishments in both Britain and the United States.

Baron Hiroshi Oshima
Oshima (1886–1975) was Japan's ambassador to Germany during World War II. He sent messages on the broken Purple cipher.

THE PURPLE CODE

In 1939 the Japanese began using a new cipher machine for sending diplomatic messages. They called it the Alphabetic Typewriter 97, but in the United States it was known by the codename Purple. The Purple machine was a development of an earlier one codenamed Red.

American code-breakers had already cracked the Red system, and now the cryptographer William Friedman and the US Army Signals Intelligence Service began work to break the new cipher. The cryptographers were aided by the interception of a message that had been enciphered on both the Red and Purple machines.

This message, and other intercepted messages sent using Purple, were the only information the code-breakers had to help them build a Purple machine of their own. A breakthrough came when they tried using stepping switches – part of the telephone technology of the time. By a lucky coincidence, these worked in exactly the same way as the switches in the Purple machine.

By late 1940, Friedman and a team of US Navy code-breakers were able to construct a Purple machine. It was so efficient that Japan's declaration of war – sent to the embassy in Washington a day ahead of the attack on Pearl Harbor to allow time for decipherment – was read by American intelligence before it was presented to the US Secretary of War.

HOW THE ENIGMA WAS CRACKED

In 1939, the British began investigating the German Enigma cipher machine (see p. 122). The Government set up a Code and Cipher School at Bletchley

WILLIAM FRIEDMAN

A Soviet émigré to America, William Friedman (1891–1969) was the author of a series of pioneering papers that set out the main principles of modern cryptography. Friedman's wife, Elizabeth, was also an expert cryptographer, and sometimes they collaborated. William Friedman was largely responsible for breaking the Japanese Purple cipher in 1940. After World War II, his work culminated in the formation of the US National Security Agency (see p. 46), an organization that specializes in signals intelligence and cryptography.

Switching unit

Housing for stepping switch

Stepping switch removed from housing

Purple cipher machine
In this Japanese device, two electric typewriters were connected via two switching units. Plain text typed into one of the typewriters would emerge from the other in the Purple cipher.

The Enigma cipher machine
The Enigma's rotors (the early models had three but this one has four), its complicated internal wiring, and its changing set-up produced a cipher that the Germans considered unbreakable.

Bletchley Park, England
At this country house, and in prefabricated huts on its grounds, over 1,000 staff worked during World War II to break German ciphers.

ALAN TURING

A mathematical genius, Alan Turing (1912–54) played a leading role in the breaking of the Enigma ciphers. At the age of 24, Turing had written a paper that set out the principles by which modern computers work. During World War II, Turing was set to work at the Government Code and Cipher School at Bletchley Park. While there, he conceived the idea behind Colossus, the first electronic computer in the world. The computer helped British code-breakers to meet the challenge presented by the new, more complicated German cipher machine, the ten-rotor Geheimschreiber (see p. 123).

Park, a short journey outside London, where a community of mathematicians, linguists, and creative thinkers in other disciplines worked at first on breaking the Enigma ciphers, and later on breaking other enemy ciphers.

The chief problem they faced was to discover the key settings that had been selected when setting up each Enigma machine for its daily use. A further problem was that the equipment itself differed between the various German organizations that used it.

"BOMBES"
Before the war, Polish code-breakers had developed machines called "bombes" that had successfully deciphered some of the Enigma messages. Unfortunately, the Germans were continually making the Enigma more complicated.

At Bletchley Park, new versions of the bombes were developed. At first, these failed to keep pace with the increasing complexity of the Enigma cipher. Then the mathematician Alan Turing added 26 electrical relays that speeded up the process of deciphering a message.

Even then, success was achieved only by means of educated guesswork. Using a process of hypothesis and experiment, code-breakers were able to deduce the wording of the part of the message that spelt out the key settings in use.

Mathematician Gordon Welchman developed a procedure known as traffic analysis, which made it possible to sort messages according to the organizations that sent them. This would identify the type of Enigma machine used, and again reduce the number of variables that the bombes had to cope with.

Naval Enigma signals were broken from 1941 to 1945, partly with the help of captured machines and documents, yielding vital information for Britain.

Ian Fleming
James Bond's creator, Fleming (1908–64) worked for British naval intelligence in World War II. He was involved in plots to steal Enigma documents.

Soviet spy networks

DURING WORLD WAR II, the top priority for Soviet espionage was to help defend the Soviet Union against its enemies, Japan and Germany. From the 1930s, Soviet Military Intelligence's Fourth Department (formerly and again later called the GRU) set up spy networks in Japan and Europe. The largest of these was in Western Europe, run from Brussels and later Paris. It was nicknamed the Red Orchestra (Rote Kappelle) by German counterintelligence.

Leopold Trepper
Nicknamed "Big Chief", Trepper (1904–83) went to Brussels in 1938 to launch and operate the Red Orchestra. He later moved to Paris.

The Red Orchestra was headed by Leopold Trepper and had agents at high levels throughout enemy civil and military structures. It was, however, often frustrated by the poor quality of its clandestine radios, which meant that sometimes the network had to depend on vulnerable human couriers. The network suffered badly from German counterintelligence: the Germans captured important messages from Moscow that led them to identify key members of the network; they

Schulze-Boysen
Soviet agent Harro Schulze-Boysen (1909–42, left) was an officer in the German air force. This picture was taken at the German air ministry.

THE RED ORCHESTRA

The Red Orchestra was the part of the the Soviet spy network that covered Western Europe. It was led by Leopold Trepper and conducted its business under the cover of the Foreign Excellent Raincoat Company. All units reported to Moscow, but not all were in contact with one another. After Trepper's arrest by the Gestapo in 1942, the Red Three unit was the most productive element of the Red Orchestra. This unit was run by Alexander Rado and operated from Switzerland. Its most important agent was Rudolf Rössler (codename Lucy). Today, the Red Orchestra is studied as a classic example of a Soviet intelligence network.

Trepper/Sukolov group
The chain of command is shown by solid lines; the dotted lines represent acquaintance only. The network was always changing as agents were arrested or moved to another country. This diagram applies to the period December 1938–July 1940.

Richard Sorge
This Soviet stamp shows Sorge
(1895–1944) with a Hero of
the Soviet Union's star.

also captured the cipher used for messages from Brussels. Another difficulty was that the Soviet leader Josef Stalin distrusted intelligence that came from Britain and America. This led him to make very heavy demands on the Soviet Union's intelligence resources and meant that although the Red Orchestra sent a lot of information to Moscow, not all of it was believed by the Soviet authorities.

UNHEEDED WARNINGS
When the Germans invaded France in 1940, Trepper moved to Paris. He went into business as a contractor for the German army. Sources gained in this way enabled Trepper to forewarn Stalin of Hitler's plan to invade the Soviet Union in June 1941 but, like other warnings, this was ignored. Warning

of the attack also came from two other Soviet agents in Germany, Harro Schulze-Boysen and Arvid Harnack. They sent German secrets to Moscow by radio, until their arrest and execution in 1942. Trepper himself was arrested soon afterwards. He tricked the Germans into believing that he was a double agent, escaped in 1943, and lived out the war in hiding.

RICHARD SORGE
Long before Japan entered the war in 1941, Moscow feared a Japanese invasion. The Fourth Department sent Richard Sorge, a spy who was half German, to Tokyo in 1933. Posing as a German journalist, Sorge befriended the German military attaché in Tokyo, Eugene Ott, and a Japanese

Hotsumi Ozaki
Recruited by Sorge in 1930, Ozaki gathered intelligence from Japanese political circles.

journalist named Hotsumi Ozaki. In July 1941, Sorge learned from these sources that Japan was more inclined to begin its military campaign in southeast Asia than to attack the Soviet Union. If it was true, this information would enable some Soviet armies to be moved from defensive duties on the Soviet Union's eastern borders and used to fight the Germans attacking Moscow. Josef Stalin did not believe it, however, just as he had disbelieved Sorge's warning of Germany's attack in May 1941. Only later in 1941 was Stalin ready to believe Sorge's information about Japan, when signals intelligence confirmed it. Stalin was then able to move more troops from the east to halt the German invasion. Sorge was arrested and executed in 1944.

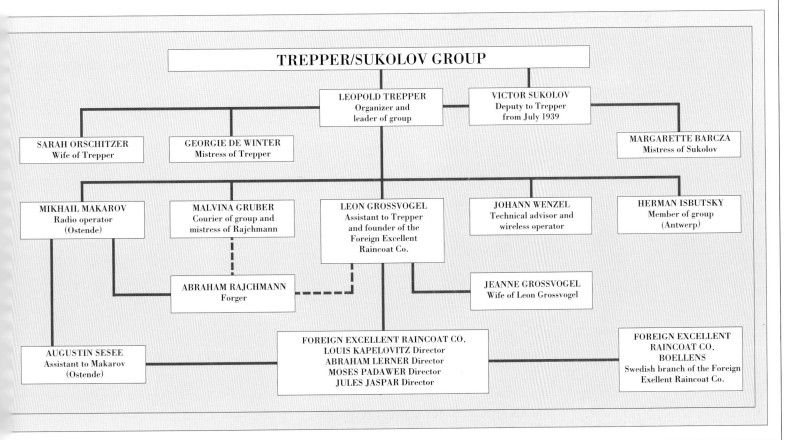

TREPPER/SUKOLOV GROUP

Japanese intelligence

DURING WORLD WAR II, Japan's intelligence organization had several elements. Abroad, embassies played a key role coordinating intelligence-gathering. Within Japan, the Tokko – a special bureau of the Tokyo police force – was responsible for domestic counterintelligence. The armed services also had their own intelligence sections, with the military police (Kempei Tai) covering counterintelligence activities in territories occupied by the Japanese.

Admiral Yamamoto
Yamamoto (1884–1943) planned the attack on the Pearl Harbor base of the US Pacific Fleet, making use of intelligence obtained from a Japanese spy.

The Tokko was formed in 1911 with the purpose of suppressing "subversive thoughts" and defending Japan's strictly regulated political system. It did much to prevent the rise of communism in Japan in the years after World War I.

COUNTERINTELLIGENCE

By 1932, the Tokko had become Japan's chief internal counterintelligence organization. It was divided into four sections: the first monitored left-wing political activists; the second maintained files on the right wing; the third section watched foreign residents and embassies; and the fourth monitored friendly embassies, like that of Germany.

The domestic responsibilities of the Kempei Tai were officially limited to matters concerning members of the armed services. However, the right-wing military movement that dominated Japanese politics used the Kempei Tai to intimidate opposition politicians, arresting those who campaigned against the political order of the time as "terrorists". During the war, the power of the Kempei Tai was enhanced by the patronage of the prime minister,

Hideki Tojo (1884–1948), who had been one of its officers early in his career. In territories occupied by Japan during the war, such as parts of China and southeast Asia, the Kempei Tai operated with extreme ruthlessness, gaining a brutal reputation similar to that of the Gestapo in Germany (see p. 34).

ACHIEVEMENTS AND FAILURES

Immediately after the Japanese capture of Singapore in February 1942, the Kempei Tai arrested hundreds of Chinese Singaporeans, whom it considered to be security risks, and executed them at night on beaches near the city centre. Later, in 1944, naval Kempei Tai units were responsible for hunting down and executing a team of saboteurs from Allied countries, who had attempted to raid Singapore harbour (see p. 99). Despite the zeal of Japanese counterintelligence efforts, a major spy ring working for the Soviet Union managed to flourish in Tokyo in the late 1930s and early 1940s. This spy network, created by Richard

The attack on Pearl Harbor
A Japanese naval officer in Hawaii provided intelligence on American ship movements until hours before the attack on 7 December 1941.

Consul-General Nagao Kita
As Japanese consul-general in Honolulu, Hawaii, Kita provided the enciphering facilities for the naval spy Takeo Yoshikawa.

Sorge (see p. 39), passed a great deal of highly important information to Moscow before it was discovered in 1944. One reason for Sorge's great success may have been that the Tokko was overburdened by the enormous volume of meaningless reports that it received from over-eager informants.

INTELLIGENCE IN THE PACIFIC

During the months before Japan's entry into World War II, Japanese army intelligence established its agents throughout southeast Asia, as part of what was known as Organization F. Meanwhile, Japanese naval intelligence scored a major success in securing information on the US Navy base at Pearl Harbor in Hawaii, which Japan intended to attack. In March 1941, Japanese naval ensign Takeo Yoshikawa travelled to the Hawaiian islands under

Purple cipher machine
The Japanese diplomatic service used the Purple machine to encode correspondence (see p. 36).

SABOTAGE BALLOONS

Throughout World War II the continental United States lay outside the range of bombers from either Germany or Japan. Nevertheless, the Japanese brought the United States under an unusual kind of aerial bombardment. Between 1944 and 1945, some 6,000 balloons bearing incendiary charges were launched from Japan.

The balloons were carried by the prevailing winds, and dropped their charges over the heavily forested northwest of America. At least 369 balloons completed the 9,700-km (6,000-mile) journey. The only fatalities, however, were a family of seven, who were killed by a single balloon.

Japanese sabotage balloon
The Japanese used balloons carrying incendiary devices to bombard the United States. They were wind-borne, and were primarily intended to cause forest fires.

an assumed name. From then until Japan's surprise attack on the base on 7 December 1941 he sent weekly reports on the dispositions of American warships. Although not a trained spy, Yoshikawa was familiar with the organization and structure of the US Navy. He possessed no code of his own but sent his messages through diplomatic channels, under the signature of Japanese Consul-General Nagao Kita. American code-breakers could read the coded Japanese diplomatic mail, sent by cable (see p. 36), but the cable authorities in Hawaii, for reasons never explained, did not pass on the relevant cable traffic to the American authorities. Yoshikawa's last message was transmitted just 12 hours before the Japanese began their attack on Pearl Harbor.

INTELLIGENCE IN EUROPE

Another Japanese intelligence operation was run from Spain, a neutral country. This group was the TO network, which gathered intelligence on Allied shipping from agents in the United States and elsewhere. The coordinator of TO was Yakichiro Suma, who held the rank of a minister in the Japanese embassy in Madrid. Intelligence from TO was used by the Germans as well as the Japanese.

SPY PROFILE **Dusan Popov**

Dusan "Dusko" Popov (1912–81) was a Yugoslav double agent, ostensibly working for the German Abwehr (see p. 34) but actually controlled by British intelligence. In 1941, the Abwehr sent him to the United States to gather information on Pearl Harbor. FBI director J. Edgar Hoover, however, disliked Popov and avoided dealing with him. As a result, the potential significance of this interest in Pearl Harbor was overlooked.

COLD WAR

U-2 spy plane
Introduced in 1956, the U-2 operated at such a high altitude that it was out of range of the Soviet aircraft and missiles of the time.

T HE PERIOD OF CONFRONTATION between East and West that ran from 1945 until the fall of communism in the early 1990s is known as the Cold War. At the very beginning of this period, the Soviet Union's former wartime allies in the West were shocked to discover the extent of Soviet espionage activity that was directed against them. America responded by creating its own foreign intelligence organization, the Central Intelligence Agency (CIA). Later, the National Security Agency (NSA) was set up as a central body responsible for signals intelligence and cryptography. Counterintelligence within the United States remained the responsibility of the Federal Bureau of Investigation (FBI).

National Security Agency emblem
America's NSA is responsible for information security, foreign signals intelligence, and cryptography.

HUMAN INTELLIGENCE

The divided city of Berlin was in the forefront of espionage operations in the Cold War. Surrounded by the Soviet sector (later East Germany), it became an international centre of intelligence activity. One of the most notable incidents was the digging of a tunnel by the CIA and MI6 to intercept a cable carrying military communications to Moscow (see p. 44).

The capture of Berlin in 1945 had given the Soviet state intelligence organization, the NKVD, control of Nazi records, which enabled its successor agency, the NKGB (later KGB), to blackmail many West German citizens into becoming spies. The secret police files of other states also provided blackmail material, as in the example of the Czech spy known as Anna (see p. 48).

The Soviet Union was also successful in operating a number of spies in Britain. Notable among these were George Blake, Gordon Lonsdale and his network of agents, and, most damagingly, the five members of the Cambridge ring (see p. 165). Most of these early Soviet spies were motivated either by ideology or

MICRODOT READER
(ENLARGED 1.5 TIMES)

MICRODOT FILM
(ACTUAL SIZE)

Microdot film and reader
During the Cold War, microdots were much used to convey intelligence in a miniaturized form. They can be read only under powerful magnification.

by the threat of compromise. Later, however, the KGB found that the lure of money was the easiest way to recruit agents. The two most important KGB agents to be exposed in the United States in recent times, John Walker and Aldrich Ames, both offered their services for money. Ames operated as a mole inside the CIA, while Walker sold secrets from within the US Navy.

Control unit in pocket

Remote cable to control unit

Camera

Harness is fastened around chest

Necktie camera
Worn inside an intelligence officer's clothing, this KGB camera took photographs through a fake tiepin. It was operated by a remote shutter release that was concealed in the pocket.

SPIES IN THE SKY

Another major element of the Cold War was the arms race, a contest for nuclear weapons supremacy between East and West. In this struggle the CIA found that its existing techniques for intelligence-gathering were inadequate for assessing the nuclear strength of the Soviet Union. This led to the development of the U-2 spy plane, which was able to conduct high-altitude photographic reconnaissance. Besides flying over the Soviet Union, the U-2 was used in 1962 to monitor developments on the island of Cuba, revealing the presence of Soviet medium-range nuclear missiles. This precipitated the Cuban Missile Crisis, the most dangerous event of the Cold War, resolved only by a firm American stance.

Soviet stamp
This postage stamp commemorates 50 years of Soviet security services.

Another technological race arose from the Soviet Union's launch of the first satellite in 1957. By 1961, satellites were being used for photographic reconnaissance, although the early technology necessitated jettisoning the film for recovery and development on Earth. In 1976 the Americans began using digital technology, which enabled satellites to beam high-definition images back to Earth as soon as they were taken. Such developments in technology have become a prime target for espionage.

KGB gas gun
Developed during the Cold War for assassinating political opponents of the Soviet regime, this weapon emitted cyanide gas, capable of causing almost instant death.

Berlin: spy city

THE GERMAN CITY OF BERLIN occupied a unique position during the Cold War years that followed World War II. After the end of the war, the victorious Allies – America, Britain, France, and the Soviet Union – divided Germany into zones of occupation. The old German capital, Berlin, was similarly divided into four zones, even though it was surrounded by the Soviet zone of occupation, which became the German Democratic Republic, or East Germany.

☐ *French sector*	☐ *US sector*
☐ *British sector*	☐ *Soviet sector*

A divided city
Isolated within Soviet-occupied territory, later to become East Germany, Berlin was divided by the wartime Allies into four zones of occupation. The arrow shows the position of the Berlin tunnel, used to tap into Soviet military communications.

The Soviet Union soon sealed off its own zone from Western interference. Within the Soviet sector, the NKVD (state security) and GRU (military intelligence) operated without restriction, confiscating German industrial machinery, even whole factories, to be sent back to provide jobs in Soviet towns. German scientists were rounded up and made to work for Soviet industry.

INTELLIGENCE ACTIVITY
Meanwhile, agents were recruited to begin spying in the West. Captured Nazi records provided plenty of material with which to blackmail potential agents. West Germans with relatives in the East could also be coerced, by threats to their families, into

assisting the Soviet Union. As a result, between 1950 and 1969 a total of 2,186 agents were convicted of espionage in West Germany, and 19,000 admitted espionage but were not prosecuted.

The head of the West German Foreign Intelligence service for most of this period was Reinhard Gehlen. During the war, he had headed the section of

Reinhard Gehlen
A German intelligence officer during World War II, Gehlen (1902–79) worked for the Americans after the war. He became head of the West German intelligence service.

Road above telephone cables

Soviet–East German telephone cables

Nitrogen-filled tube to detect taps by loss of pressure

Wall of Rüdow cemetery

East–West border fence

American "Radar Station Rüdow" – a concealment for tunnel entrance

Sandbags

"No entry" sign to delay pursuers momentarily

Narrow-gauge railway for moving equipment

Steel door

Amplifying and monitoring equipment

Nitrogen-filled chamber to avoid detection

The Berlin tunnel
From a nondescript building disguised as an American radar installation, the CIA and MI6 constructed a 450 m (1,476 ft) tunnel, mostly under East Berlin, to a chamber where Soviet military communication lines were tapped.

Checkpoint Charlie
This famous crossing place in the Berlin Wall was the site of several successful escapes from the East, some failures, and a dangerous confrontation between American and Soviet tanks in 1961.

German military intelligence responsible for the Soviet Union. He was captured by the Americans in 1945 but persuaded them to employ him and his staff as spies in return for files and names gathered by his wartime espionage network.

In 1949 Gehlen was appointed head of the new German Federal Intelligence Service (later the West German Foreign Intelligence Service – BND). Gehlen remained in this position until 1968, when his reputation was tarnished by the discovery of double agent Felfe (see p. 105) among his headquarters' staff.

UNDERGROUND INTERCEPTION
One of the Cold War's most ambitious intelligence operations was mounted in Berlin in 1954 by the CIA and Britain's

MI6. From just inside West Berlin, the CIA dug a tunnel 450 m (1,476 ft) long to reach a point directly beneath the underground telephone lines by which the Soviet military HQ in East Berlin communicated with Moscow. MI6 then tapped into these lines. The tunnel functioned for a year before it was found by East German repair men. The intelligence gathered was mainly about the disposition of Soviet army units. Had the Soviets planned an invasion of the West, the tap might have provided a warning.

In later years, it emerged that the KGB spy George Blake (see p. 159) had warned his controllers about the tunnelling operation. However, since the controllers were unaware that the CIA could decipher the coded messages, they did not inform the GRU.

THE BERLIN WALL
On 13 August 1961, the East German police began constructing a fence between East and West Berlin. This grew into a 99 km (62 mile) concrete structure, fortified by watchtowers and minefields. Roads were allowed through the wall, controlled by army checkpoints. On 27 October 1961, at the American Checkpoint Charlie, a confrontation took place over Soviet attempts to deny American representatives access to the Eastern zone. For 16 hours American and Soviet tanks faced each other across no man's land, until the representatives were finally allowed through.

Lipstick pistol
This KGB 4.5 mm single-shot firing device was found in the purse of an East German spy arrested in West Berlin.

US security agencies

AFTER WORLD WAR II, the United States established a number of new organizations to meet the Cold War intelligence threat. The main three, the Central Intelligence Agency (CIA), the National Security Agency (NSA), and the Defence Intelligence Agency (DIA – see p. 56) were concerned with collecting and analysing foreign intelligence. A fourth key organization, the Federal Bureau of Investigation (FBI), was already in charge of counterintelligence within the United States. Only one other country had a larger security system than America – the Soviet Union (see p. 38). But in intelligence-collection systems the United States had the edge.

CIA CREST

Apart from these major American security organizations, there are also many other agencies of the United States government that are responsible for aspects of security. While some are often in the public eye, others operate in the closest possible secrecy.

FEDERAL BUREAU OF INVESTIGATION

Established in 1909 as part of the US Department of Justice, the FBI became a national agency in 1934. Since 1939, it has been the primary organization responsible for the various aspects of domestic counterintelligence: it is charged with detecting and neutralizing all espionage, sabotage, and other clandestine activities being carried out within the United States by hostile foreign intelligence services. The Washington Metropolitan Field Office of the Bureau has been involved in resolving a number of major spy cases, including the very damaging Walker case (see p. 54). The FBI works closely with the CIA, which is responsible for counterintelligence overseas. The CIA has no powers of arrest, and cooperates with the FBI to deal with traitors and spies within CIA ranks. Since the arrest in 1994 of KGB mole Aldrich Ames in the CIA, this relationship has become even closer; the CIA Counterintelligence Center is headed by an FBI agent.

CENTRAL INTELLIGENCE AGENCY

Created under the National Security Act of 1947, and based on a concept formulated in 1944, the CIA is made up of several directorates. The Directorate for Operations is responsible for the clandestine collection of all foreign intelligence, and for counterintelligence outside the United States. Analysis of intelligence and the production of finished reports are carried out by the

J. Edgar Hoover
Hoover (1895–1972) directed counterintelligence during World War II, and tried in vain to bring foreign intelligence-gathering under FBI control.

FBI emblem
This is an emblem from the FBI headquarters in Washington, DC. The FBI is part of the US Department of Justice.

Allen Welsh Dulles
An OSS veteran and Director of the CIA from 1953–61, Dulles (1893–1969) ran covert operations in Iran and Central America, as well as the disastrous Bay of Pigs operation in Cuba.

Directorate for Intelligence. Sections of the Directorate for Administration include the Office of Security, which is responsible for personnel and for the physical security of the CIA. There is also a Directorate for Science and Technology, comprised of various offices. (The Office of Technical Services is described on p. 83.) The Office of SIGINT Operations assists the NSA in gathering signals intelligence (see below). The National Photographic Interpretation Center provides the United States intelligence community with analysis of overhead reconnaissance photographs, which may be taken either from satellites or from aircraft. Another office of this directorate is the Foreign Broadcast Information Service (FBIS),

NSA CREST

which monitors radio broadcasts and television stations around the world and produces transcripts of broadcasts, some of which are available to the media and the public.

NATIONAL SECURITY AGENCY

The NSA was established in 1952 and has three main areas of activity. The first is information security, which means the protection of all national security systems and information, including computer systems. The second is the collection of foreign signals intelligence (often called SIGINT). Third, the NSA is the main organization in the United States for creating codes and ciphers for use by national intelligence agencies and the military. It also attempts to break the codes and ciphers of foreign powers.

AIR AMERICA

Air America was an outwardly normal American commercial airline that was covertly operated by the CIA to support its operations throughout southeast Asia. It evolved from a little-known organization, Civil Air Transport (CAT), which had been formed in China in 1946 to support American covert operations. At its peak during the Vietnam War (1961–75), Air America operated the world's largest commercial fleet of aircraft. Its pilots were often ex-military personnel, attracted by generous wages. They flew a variety of aircraft in support of CIA operations, sometimes (in great secrecy) carrying agents across national borders. One group, using U-2 and SR-71 jets, flew secret reconnaissance missions from Thailand. Air America was sold after the war and operates simply as a small-scale air charter company.

BADGE WORN BY AIR AMERICA PILOTS

Air America in action
At the end of the Vietnam War in 1975, the southern capital, Saigon, finally fell to North Vietnamese forces. Here, some South Vietnamese intelligence officers are being evacuated by an Air America helicopter from the residence of the CIA Deputy Chief of Station in Saigon.

Codename Anna

ANNA WAS THE CODENAME given to the Czech spy Alfred Frenzel. A member of the Czech Communist Party in the 1930s, Frenzel went to England as an agent of the Czech government in exile when Germany invaded Czechoslovakia in World War II. At the end of the war, Europe was divided into a "democratic" West and an eastern bloc of countries dominated by the Soviet Union. Frenzel emigrated to the newly created state of West Germany, where he eventually became a member of parliament.

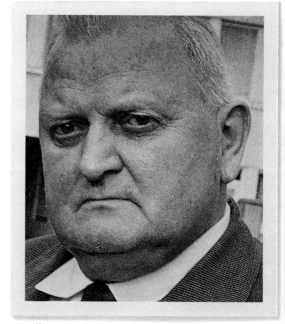

Intelligence coup
Alfred Frenzel (1899–1968) became Czechoslovakia's most important spy in West Germany during the late 1950s, operating under the codename Anna.

Czechoslovakia, in the meantime, became a communist state. The new state intelligence service (Statni tajna Bezpecnost or StB), examined the files of the pre-war military intelligence and political police, and found information on Frenzel's past activities.

In West Germany, Frenzel had now been appointed to the parliamentary defence committee, which was responsible for the re-establishment of the West German armed forces, and for their future role in NATO.

The StB investigators saw that Frenzel's position could be exploited and sent his file to the head of StB's First Directorate, known as I Sprava. This body was in charge (under the control of the Soviet KGB) of foreign intelligence-gathering. I Sprava decided to recruit Frenzel as a spy and assigned the task to StB Major Bohumil Molnar in Vienna.

RECRUITING THE SPY

In April 1956, Frenzel was visited by an old friend who had become an employee of the Czech government. He offered Frenzel a job working for the Czech government, and threatened to expose Frenzel's past political and criminal record if he refused. In addition, he made certain threats regarding the safety of Frenzel's wife, who was visiting Prague at the time. Forced to agree, Frenzel travelled to Vienna for a meeting at which he received 1,500 West German marks and was given

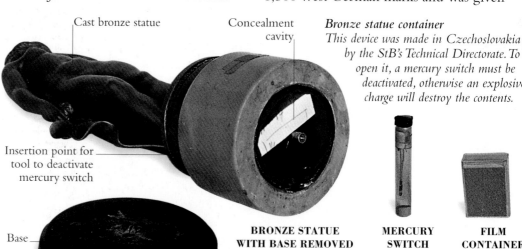

Cast bronze statue

Concealment cavity

Bronze statue container
This device was made in Czechoslovakia by the StB's Technical Directorate. To open it, a mercury switch must be deactivated, otherwise an explosive charge will destroy the contents.

Insertion point for tool to deactivate mercury switch

Base

BRONZE STATUE

BRONZE STATUE WITH BASE REMOVED

MERCURY SWITCH

FILM CONTAINER

Battery film container
This battery could power a torch, but could also be used to hide film. If the battery container was not opened correctly, the film was destroyed by acid.

the codename Anna. In July he put his signature on a document that showed that he had links with the StB. Having signed this, Frenzel was now trapped: the Czechs could blackmail him if he did not spy for them.

Frenzel began to pass information to his handlers, including a copy of the entire West German defence budget. In return, he was promised a large salary, to be paid into a Czech bank account, and a villa and car in Czechoslovakia should he eventually choose to defect. Frenzel also received money for each batch of information he provided. Subsequent batches included West German Air Force plans, and details of new American and and German aircraft and missiles. In September 1959, control of Anna was passed to a new StB officer operating as

an illegal (see p. 169) under the assumed name of Franz Altman. For transporting secret information, Altman used a range of containers that had been disguised as everyday objects by the StB's Technical Directorate, known as IX Sprava. The containers were designed in such a way that their contents would be destroyed if tampered with.

THE UNMASKING OF ANNA

Altman's method was to pass his disguised containers to Czech diplomatic couriers, who would carry them, with all Frenzel's information, out of West Germany. In October 1960, the West German

counterintelligence service, the BfV, started to watch Altman after the tax authorities became suspicious of him. This led to the discovery of his role as a spy. Altman was arrested while trying to leave the country with six rolls of film in a fake baby powder tin. The tin had to be disarmed before opening (see below).

When developed, the film revealed papers that were traced back to Frenzel, who had photographed them with his registration numbers visible. He was arrested and given a 15-year sentence, but was exchanged for four West German spies in a swap five years later. He died in Czechoslovakia in 1968.

Film container in a baby powder tin
An internal electrical circuit had to be turned off before this container could be opened, otherwise it fired a flash bulb, which would ruin the film.

Bohumil Molnar

Bohumil Molnar was a major in the First Directorate of the Czech state secret security, StB. He was entrusted with the recruitment of Anna and the supervision of his activities. For five years, this operation produced large quantities of intelligence information for the StB and the KGB. The StB's penetration of the West German government was a major coup. Molnar's reward was promotion to deputy director of the StB.

Straightened paper clip inserted to deactivate the device

Container for powder surrounded by protective wax paper

Switch

Battery

Flash bulb

Film holder

Switch

DEVICE INSIDE TIN

BABY POWDER TIN

House of spies

NUMBER 45 CRANLEY DRIVE, a small bungalow in the west London suburb of Ruislip, provided the technical support for a Soviet spy network. The head of the network was Konon Trifimovich Molody, alias Gordon Lonsdale. As a KGB "illegal" officer without embassy protection, Lonsdale reported direct to Moscow and operated under a legend (see p. 162). He arrived in London in 1955 and, using KGB funds, set up a slot-machine leasing company which was so successful (as he later claimed) that it generated a profit for the KGB. For six years, Lonsdale lived the life of a well-to-do businessman and surrounded himself with beautiful women.

45 Cranley Drive, Ruislip
This unremarkable bungalow, in a residential London suburb, was the Krogers' home and base for Lonsdale's communications with Moscow.

At the same time, Lonsdale ran a network of agents in Britain. He did not recruit agents himself but used those who had already been recruited. The Cohens, for example, had been active as Soviet agents in New York. Houghton had been recruited by Polish intelligence.

THE KROGERS

The couple who lived apparently normal lives at 45 Cranley Drive were Lona and Morris Cohen, operating under the alias of Helen and Peter Kroger.

HELEN AND PETER KROGER

KGB FIRST CHIEF DIRECTORATE

The KGB was divided into a number of directorates, the most prominent of which were the First Chief Directorate, known as the FCD, and the Second Chief Directorate, which was in charge of domestic security. The FCD was responsible for overseas operations, and had several sub-directorates. Directorate T gathered scientific and technical intelligence. Directorate K infiltrated foreign intelligence services and was in charge of the security of Soviet embassies. Directorate S was the office that ran Soviet illegals (see p. 162) worldwide, including Konon Molody, alias Gordon Lonsdale.

KGB FIRST CHIEF DIRECTORATE EMBLEM

They provided Lonsdale with the technical support he needed to pass on his intelligence information to the KGB headquarters in Moscow. The Krogers ran their own small business as antiquarian book dealers, and this provided them with opportunities to smuggle microdots hidden in the books that they were buying and selling internationally. They sent these books to various addresses abroad, from which they were then forwarded to the Soviet Union. The Krogers' radio and burst transmitter (see p. 118) were reserved for urgent communications with Moscow.

ETHEL ELIZABETH "BUNTY" GEE   HARRY FREDERICK HOUGHTON

Talcum powder tin concealment
The British security services MI5 and Special Branch found this concealment after searching the Krogers' bungalow. Inside the tin of talcum powder were hidden radio communication schedules recorded on microfilm.

Searching the Krogers' cellar
This trapdoor led to a small cellar beneath the kitchen at 45 Cranley Drive. A search carried out by MI5 personnel revealed the KGB agents' radio and burst transmitter attachment used by the Krogers to send urgent messages to Moscow.

SPY GADGETS

The Krogers' bungalow contained the espionage equipment needed to support Lonsdale's spy network. In a space under the kitchen floor, entered by a hole only just large enough to crawl through, an agent's radio and burst transmitter were kept. Microfilm was hidden in a can of talcum powder, while one-time pads and signal plans were concealed inside a torch battery (see p. 128 for a similar concealment) and a cigarette lighter. A box of face powder held a tiny microdot reader (see p. 131). As well as equipment to make microdots, the Krogers also had false passports and thousands of dollars.

BETRAYAL OF THE RING

The Lonsdale spy network was finally broken when the British security service MI5 (see p. 164) received information from a Polish defector. MI5 placed the so-called Portland spies under watch, and this led them to Lonsdale and subsequently to the Krogers.

The Portland spies were Harry Houghton, a clerk at a weapons research establishment in Portland in Dorset, and his lover, Ethel Gee, a filing clerk who also had access to secret information. In return for money, these two passed Lonsdale details of NATO plans, naval manoeuvres, and a new submarine-detection system. On 7 January 1961 Lonsdale was arrested as he received a package of information from Houghton and Gee, who were also arrested soon afterwards.

At his trial, Molody refused to reveal his identity. His legend as Lonsdale, prepared by the First Directorate of the KGB, was flawless except for one detail. The real Lonsdale had been circumcised at birth, whereas Molody had not.

Molody and the Krogers were jailed, but Molody was freed in a spy swap in 1964. Houghton and Gee were given 15-year sentences. They were married after their release. Molody had probably controlled other spies, but their number and identities are not known.

SPY PROFILE   Konon Molody

Born in Canada, Konon Molody (1924–70) was brought up in America. In 1938 he went to the Soviet Union and joined the NKVD (see p.27). Molody went to Britain in 1955 after adopting the identity of Gordon Lonsdale, a dead Canadian. He became a highly successful businessman, a cover for his espionage activities. Lonsdale is believed to have controlled many agents, but only four of them were arrested.

U-2 spy aircraft

CONVENTIONAL INTELLIGENCE-GATHERING by the Americans in the early 1950s had failed to provide effective monitoring of the growing Soviet nuclear capability. The first Soviet nuclear bomb had been tested in 1953, and Moscow was building jet bombers that were believed to be capable of attacking America. Aerial photographs providing clear information about the new Soviet military threat were urgently needed, and in late 1954 the CIA commissioned the design and construction of an advanced spy aircraft that could be used to obtain them.

Krushchev inspects U-2 wreckage
Soviet Premier Krushchev (in light suit) examines equipment salvaged from the wreckage of Powers' aircraft after it crashed in Soviet territory.

The new spy aircraft, the U-2, was designed to photograph Soviet military installations from a very high altitude. Operating at over 24,000 m (80,000 ft), the U-2 was immune from attack by all the Soviet interceptors and anti-aircraft missiles of the early 1960s. The U-2 Hycon Model 73C camera that was carried in U-2s was capable of recording details as small as 30 cm (12 in) across, and the 73B Pan Camera, also carried by U-2s, could take more than 4,000 pictures in the course of a single mission. The aircraft looked much like a motorized glider. It had a wingspan of 23.5 m (79 ft), and was powered by a single engine. Operating at high altitudes where there was little oxygen, the U-2 risked engine failure through lack of oxygen, known as a "flame-out". To relight the engine, the pilot would have to glide down to an altitude where there was more oxygen.

OPERATION OVERFLIGHT

The first U-2 unit to be formed was the 1st Weather Reconnaissance Squadron (Provisional). By 1960, ten U-2s were operational, all under the cover of an organization called the National Advisory Committee for Aeronautics, which was supposedly engaged in meteorological research. The U-2 missions were codenamed Operation Overflight and flew from bases in the United Kingdom, Turkey, and Japan. Although the Soviet Union knew of the violations of its airspace, it was unwilling to admit publicly that its fighter aircraft and anti-aircraft missiles were incapable of stopping them. Once the U-2 reconnaisance had established that the Soviet bomber threat was imaginary, attention was switched

Francis Gary Powers
CIA pilot Francis Gary Powers is shown here in captivity, shortly after his U-2 spy aircraft was shot down over Soviet territory.

A crashed U-2
Russian citizens examine the wreckage of Francis Gary Powers' U-2 after its crash near Sverdlovsk, 1,120 km (700 miles) east of Moscow in the Ural Mountains.

U-2 in Moscow
The wreck of Powers' U-2 was put on public display to embarrass the Americans. Here, residents of Moscow inspect the wreckage.

to the Soviet Union's nuclear missile programme. Information on this was needed by US President Eisenhower before attending the Paris Summit with Soviet Premier Krushchev. Eisenhower consulted the CIA director, Allen Dulles, who assured him there was no chance of a U-2 pilot being captured alive. On 1 May 1960, confident that neither the U-2 nor the pilot would fall into Soviet hands, Eisenhower authorized a flight over the Soviet inter-continental ballistic missile test centre at Tyuratam.

POWERS CRASHES
The mission was flown by CIA pilot Francis Gary Powers. Powers took off from Peshawar in northern Pakistan, intending to fly over the missile test sites, as well as over other military and industrial areas, and land in Norway. Near the Soviet city of Sverdlovsk, his U-2 suffered an engine flame-out that forced him to descend to an altitude low

enough for him to relight his engine. This brought the aircraft within range of a newly developed type of Soviet anti-aircraft missile, the SA-2.

One of the missiles fired went off close to the aircraft, causing the fragile wing of the U-2 to buckle and sending the aircraft into a spin. Powers was thrown from the aircraft before he could set its self-destruct mechanism. He parachuted to safety and the U-2 crashed. However, the aircraft's systems remained intact and were available for the Soviets to inspect. Believing that the U-2 and its pilot had been destroyed, the US government announced that

U-2 spy aircraft
Powered by a single jet engine, the U-2 had a wingspan of 23.5 m (79 ft), optimizing its performance at extreme altitudes.

an aircraft on a weather reconnaissance mission had been lost after it had strayed into Soviet airspace. Krushchev then revealed that Powers was in Soviet hands and had admitted aerial espionage, catching the Americans in a very embarrassing lie. The Paris Summit ended in disarray, to the Soviet Union's political advantage. Powers was found guilty of espionage at a Moscow trial; he was later exchanged for a KGB spy in American hands (see p. 164).

U-2S AND THE CUBAN MISSILE CRISIS

During the early 1960s, the CIA focused on gathering intelligence from Cuba because it had a communist government that was on friendly terms with the Soviet Union. On 14 October 1962, a U-2 spy aircraft photographed evidence of the installation of Soviet missiles near Havana, the Cuban capital. The missiles appeared to be medium-range nuclear SS-4s, easily capable of reaching the United States. On 22 October President Kennedy announced a maritime quarantine of Cuba, to prevent additional stockpiling of the missiles. Tension between the United States and the Soviet Union escalated, reaching a peak on 27 October, when a U-2 flying over Cuba was shot down. There was the prospect of war. However, on 28 October the Soviet Union announced that it would withdraw the missiles. U-2 missions were later flown to verify this withdrawal.

Airfield in Cuba with 21 Soviet bombers

Closer shot confirms identity of bombers

Soviet bombers in Cuba
U-2 pictures proved that not only missiles, but Soviet Il-28 nuclear bombers were present in Cuba, well within range of the United States.

Walker spy ring

THE KGB'S MOST IMPORTANT SPY in America in the 1970s was John Anthony Walker, Jr. He was a chief warrant officer in the US Navy who had access to naval secrets, and decided to become a spy because he needed money after a series of business failures. Walker made his first contact with the KGB in early 1968 by asking to see "someone from security" at the Soviet embassy in Washington, DC. He had calculated correctly – the Soviets were willing to reward him, as they did in similar cases, with cash payments.

Walker's Minox camera
In the course of his long career as a spy, Walker photographed so many secret documents that his Minox C camera wore out.

John Walker
As part of his cover, Walker espoused a variety of anti-communist political causes and joined fringe groups such as the Ku Klux Klan (KKK).

Walker took with him a month's key settings for the KL-47 cipher machine used at the US Navy's command centre for Atlantic submarine forces, where he worked. Announcing that he had easy access to such settings, Walker demanded $1,000 per week. He was given some cash in advance and, at a later meeting, received $5,000 in return for a series of cipher key settings' cards. Walker was also given a Minox camera (see p. 70) to copy secret documents and cipher material.

DEALINGS WITH THE KGB

During the next 17 years, Walker gave the KGB more cipher key cards as well as various technical manuals. These items enabled the Soviets to obtain important naval secrets, including the movements of the American nuclear submarine fleet. Besides this, the Soviets gained advance knowledge of American bombing raids on North Vietnam in the early 1970s.

The KGB gave Walker a rotor reader with which to analyse the inner wiring of US Navy cipher machine rotors. They also trained him in espionage tradecraft at a series of secret meetings in Austria. In America, Walker seldom met his KGB handler personally, but used a series of dead drops (see p. 132) to pass over information and receive payment.

FAMILY AND FRIENDS

When Walker saw his access to secret material ending because of his imminent retirement from the navy, he drew his family into the spy ring. He recruited his brother Arthur and his son Michael, who was serving in the navy. John Walker also recruited his friend Jerry Whitworth, a navy communications specialist.

ROTOR READER

Walker was given this device by the KGB to trace the internal wiring of the rotors used in the US Navy's KL-47 cipher machine. Walker removed the rotors from the KL-47 and placed them over the disc of the rotor reader. Contacts inside the disc sent signals through the rotor reader's internal circuitry to light up numbers on a display board. Walker was taught how to interpret these numbers so as to work out the internal wiring of the cipher rotors.

The KGB already had lists of the key settings of the KL-47, as these had been stolen by Walker. Knowledge of both the key settings and the internal rotor wiring enabled the KGB to decipher some of the US Navy's radio messages.

KL-47 ROTOR MOUNTED ON READER

X-RAY OF READER SHOWING WIRING

THE VIENNA PROCEDURE

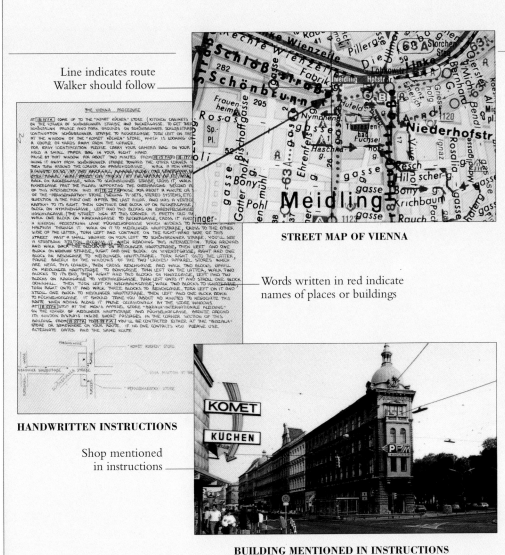

Line indicates route Walker should follow

STREET MAP OF VIENNA

HANDWRITTEN INSTRUCTIONS

Words written in red indicate names of places or buildings

Shop mentioned in instructions

BUILDING MENTIONED IN INSTRUCTIONS

Once Walker was established as an agent, the KGB avoided direct meetings with him in America for security reasons. Instead he was instructed to travel abroad, usually to Vienna (or sometimes to Hong Kong), for training, instructions, and payment from his KGB case officer.

Vienna was often used for such purposes by the KGB, because of both its status as an international city and the neutrality of its counterintelligence service. To direct him to his meetings, Walker was given maps and written instructions. Complex routes were used to give the KGB time and opportunity to detect whether Walker was under surveillance.

Along his route he was watched by KGB agents with body-worn surveillance radios (see p. 106). All likely frequencies were monitored for signs of any unusual activity by Austrian counterintelligence or the CIA, which operated from the American embassy. If any of the KGB agents involved noticed anything suspicious, the meeting would be aborted. Walker was given back-up instructions for an alternative meeting in case this happened.

The instructions and map shown here were used on a trip Walker made to Vienna in 1978. It is known that during the course of a 40-minute meeting with his handler he received money and instructions, and handed over cryptographic secrets stolen by his accomplice Jerry Whitworth.

Walker's wife knew for many years that he was a spy, but she kept silent. After the couple divorced, she eventually did inform the FBI. One evening in 1985, FBI personnel followed John Walker to a dead drop site outside Washington, where Walker left a package of secret material obtained from his son.

The FBI intercepted this material, missed a chance to pick up the KGB handler, and arrested Walker later that evening at a nearby hotel.

John Walker was sentenced to life imprisonment; his accomplices also received prison terms. What the ring's activities had cost America in terms of security remains beyond calculation.

MICHAEL WALKER: CODENAME S – ON ACTIVE SERVICE IN THE US NAVY

JERRY WHITWORTH: CODENAME D – NAVY COMMUNICATIONS EXPERT

ARTHUR WALKER: CODENAME K – ELDER BROTHER OF JOHN WALKER

Spying from space

THE LAUNCH OF THE FIRST man-made satellite, by the Soviet Union in 1957, opened up new opportunities for intelligence-gathering. A camera on a satellite could carry out surveillance of any part of enemy territory that lay beneath its orbit. The first spy satellite was launched by the Americans in 1961. For 15 years, pictures from a satellite took longer to reach the analyst than those from a spy plane, although, of course, they could cover a far greater area. All this changed in the 1970s, when digital technology made pictures immediately available.

American satellite image
KH-11 satellite image of a Soviet aircraft carrier under construction. A US naval intelligence analyst was jailed for releasing this image.

The early satellites had to jettison their film in a container to be retrieved and flown to a processing point, often over long distances. This process was known as "bucket dropping" and was so slow that the Arab-Israeli Six-Day War of 1967 was over before the first satellite photographs of it reached Washington. Satellites were for strategic (long-term) surveillance, while tactical (day-to-day) observation was done by spy planes.

THE KH-11

The Americans initiated a top secret programme to produce better satellites. The result, the KH-11 satellite, became operational in 1976. It was different from earlier models in that it carried no film. Instead, it beamed its images in digital form to ground stations as soon as they were taken. As well as making pictures rapidly available for analysis, this system has other advantages. The digital images are capable of extremely high definition. From its orbit 322 km (200 miles) above the Earth, the KH-11 could resolve detail as small as 15 cm (6 in) across. Images of this sort can be enhanced even further by computer manipulation. At America's National Photographic Interpretation Center, a library of visual

THE US NATIONAL RECONNAISSANCE OFFICE (NRO)

This office was officially declassified as a secret organization in 1992. It was formed in the early 1960s to manage the US Photographic and Electronic Listening Satellites Program and the US Airborne Reconnaissance Program. Its powerful computers were used in the Gulf War (1990–91) to identify Iraqi weapons systems from photographs.

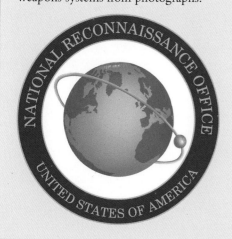

The Rhyolite satellite
This American telecommunications interception satellite was advanced for its time, the middle 1970s. It targeted the Soviet Union and China, eavesdropping on secret communications traffic and providing intelligence on ballistic missile tests. The 680 kg (1,500 lb) satellite had a large antenna dish, which was capable of picking up "leaked" transmissions from Earth over 35,000 km (22,000 miles) away. These were then relayed back down to a ground station for analysis.

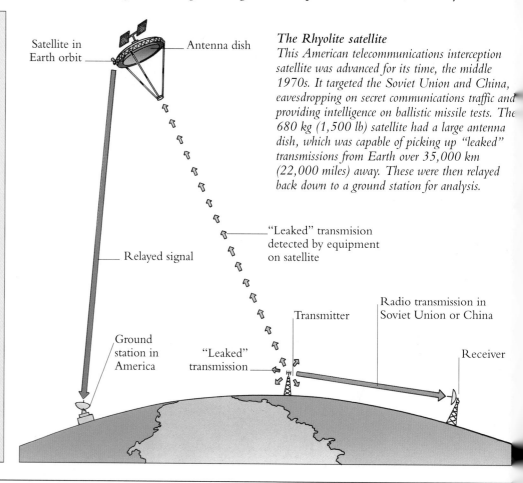

Satellite in Earth orbit — Antenna dish

Relayed signal

"Leaked" transmission detected by equipment on satellite

Radio transmission in Soviet Union or China

Ground station in America

"Leaked" transmission

Transmitter

Receiver

Soviet satellite image
The CIA obtained this Soviet satellite image of Washington, DC and their own headquarters; it was later displayed in an agency internal poster.

interpretation keys is maintained. An intelligence analyst can check a satellite image against the visual keys in order to recognize a major weapons system.

A satellite codenamed Lacrosse was launched in 1988, using radar to "see" through clouds. It was joined in 1989 by an infrared version, giving night vision. With these capabilities, satellites have continued to be the chief means of monitoring Strategic Arms Limitation Treaties between the United States and the Soviet Union (and now Russia).

SATELLITE SPIES
Inevitably, satellite technology became the target of espionage, and its secrets have to be closely guarded. American agencies do not release their satellite images for public use until the pictures have been modified in such a way as not to reveal too much of the technology involved.

A major spy scandal did, however, occur in America in 1977, which showed that security in some satellite companies was not tight enough. The scandal concerned a pair of self-taught and somewhat amateurish, though mercenary, spies: Christopher Boyce and his childhood friend Andrew Lee.

Through the influence of his ex-FBI father, Boyce had obtained a job with TRW, the company that produced and operated the Rhyolite satellite for the CIA. The Rhyolite was a spy satellite that monitored Soviet and Chinese secret telecommunications.

Boyce's job was in a top-secret office, known as the Black Vault, where he helped to coordinate communications between TRW, the national intelligence agencies, and the satellite monitoring stations. Security in the Black Vault was so lax that Boyce found he had easy access to classified material.

Lee's role was to make contact with the KGB. He would travel to Mexico City, and sometimes as far as Vienna, to sell the information to the Soviets.

Christopher Boyce

Christopher Boyce (b.1953) took a job with the American satellite company TRW and used it to obtain information about America's satellites. The information he and Lee sold to the KGB alerted the Soviet Union to the vulnerability of its military communications to eavesdropping by American satellites. Arrested in 1977, Boyce was sentenced to 40 years, escaped, and received 20 more years on recapture.

The material he sold concerned, among other things, the Rhyolite programme, the KH-11 satellite, and various ciphers.

The pair were brought to trial after Lee was arrested by the Mexican police for suspicious activity outside the Soviet embassy. He was carrying a pocketful of satellite secrets on strips of Minox film.

Andrew Daulton Lee

Andrew Lee (b.1952) is a documented example of a spy whose motive was to find money to pay for his drug habit. In 1975 he began to sell satellite secrets, provided by his friend Christopher Boyce, to the KGB. Lee travelled to Vienna and Mexico City to carry out these transactions. After his arrest in Mexico, he was handed over to the FBI, tried, and sentenced to life imprisonment in the United States.

Camera pod from a spy satellite
A Soviet camera pod lies on the ground in Kazakhstan, after its film has been extracted for processing. Soviet satellites relied on cameras that used conventional film long after the Americans introduced digital transmission.

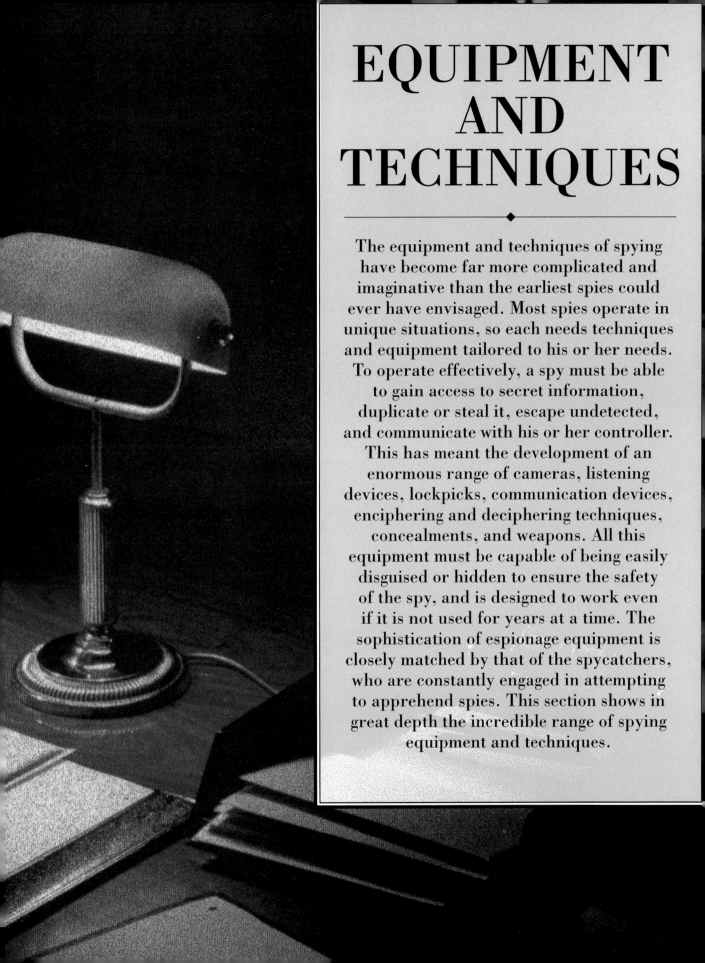

EQUIPMENT AND TECHNIQUES

◆

The equipment and techniques of spying have become far more complicated and imaginative than the earliest spies could ever have envisaged. Most spies operate in unique situations, so each needs techniques and equipment tailored to his or her needs. To operate effectively, a spy must be able to gain access to secret information, duplicate or steal it, escape undetected, and communicate with his or her controller. This has meant the development of an enormous range of cameras, listening devices, lockpicks, communication devices, enciphering and deciphering techniques, concealments, and weapons. All this equipment must be capable of being easily disguised or hidden to ensure the safety of the spy, and is designed to work even if it is not used for years at a time. The sophistication of espionage equipment is closely matched by that of the spycatchers, who are constantly engaged in attempting to apprehend spies. This section shows in great depth the incredible range of spying equipment and techniques.

CAMERAS

S INCE ITS INVENTION in the middle of the 19th century, photography has played an increasingly important role in intelligence-gathering. Spies use cameras for taking photographs of people; places such as airfields or other military installations; and objects such as bridges, military equipment, aircraft designs, or documents. To be most effective, a spy may need to avoid taking photographs openly. In these cases, a small, easily concealed camera capable of taking high-quality pictures is needed. The intelligence services use three main types of camera, each suited to a specific requirement.

SUBMINIATURE CAMERAS

These cameras are small enough to carry in the pocket and can be adapted for various uses, among them surveillance photography and document copying. For ease

Miniature cassettes
These modern film cassettes are designed for clandestine cameras. They are shown here at actual size.

of concealment, some subminiature cameras are made without a viewfinder, and must be aimed instinctively. The most famous and successful of the whole class of subminiature cameras is the Minox, which was first made in Latvia in 1938. Although the Minox was not in the first place conceived for use in espionage, its excellent lens, small size, and quality of construction made it eminently suitable. A range of accessories devised for Minox cameras enables them to be used in concealments or for document photography, and the brand has been widely used by intelligence services. Other brands of commercially produced subminiature cameras include the Echo 8 cigarette-lighter camera and the Steineck wristwatch camera, which were both used in the Cold War. During World War II, intelligence services developed their own cameras, notably the matchbox cameras of the French secret service and the OSS (see p. 32).

Photo-surveillance briefcase
A Robot camera is concealed in a briefcase for surveillance use. The camera has to be aimed instinctively – without the use of a viewfinder – while the case is held under the user's arm.

Minox film canister
First produced in 1938, the Minox camera used pre-loaded cassettes of film providing 50 exposures.

CONCEALED CAMERAS

Unobtrusive photography often plays a part in espionage operations. Cameras may be hidden inside an object such as a handbag, or strapped to the body, with the lens hidden behind a fake tiepin or button. With the latter, pictures are taken by means of a remote shutter release hidden in a pocket. Two commonly used concealed cameras were the Soviet F21 and the West German Robot. Both were developed from a pre-World War II German design, and used spring-driven motor winding mechanisms. A wide variety of concealments have been devised by both Soviet and Western intelligence agencies, as well as by the Robot factory itself (see p. 64).

Steineck ABC wristwatch camera
This camera could take six pictures, under the pretence of checking the time.

KGB surveillance camera
Designed to be concealed in the hand, or worn by the spy in a body harness, this camera was operated by pressing the actuating rod.

COPY CAMERAS

A special class of cameras exists for the task of photographing documents. They are often custom-made, but commercial copy cameras are available, with special accessories. A standard camera can be used when necessary, but skill and practice are needed to obtain acceptable images. Most intelligence services issue special copy camera kits, housed in unobtrusive boxes or attaché cases, which can be used by agents who do not have specialized photographic skills. The KGB developed a miniature copy camera the size of a Minox film cassette for smuggling past security checks. Later, the same agency issued a "brush" camera, which is swept across documents like a hand-held photocopier, photographing as it goes.

Czech copy camera
Used for document photography by personnel of the Czech security agency StB, this camera was housed in an anonymous-looking wooden case.

Concealed cameras

SPIES USE CONCEALED CAMERAS for covert photography. The camera may be hidden under a spy's clothing, or disguised as another object. While some subminiature cameras have only one fixed disguise, there

VEHICLE PLATE CONCEALMENT

are concealed cameras that may be disguised in various different ways. For example, the Tessina, Robot (see p. 64), and F21 (see p. 66) each have a special range of concealments. Standard cameras can be used clandestinely if equipped with special attachments like the vehicle nationality plate (left) with one-way glass in the "A" through which pictures can be taken.

MODIFIED LEICA LENS CAP

The word "Leica" has been cut out of this standard camera's lens cap. Pictures can be taken through the cut-out while the lens cap is on and it appears as though the camera is not being used.

Cut-out

MODIFIED LENS CAP

Shutter release button · Lens

STANDARD LEICA CAMERA

TESSINA CAMERA IN CIGARETTE PACKET

The world's smallest motor-driven 35 mm camera, the Swiss Tessina fits in a cigarette packet (this should be a brand recognized in the country where it will be used). An internal frame holds the lens aligned with tiny holes in the packet. The shutter release is pressed through the packet, to take up to 10 pictures before rewinding is necessary.

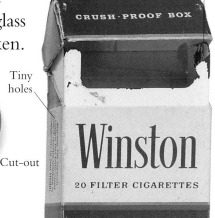

Internal metal frame

Tiny holes

CIGARETTE PACKET CONCEALMENT

Shutter release button
Focusing dial

Lens

Frame counter · Exposure table

TESSINA CAMERA

TESSINA CAMERA CONCEALED IN BOOK

The tiny Tessina camera may alternatively be hidden inside a cut-out section of a book. Pictures can be taken through the side of the book by applying pressure to the cover, and thereby operating a shutter release plate.

Book concealment

Shutter release pressure plate

Opening for lens

TOYKA 58-M NECKTIE CAMERA

This KGB camera was designed to be strapped to a spy's body and take pictures through a special tiepin. There are two identical-looking tiepins, one for use with the camera and a standard one for everyday use. A spy would wear the standard tiepin regularly, so that people would become used to seeing him wearing it. The special tiepin would be worn with the camera when he needed to take pictures. The camera is spring-wound and almost silent.

Remote shutter release

Control unit in pocket

Remote shutter speed adjustment

Cloth harness that straps around chest

Fastening hook for attaching strap

Harness adjustment D-ring

Lens

Mechanism for locking camera to baseplate

Camera shown with baseplate

K-№657514

KGB NECKTIE CAMERA

Remote cable to control unit

Necktie camera in use
The camera is held by an aluminium bracket to a cloth harness, worn under the agent's shirt. The remote cable runs to the agent's trouser pocket.

Camera shown in position

Film take-up adjustment tool

Standard tiepin with transparent stone

Film case

Film slitter

Lens cap

Film cassette

9,5

FILM LOADING EQUIPMENT

TIEPIN

● ● ● ● ● ●	**TECHNICAL DATA**
Negative size	8.5 x 11 mm
Film	9.5 mm Minox cassette format; special film slitter provided for reduction of 35 mm film
Cassette	Standard Minox cassette with 50 exposures
Shutter speeds	1/10, 1/50, 1/50, and 1/400 second
Winder	Spring-wound; 27 exposures in sequence
Dimensions	8.3 x 3 x 1.5 cm (3¼ x 1¼ x ⅝ in)

Robot camera

THE ROBOT CAMERA, dating from 1934, was powered by a spring-driven motor that allowed successive pictures to be taken without the user having to wind on manually. It was used in World War II by the German air force to provide proof of destroyed targets, and by the German intelligence service (see p. 34). In the early years of the Cold War, spies in both the communist bloc and in the West used it because, with no need for hand winding between photographs, it could be used in a variety of concealments.

(see p. 34)

	TECHNICAL DATA
Date	1969
Lens	Xenon 40 mm f1.9
Negative size	24 x 24 mm
Film	Standard 35 mm or special film, depending on application; 50 exposures
Shutter	Rotating shutter, ¼ to ⅟₅₀₀ second plus B
Motor	Double spring-wound
Options	Special silent, slow-winding model available from factory

ROBOT STAR 50 CAMERA

The Star 50 was the last Robot model to evolve from the World War II design. It could take 50 pictures and the short focal length of its lens meant good depth of field, with sharp pictures.

Shutter release button

Viewfinder (not used in covert operations)

ROBOT STAR 50

Lens

Shutter speed dial

HANDBAG CONCEALMENT KIT

The Robot factory owners were aware of the different intelligence applications of its range of cameras, and made kits that enabled them to be installed in a variety of concealments. This kit allows the user to hide a Robot Star 50 inside a handbag. The hidden camera takes the photographs through a decorative metal ornament, of which a wide selection was available from the manufacturer.

Remote shutter release, placed out of sight

Cable

Attachment holding camera lens to bag

Solenoid

Metal ornament hides the opening for the camera's lens

Internal frame

Battery

Remote shutter release

Solenoid switch for remote operation of shutter

Internal frame to hold camera inside bag

Battery to power solenoid

METAL ORNAMENTS

Handbag concealment
The Robot concealment kit could be fitted to a variety of bags. Care was taken to select a type of bag that was commonly carried in the intended country of use and that was also strong enough to support the camera.

PHOTO-SURVEILLANCE BRIEFCASE

This briefcase, with its concealed camera, was used during the 1950s and 1960s for photo-surveillance operations by the United States intelligence services. Intelligence officers would carry the briefcase under one arm and take photographs at right angles to the way they were facing. As the viewfinder could not be used, a great deal of practice was needed to take accurately framed photographs. The officer had to learn instinctively how to position the briefcase correctly in order to photograph the desired subject. The camera is operated by pressing the shutter release lever through the briefcase.

Lever squeezed through the case to take photograph

Cable release

Robot Star II camera

Standard latch

Camera lens takes photograph through latch

In 1968 Philip Agee, a CIA officer, resigned. In a book published in 1975, he exposed details of every CIA officer and operation that he had ever encountered during his 12-year career. Agee denied cooperating with any hostile agencies, but former KGB officers revealed he had worked with the KGB. Under surveillance after resigning, Agee was secretly photographed by means of a Robot camera hidden in a briefcase.

WAIST-BELT SURVEILLANCE CAMERA

A waist-belt concealment lets a Robot camera take photographs through a false button. It was intended for the unobtrusive surveillance of people. Spare buttons were provided, so that all the buttons on the user's coat could be replaced and would match the false one.

False button mounted in front of the camera lens

Front piece of belt hides camera

Hole over camera lens

Belt strap

Hook

Hook hole

Robot Star II camera

Back piece of belt supports camera

Cable release

False button

Surveillance camera in position
When the Robot camera is worn on a waist belt hidden under a coat, it is virtually impossible to detect.

F21 concealed camera

BELT BUCKLE CONCEALMENT

THE SMALL, LIGHTWEIGHT F21 camera was adapted from the German Robot camera (see p. 66) in 1948 by the KGB. The F21 was used for surveillance photography; it could take several pictures in quick succession with a spring-driven winder, and it had many concealments, so spies could use the camera in a wide variety of different situations. A version of the F21, the Zenit Model MF1, has been sold commercially without concealments since the end of the Cold War.

Lens aperture adjustment lever

Remote shutter release

POCKET REMOTE CONTROL UNIT FOR F21

Cable to concealed camera

F21 CAMERA AND ACCESSORIES

The F21, with lenses, accessories, and concealments, makes a versatile kit for clandestine photography. Its small size (it is shown here full size) and quietness make it unobtrusive. Because it has no viewfinder, it must be aimed instinctively.

ALTERNATIVE FACEPLATE AND LENS FOR CAMERA

Winder

Frame and film counter adjustment

Shutter release

N°72749

Lens

F21 CAMERA

```
• • • • • •   TECHNICAL DATA
         Lens   28 mm f2.8
Focusing range   3 m (10 ft) to infinity
Negative size    18 × 24 mm
         Film    Standard issue, 21 mm
     Cassette    14–100 frames, depending
                 on thickness of film
Shutter speeds   1/10, 1/30, 1/100 second
  Dimensions     77 × 41 × 55 mm
                 (3 × 1⅝ × 2⅛ in)
       Weight    180 g (6⅜ oz)
Temperature range −20 °C to 55 °C
                 (−4 °F to 131 °F)
```

Special F21 camera

Winder

Shutter release

N°72652

Lens

Wooden block

F21 UMBRELLA CONCEALMENT (INTERIOR)

JACKET CONCEALMENT

The jacket shown here is one of many styles used with the F21 by Soviet intelligence services. A faceplate attached to the F21 carries a false button that covers the lens. The camera is suspended inside the lining, while the false button protrudes through a hole in the front of the jacket. When the remote shutter release – held in a pocket – is gently squeezed, the centre of the false button opens briefly to allow a photograph to be taken.

POSITION OF F21 CONCEALMENT

False button protrudes here

Attachment for suspension harness

Faceplate

Faceplate locking lever

False button

F21 CAMERA WITH FALSE BUTTON FACEPLATE

Facing adapts button for use on a different jacket

NORMAL BUTTON

ALTERNATIVE FACING FOR FALSE BUTTON

INSIDE VIEW OF F21 CONCEALMENT

CAMERA CASE CONCEALMENT

A spy would wear this camera case around the neck as though the camera was not being used. But inside, an F21 was mounted sideways to take pictures at right angles to the front of the case. As the spy pressed a button, a flap opened and a picture was taken.

Strap

Location of flap

Metal frame

Pulley operating flap

Location of shutter release button

F21 camera mounted sideways

35mm camera case

UMBRELLA CONCEALMENT

It was possible for a spy to take pictures through a tiny hole in an inconspicuous object such as an ordinary telescopic umbrella without attracting any attention. The F21 camera was mounted in a shaped wooden frame that fitted inside the umbrella, with the camera lens aligned with a hole in the umbrella cover. A spy would carry the umbrella in his hand and take a photograph by pressing the shutter release through the umbrella fabric.

Strap

Prongs position camera to align with lens opening

Opening in umbrella fabric for lens

F21 UMBRELLA CONCEALMENT (EXTERIOR)

Subminiature cameras

SUBMINIATURE CAMERAS are a class of pocket-sized cameras that use small film sizes, often 16 mm or 9.5 mm. They are useful for gathering photographic intelligence, and many are built into an outer casing that disguises the camera as a different object. To ensure that the disguise is effective, certain features of normal cameras, like the viewfinder, may be omitted. Spies may need a considerable amount of training to use subminiature cameras, because pictures have to be taken surreptitiously, and often under very difficult circumstances. Intelligence agencies sometimes have subminiature cameras specially made for their own use. On other occasions they use models that are available commercially and are suitable for espionage photography.

WORLD WAR II FRENCH MATCHBOX CAMERA

WRISTWATCH CAMERA

The Steineck ABC camera was made to resemble a wristwatch. It uses a circular piece of film with six exposures. Pictures can be taken while pretending to check the time.

Len

Shutter release

Right-angle viewfinder

Aperture setting control with bright (yellow) and dim (blue) light settings

Wrist strap

CIGARETTE LIGHTER CAMERA

Designed in Japan in 1951, the Echo 8 cigarette lighter camera was once the smallest commercially available camera in the world. It was housed inside a working cigarette lighter. This concealment made it ideal for use in social or business settings, where a cigarette lighter would not attract attention. To use the camera, the spy just needed to flip up the top and light a cigarette while aiming the camera at the subject.

16 mm film is slit in half to 8 mm

Lid

FILM SLITTER

Viewing port

Aperture setting scale

Aperture setting knob

Exposure setting lever

CIGARETTE LIGHTER CAMERA

How the camera was used
This picture is from a contemporary instruction manual. The lens, shown as a dot, has been made more clearly visible for instruction purposes.

CIGARETTE PACKET CAMERA

This is a Soviet Kiev 30 16 mm camera, which is housed inside a metal fake cigarette packet. The film is advanced and the shutter cocked by manipulating one of the fake cigarettes. A real cigarette can be carried in the packet for authenticity.

Lens opening

Shutter release

The House of John Player, Nottingham, England

The House of John Player, Nottingham, England

FAKE CIGARETTE PACKET

Fake cigarette

Internal mounting rail

Kiev 30 camera

Lens

Shutt relea

CONCEALED CAMERA

SURVEILLANCE CAMERA

This KGB surveillance camera was used from the 1950s until the 1970s. It was designed to be aimed instinctively while concealed in the hand. It could also be worn flat against the body in a body harness, enabling photographs to be taken through a fake button or brooch. The shutter is released and the film is advanced when the thumb lever is depressed.

PINHOLE CAMERA

This tiny KGB camera from the 1980s utilizes a 19th-century photographic principle: each one of its four chambers has a pinhole aperture for a lens, making it possible to photograph close-up and distant objects without focusing.

Shutter speed control

Focus scale

Connecting point for body harness

Cast metal casing

Thumb lever

Pinhole aperture

PINHOLE CAMERA

Screw to open pinhole lens

KGB TEST PHOTOGRAPH TAKEN WITH A PINHOLE CAMERA

MATCHBOX CAMERA

The Kodak company developed this 16 mm camera for use by the OSS (see p. 32) during World War II. It was made in the shape of a matchbox and could be camouflaged by adding a matchbox label appropriate for the country in which it was to be used.

Lens opening

Shutter release

Lens opening

Label glued to housing

CAMERA

CAMERA WITH MATCHBOX LABEL

Minox camera

EARLY FILM CASSETTE CASE

THE MINOX SUBMINIATURE CAMERA, in its various models, was for years the world's most widely used spy camera. It was originally manufactured in 1938 in Riga, capital of Latvia, as a commercial camera, but it was soon apparent that the small size, precision, and flexibility of the Minox made it ideal for clandestine photography. It is suitable both for general use and for close-up work, such as taking photographs of documents, and can take 50 pictures without reloading. In models produced since the end of World War II, very high resolution lenses were fitted which, when used with better-quality film, allowed a tremendous amount of detail to be obtained from the tiny negatives. With its many accessories, the Minox could be adapted for a wide range of intelligence uses, and it stayed in widespread use until the end of the Cold War in the early 1990s.

Demonstrating the Minox American KGB spy John Walker (see p. 54), following his arrest, shows how he used his Minox C camera with its measuring chain.

MODEL B MINOX AND ACCESSORIES

Produced from 1958 to 1972, this was the most widely used of all Minox cameras for intelligence purposes. It was the first model to have a built-in light meter. Since it did not need batteries, it could be hidden for long periods before use.

DAYLIGHT DEVELOPING KIT

With Minox's miniature developing tank, spies could process their film in full daylight. The tank is the size of a small drinks can and uses tiny quantities of chemicals, poured in through a light-tight opening.

Light-tight opening for chemicals

Thermometer

Thermometer case

PROCESSING
THERMOMETER

Groove for film

Cassette holder

DAYLIGHT
DEVELOPING TANK

NEGATIVE
VIEWER

RIGA MINOX ENLARGER

Early Minox enlargers were designed to produce small prints from the tiny negatives. Since World War II, improved enlargers have been developed, which make bigger prints from the higher resolution film now available.

Lamp housing

Tray for film negative

Focus adjustment

Control button for lamp

Transformer

Push button to open printing mask

Base for photographic paper

RIGA MINOX CAMERA

The original Minox camera was seen as a marvel of technology when it first became available in 1938. During World War II, the intelligence agencies found it difficult to acquire enough Minox cameras for their espionage activities. In this picture the camera is shown actual size, seen from the top.

Front of viewfinder

Lens

Focusing dial

Shutter speed dial

Frame counter

Stainless steel body

Camera opened to fit film cartridge

Shutter release

●●●●●● TECHNICAL DATA	
Lens	Minastigmat five element
Maximum aperture	f3.5
Focal length	15 mm
Negative size	8.5 × 10 mm
Film	Unperforated 9.5 mm film; 50 exposures
Shutter speeds	½ to 1/1000 second
Focusing range	20 cm (8 in) to infinity
Dimensions	79 × 27 × 15 mm (3⅛ × 1 1/16 × ⅝ in)
Weight	128 g (4½ oz)

THE MINOX INVENTOR

The Latvian engineer Walter Zapp (b.1905) wanted to create a portable camera that would fit easily in the palm of the hand and yet take high-quality, spontaneous pictures. During the 1930s, Zapp developed a mechanism that met these very strict size requirements. In 1938, the first Minox camera was produced in Riga, Latvia. It used film one-quarter the size of standard 35 mm film, with 50 frames loaded in a cassette. Although Zapp had produced the Minox for general photography, it soon became highly sought after by intelligence agencies around the world for use in espionage photography.

Early Minox design team
The 1937 design team that produced the first Riga Minox, with Walter Zapp at the centre.

Copy cameras I

SPIES OFTEN HAVE just a few moments in which to copy secret documents. They may have stolen the documents and need to replace them before the documents are missed, or they may have access to them in an office that is empty only for short periods. Normal cameras can be used for document photography but they require care and time to take good-quality pictures. Intelligence services have developed special portable copy cameras that are quick, easy, and reliable to use. Copy cameras can be either miniaturized or disguised: a fine example of the latter is the KGB rollover camera that is disguised as a notebook (see p. 74).

YELKA C-64 COPY CAMERA

This equipment was designed for the KGB and operates on a wide range of electrical voltages, including that of car batteries. It is simple to use and produces good pictures. The Yelka was built with hinges that enabled it to be folded down when not in use. The whole unit, when folded, fits inside its own base (its copy stand), which is about the size of a large book. The example shown here was used by personnel in East Germany's intelligence agency, the Stasi.

Copy light power cable

Camera support column

Copy camera

Bulk film holder

Bright copy light

Telescopic lamp arm

Lens

Cable release

Red lines coordinate with focus marks on camera lens

Copy table

Power warning light

Optional battery power cable

Whole assembly folds into base unit for storage

On/off switch

• • • • • • **TECHNICAL DATA**	
Lens	Industar 30mm f 5.6 with a 50 degree angle of view
Negative size	18 × 24 mm
Film	35 mm, high resolution b/w or colour, ASA 2 to 100
Cassette	400 frames
Shutter speeds	1, ½, ⅕, ¹⁄₁₀, and ¹⁄₂₀ second, plus B
Voltage	220 or 127 volt AC, 12 volt DC
Lighting lamps	127 volt or 12 volt
Document size	68 × 90 mm, 120 × 160 mm, 180 × 240 mm, 240 × 320 mm
Packed size	75 × 265 × 375 mm (3 × 10⅜ × 14¾ in)
Weight	Less than 5 kg (11 lb)

Das Ministerium für Staatssicherheit

East Germany's State Security Ministry was usually known as the Stasi – short for its official German title (above). In effectiveness, it was second only to the KGB among Soviet bloc intelligence organizations. As well as running a network of agents in West Germany and elsewhere, the Stasi was responsible for monitoring the activities of East Germany's own citizens. After the collapse of East Germany in 1989, the German public was astonished to learn the extent of surveillance that had been going on in their midst.

Stasi lapel badge

Stasi officers watching a public meeting or demonstration wore badges to identify themselves to each other and to informers. This Stasi badge, shown twice real size, has a revolving disc that can display four different identifying colours.

ATTACHE CASE COPY CAMERA

An attaché case forms the concealment for this American copy camera. When the case is opened, the copy lights fold out into position and operate with either mains power or batteries. The modified fixed-focus 35 mm camera uses nylon gears for silent operation. This type of attaché case copy camera has been used by a variety of American intelligence organizations.

Special Pentax camera — Housing for batteries

Cable release

On/off switch

Copy lights

Folding aluminium frame

Copy table

Carrying handle

Power cord

COPY CAMERA KIT

The components of this copy camera kit, designed for the Czech intelligence service (known by its Czech initials StB), could be quickly assembled from the small case in which they were usually carried. Coloured marks on the legs correspond to focus settings on the camera.

Focusing mark

Bulb

Voltage selector

COPY LIGHTS

Film winder — Faceplate

Lens

Power plug

LEGS OF STAND

MEOPTA COPY CAMERA

Compartment for spare bulbs

EMPTY CASE FOR CAMERA KIT

Compartment for metal legs

CAMERA SET UP FOR USE

Camera

Cable release

Faceplate

Lens shroud

Four-legged copy stand

Voltage selector

Copy light

Focusing mark

Copy cameras II

ROLLOVER CAMERA

This KGB rollover or brush camera can copy up to 40 pages before it needs reloading. The camera is concealed in a fake notebook resembling a real one that the spy carries and uses regularly. To use the camera, the spy rolls or brushes the inner spine of the fake notebook over a document. Tiny wheels in the spine of the notebook activate the camera mechanism and its built-in light source.

REAL NOTEBOOK

ROLLOVER CAMERA DISGUISED AS NOTEBOOK

Film slitter
The slitter cuts standard 35 mm film to the correct width for use in the cassette of the rollover camera.

35 mm film

Handle is raised to allow film to be fed into the slitter

FILM SLITTER

Film cassette

Batteries for document lights

Rollers touch the document

Wheel registers film position

Counter

Hinged cover

Rollover photography
The KGB camera being rolled over a document to copy it. The camera can cross the page in any direction.

MECHANISM OF THE ROLLOVER CAMERA

MINIATURE DOCUMENT CAMERA

Shown actual size, this small KGB camera was intended for use in facilities where strict security is maintained. It has no viewfinder and few external controls – just a shutter release and film advance. A film slitter cuts standard 35 mm film down to a width of 9.5 mm for use in a Minox (see p. 70) cassette.

Shutter release

Film advance

Channel for 35 mm film

Location of lens

CAMERA

Film

FILM CASSETTE

FILM SLITTER

Crank to pull film through slitter

Camera

Using the document camera
The camera has a fixed focus, so in order to take clear photographs it must be held as shown, at a specific distance from the document. A constant light should be directed on the document.

SIMPLE COPY SET-UP

IMPROVISED COPY TECHNIQUES

Agents are trained to improvise copy set-ups so that they can obtain good copies even in circumstances in which time or equipment are limited. Because they consist of ordinary office equipment, these set-ups do not attract suspicion when dismantled.

Simple copy technique
This technique was developed by Victor Ostrovsky (see p. 62) for Mossad. The document, taped to a book, is stood in front of the camera, which is stuck to another book with chewing gum. Desk lamps are used for illumination. A remote shutter release is used to avoid shaking the camera.

HIGH-VOLUME COPYING: SIDE VIEW

35 mm camera taped between two rulers

Ruler

TOP VIEW

High-volume copying
Large quantities of documents can be copied quickly with this technique because once the equipment is set up, each document can be rapidly placed in the correct position and photographed. A standard 35 mm camera is used, along with books, adhesive tape, rulers, and desk lamps. With practice, the best combination of exposure time, focus, and lighting can be established. The set-up is then exactly reproduced for each copying session.

SECRET OPERATIONS

Bugs in plugs
Items of electrical equipment, such as plugs, make good hiding places for listening devices. They draw their power from the electrical socket and can work for years unless detected.

T HE CENTRAL TASK of an intelligence agency is to obtain secret information, but this is only one of a range of secret operations that are vital to it. Others include communications, countersurveillance, sabotage, and escape and evasion (avoiding capture or recapture by the enemy). For all these activities, the large intelligence agencies train skilled personnel and develop special techniques and equipment. In the KGB, this used to be done by a Directorate known as OT (this stood for Technical Operations). The CIA counterpart is the Office of Technical Services. In Israel, Mossad employs technical experts known as *marats* for the same purpose.

WATCHING AND LISTENING

A major role for the technical experts in an intelligence agency is to provide the means of carrying out surveillance. Photographic and video cameras may be employed to monitor the activities of foreign agents. A number of notable spies have been caught as a result of visual surveillance operations. Audio surveillance, too, can yield much valuable intelligence. Specialists are trained to place listening devices – known as bugs – in locations where secret conversations or meetings may take place. In certain circumstances the listening devices are linked by wire to a nearby listening post. Alternatively, the bug may be coupled with a transmitter, which sends the sound in the form of a radio signal. The signals are picked up by special receivers, some of which incorporate a recording device. Another branch of audio surveillance entails taking the listening device personally to where it is needed. Microphones and recording devices that can be hidden in an agent's clothing have been developed for this purpose.

Miniature monocular
This KGB monocular, held between the fingertips when used, is small enough to be stored inside a 35 mm film canister.

Wire recording device
The KGB Mezon recording device is sufficiently compact to be hidden in the clothing and activated by a control switch in the pocket. The device uses thin wire instead of tape to store its recordings.

GAINING ENTRY

In order to plant a listening device or gain access to secret material, it may be necessary to make a surreptitious entry. The value of whatever intelligence is gained will be reduced if the targets suspect a breach of security. The first step in carrying out a surreptitious entry is reconnaissance. One or more visits must be made to the target location. Using specialized equipment, it is even possible to see under doors and through keyholes. A key will be needed, and the best way is to "borrow" a key that can be copied and then returned. If this cannot be done, a lock will have to be picked, and this again is a specialist skill.

Lockpick and tension wrenches
The type of lock found in the target location will determine which of the many different tools are selected for use.

WARTIME OPERATIONS

In wartime, personnel sent to operate behind enemy lines are equipped and trained to escape from, or evade capture by, the enemy. During World War II, many concealments were devised for escape aids, such as the maps and compasses that were issued to aircrew flying missions over enemy territory.

World War II also led to increased development of tools and techniques for sabotage behind enemy lines. Many forms of explosive device were produced. Some were disguised as coal or animal droppings. Some had delay devices, such as pencil fuses, facilitating controlled detonation. Enemy ships in harbour were attacked using special small boats and canoes, and limpet mines were attached magnetically to the hulls. Sabotage is not merely profitable in terms of the destruction it causes, but also because of the large numbers of troops the enemy is forced to divert to guard transport, communications, and industrial installations.

Concealed blades
Special concealments were devised for escape aids. Here, leather inner soles provide hiding places for a blade and five gold coins.

Pencil fuses
These devices were used by saboteurs during World War II to delay the detonation of explosives. The delays gave the saboteurs enough time to escape in safety (see p. 97).

Visual surveillance I

VISUAL SURVEILLANCE is the art of watching without being detected. Intelligence agencies train and employ special teams to perform this role, using such equipment as hand-held optical devices (including night vision equipment) and film and video cameras. Cameras may be set up for long-term surveillance, or miniaturized for concealment on the spy's person. In American and British agencies, visual surveillance experts are called watchers; their talents are employed in internal security and counterintelligence operations. In the Soviet Union, the KGB designated a whole directorate (the seventh) for the role of surveillance.

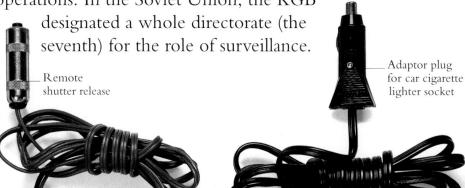

— Remote shutter release

Adaptor plug for car cigarette lighter socket

Photographic evidence
In this KGB surveillance photograph Penkovsky, working as a mole for the West in Moscow, enters a building used as a dead drop site (see p. 132).

AUTO CAMERA MARK 3

This fixed surveillance camera was produced in Britain during the 1950s and is such an effective surveillance tool that it is still used today. The large film chambers hold enough 35 mm film to take up to 250 pictures before reloading. It may be powered by a 12 volt power pack or through a car's cigarette lighter socket during mobile surveillance.

SURVEILLANCE BINOCULARS

Made in France in the 19th century, this pair of binoculars has an angled mirror inside its right hand side. This enabled the user to pretend to be looking straight ahead, while covertly looking to the right. The left side gave a normal view.

Bulk film chamber   Mounting attachment

36 mm
f3.5 lens

Side viewing port

Normal view

Right angle vi[e]w through side por[t]

FOLDING MONOCULAR

Members of the KGB used this folding monocular for secret visual surveillance. The monocular was jointed so that it could be unfolded (as shown here) and held in the fist for surreptitious surveillance without attracting attention.

Objective lens

Joint to fold monocular

Eyepiece

MINIATURE MONOCULAR

Shown here at its actual size, this monocular was so small that its KGB users were able to conceal it in an empty 35 mm film container. The monocular had a magnification of 2.5 times. The finger ring enabled the spy to hold the instrument, when it was not in use, in one hand while not appearing to be concealing anything.

Focusing dial

Eyepiece

Objective lens

Finger ring

KGB BORDER GUARDS

The Border Guards of the Soviet Union formed a separate directorate within the KGB. This was a fully equipped military force, with its own artillery, armoured fighting vehicles, and patrol boats. The force comprised 300,000 to 400,000 personnel at its peak. It fulfilled the dual role of keeping foreign intruders out of the Soviet Union and preventing any unauthorized exits. To help them with these duties, the Border Guards were issued with specialized visual surveillance equipment, such as the passive PN-1A night vision device (shown below left).

BORDER GUARD'S MEDAL (REVERSE)

FRONT OF MEDAL WITH CERTIFICATE

PASSIVE PN-1A NIGHT VISION DEVICE

Modern passive night vision devices amplify existing light, such as starlight, so that the user can see in almost total darkness. This hand-held device works almost silently and it is extremely difficult for anyone to detect it being used.

Eyepiece for viewing

Objective lens

Activation trigger

Battery compartment

Wrist strap

Pistol grip

FIBRESCOPE

Derived from medical equipment, the fibrescope receives images through 7,500 strands of fibre-optic cable. It is used to conduct surveillance beneath a door, or through a small hole drilled in a wall.

Eyepiece

Bundle of fibre-optic cables

Handle

Lens

Visual surveillance II

FIXED SURVEILLANCE CAMERA

The KGB designed this fixed surveillance camera to be mounted in a variety of concealments. This example is hidden inside a decorative mask and coupled with a timing device (an intervalometer) that triggered the camera to take photographs at preset intervals. In a different housing, cameras of this type were used to take compromising photographs of people who could then be blackmailed.

Film tension adjustment dial

№78267

SPARE CASSETTE

Lens

LENS CAP

Film cassette

№78267

№78267

FIXED SURVEILLANCE CAMERA

OTKP
3akp

3akp
OTKP

CAMERA LID

Hole for camera lens

CONCEALMENT MASK

Intervalometer

Elastic to hold equipment in position

Camera

CAMERA HIDDEN BEHIND MASK

Power and control cables

Connector

ПЕРЕМОТКА

ЦИКЛ

ВКЛ.

Timing dial

Hinged cover

INTERVALOMETER

Connector

BUTTONHOLE MOVIE CAMERA

This device was used by the KGB during the 1960s and 1970s. It was the movie equivalent of the KGB's F21 camera (see p. 66), and like the F21 it filmed through a false button, which opened to reveal a lens. It used a film cassette that was mounted on the camera at right angles to the lens. The user turned the camera on and off with a switch hidden in a pocket. A battery pack, concealed in another pocket, powered the camera.

Locking lever for cassette

Film cassette

Power on/off switch

Camera

False button opens to reveal lens

Remote camera on/off switch

BUTTONHOLE MOVIE CAMERA

Battery pack

SPARE FILM CASSETTE

MICRO-VIDEO CAMERA

Modern technology, particularly the silicon chip, has made it possible to produce miniature video cameras such as this one. The size of the camera makes it easy to mount in many concealments, including a baseball cap. The camera is so sensitive that it can be concealed under a cotton shirt, taking pictures through the material.

Video connection

Battery pack

Camera (normally hidden by an extra layer of material)

CAMERA IN BASEBALL CAP CONCEALMENT

CAMERA (ACTUAL SIZE)

Pinhole lens

Circuit board

INTERIOR OF CAMERA (ENLARGED)

Listening devices I

INTELLIGENCE AGENCIES make great efforts to develop devices that will enable them listen to their enemy's conversations. Tiny eavesdropping microphones are coupled with miniature amplifiers, transmitters, or tape recorders, while other devices intercept signals from telephone wires. Once created, the equipment must be planted. Specialized equipment, such as the fine wire kit or the silent hammer, is available for installating microphone wires in walls. A transmitted signal from a listening device should be strong enough to be received at a listening post, but weak enough to make it difficult to locate using ordinary anti-bugging devices. Now listening devices exist that can store signals digitally and transmit them to a listening post at a predetermined time.

SILENT HAMMER

MINIATURIZED LISTENING EQUIPMENT

Many types of miniaturized equipment have been made for spying purposes: a bugged mouthpiece, ready for insertion in a public telephone; a multi-purpose bug, small enough to hide almost anywhere; and a through-the-wall device, with a plastic tube that would not be discovered by metal detectors.

BUGGED MOUTHPIECE FOR PUBLIC TELEPHONE

Antenna

Microphone

Power lead

GENERAL PURPOSE MINIATURE OUTFIT

Housing for microphone

Plastic tube

DEVICE FOR LISTENING THROUGH WALLS

FINE WIRE KIT

To hide the wires when installing a bug, American technicians developed this wire-laying tool and its accessories. The tool is capable of forcing fine wires or cables into soft building materials or cracks. A monitoring circuit warns if the circuit is broken during installation.

Blades for knife

Screwdriver

Wedges to hold cracks in walls open

Blades for wire-laying tool

Nine tubes of wax

Knife

Nylon stick for manipulating wire and wax

Needle for threading wire through wire-laying tool

Wax gun used to cement wires in place or to conceal them

Thirteen spools of very fine wire cable

Wire-laying tool

PEN AND BOOK DEVICES

During the decades after World War II, an agent who wanted to record a meeting surreptitiously might be equipped with a listening device disguised as a pen. Another ingenious device fitted into the spine of a book, which could be placed in a room without causing suspicion. These were typical bugs of the 1960s – today's devices make use of digital technology and are much smaller.

INDUCTION TELEPHONE TAP

This device can be clamped on to any single-line external telephone cable and connected either to a transmitter or tape recorder. Both sides of the conversation can be received clearly. With no physical connection to the telephone wire, the tap is difficult for counterintelligence agents to detect.

Plug to transmitter or recorder

Induction clamp to secure around telephone line

Insulated cable

Antenna wire

Microphone and transmitter

INSERTION OF TRANSMITTER INTO BOOK SPINE

Power leads

MICROPHONE AND TRANSMITTER FOR BOOK SPINE

MICROPHONE AND TRANSMITTER CONCEALED IN PEN

Sound travels along tube to the microphone

PETER WRIGHT

Peter Wright (1916–1995) was the British Security Service's first technical officer. He joined the Security Service (MI5) in 1955, having done scientific work throughout World War II. The early years of his career were spent inventing specialized listening devices for varied operations. Wright also attempted to work out how the Soviet listening devices that were found in the buildings of the Western nations worked. The "Thing" (see p. 84) was a Soviet listening device found in the Great Seal of the United States embassy in Moscow. Wright was the first person to fully understand how it worked. Having shown an aptitude for all aspects of counterintelligence work, Wright moved to D Branch, which was responsible for counterespionage, particularly Soviet activities in Britain. He eventually went on to become an Assistant Director of MI5.

MI5's chief scientist
Despite having no formal scientific education, Wright was a brilliant innovator, constantly attempting to find scientific solutions to MI5's problems.

Listening devices II

EARLY MINIATURIZED BUGS

The picture immediately below shows an American demonstration model from the late 1950s. It consists of an electrical plug with a listening device which, were it not for the transparent casing, would be invisible. Below that is a real bugged adaptor from the 1960s.

Bug — Transparent casing

Electrode (pin) of plug

DEMONSTRATION MODEL OF BUGGED PLUG

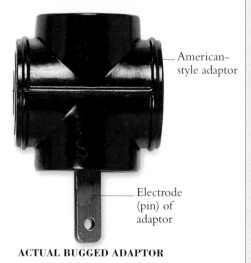

American-style adaptor

Electrode (pin) of adaptor

ACTUAL BUGGED ADAPTOR

THE "THING"

In the early 1950s, a Soviet listening device was found in the American embassy in Moscow. It consisted of a cylindrical metal object that had been hidden inside the wooden carving of the Great Seal of the United States – the emblem on the wall over the Ambassador's desk – which had been presented to him by the Soviets. The Great Seal features a bald eagle, beneath whose beak the Soviets had drilled holes to allow sound to reach the device.

Western experts were baffled as to how the device, which came to be known as the "Thing" (see below), worked, as it had neither batteries nor electrical circuits. Peter Wright (see p. 83) of Britain's MI5

Diaphragm

Sound waves

Tuning post

Cover

High-frequency radio beam

Antenna

Reflected beam with modulations

FRONT OF THE GREAT SEAL

(see p. 164) eventually discovered how it worked. MI5 then produced a copy of the device (codenamed SATYR) for use by both British and American intelligence.

The device came to world prominence when displayed at the United Nations by the American Ambassador in May 1960.

The "Thing"

BACK OF THE GREAT SEAL

How the "Thing" worked
A radio beam was aimed at the antenna from a source outside the building. A sound that struck the diaphragm caused variations in the amount of space (and the capacitance) between it and the tuning post plate. These variations altered the charge on the antenna, creating modulations in the reflected radio beam. These were picked up and interpreted by the receiver.

BELT-BUCKLE MICROPHONE

Concealed in a belt buckle, this small microphone picks up the sound of conversation through a tiny hole. The device can be linked to either a transmitter or to a tape recorder, also hidden beneath the clothing of the wearer.

Connector   Concealed wire   Microphone

MODIFIED FURNITURE COMPONENTS

Bugs can be hidden in fake furniture parts, which are then substituted for the original piece. Inside the components shown here, microphones and transmitters have been installed.

One is part of a desk, modified by Czech technicians. The other is a brace that can be adapted for any wooden furniture; it was used by an American audio-surveillance team.

Microphone   Battery   Transmitter

Tuning post to adjust frequency

DESK COMPONENT

Hole carved in the wood   Battery compartment

MULTI-PURPOSE WOODEN BRACE

ADAPTOR LISTENING DEVICE

This microphone-and-transmitter set concealed in a British adaptor allows unlimited transmitting time without concern for battery drain, because its power is taken directly from the mains. A distinct disadvantage of this device is that the transmitter is permanently powered, which would enable a trained counterintelligence "sweep team" to detect it easily.

Transmitter

INTERIOR OF ADAPTOR   **FRONT OF ADAPTOR**

TEMPORARY TELEPHONE TAP

This telephone bug can be installed rapidly and is used where there is little time to fit a more sophisticated device. The bug needs no batteries, drawing its power from the telephone. As it is not integral with the circuitry of the telephone, this bug is relatively easy to discover once the case is opened.

Leads for quick installation   Telephone bug

Base of telephone

Receivers I

LISTENING IN ON AND RECORDING conversations is an important part of surveillance; its usual end product is a tape recording. Bugs (see p. 82 and p. 84) are hidden listening devices that either transmit a conversation to a listening post some distance away or are connected to a recording device. Shown here are two further categories of audio-surveillance gear. The first is the equipment used at the listening post: radio receivers, tape recorders, and other electronic hardware. The second consists of the devices carried on the person of a spy to record a conversation on the spot. These are mostly miniaturized microphones and tape recorders. The earpiece microphone shown above is a variation on this theme, designed for making recordings of telephone conversations.

EARPIECE MICROPHONE

LISTENING POST RECEIVER

This is a portable radio receiver of American make, designed in the 1960s. Its function was to receive signals from bugs in a target location nearby. Its output was carried by cable, either to a tape recorder or to other types of monitoring equipment.

TRIGON AND PETERSON

Alexsandr Ogorodnik, codenamed Trigon, was a Soviet diplomatic service secretary who supplied information to the CIA from 1974. In July 1977, the KGB arrested his CIA case officer in Moscow, Martha Peterson. She asked for a US embassy representative, who on arrival, as the KGB noted, wore two watches – one of them a disguised microphone. Peterson was expelled from the Soviet Union. Trigon, also arrested, committed suicide.

Microphone wristwatch
The microphone inside is linked to a miniature tape recorder hidden in the operative's clothing.

Antenna receives signal transmitted by bug

Band selector is adjusted to the frequency at which the bug transmits

Output socket connects receiver to monitoring equipment

PEN WITH MICROPHONE

The KGB had fountain pens made that contained small microphones, allowing spies to record conversations. The signal was passed to a small tape recorder or transmitter hidden in the spy's clothing. A selection of different styles of pen was available to match the different types of cover under which spies operated.

MICROPHONE IN POSITION

"MOTEL KIT"

The contact microphone of this kit is firmly taped or glued to a wall or door and lets the user eavesdrop on a conversation in the next room. The microphone picks up sound waves and converts them into an electronic signal so that the conversation can be sent, via an amplifier that filters out some background noise, to a tape recorder or headphones.

CONTACT MICROPHONE

Input for microphone

Output to tape recorder

Headphone socket

PHONES

NOTCH

GAIN

Sound filter

Amplification control

AMPLIFIER

Earphones used for monitoring conversation

Connection to tape recorder or radio transmitter

Position of sound hole under clip

Pen clip

Cable runs through hole in pocket

PEN-TOP MICROPHONE

LEAD TO TAPE RECORDER

HEADPHONES

KANG SHENG: ELECTRONIC EAVESDROPPER

During the 1920s, the fledgling Chinese Communist Party formed its own secret police force in imitation of the Soviet OGPU. The head of this organization (and its successor organization, the Social Affairs Department or SAD) was Kang Sheng (1898–1975). Kang lived the life of a gentleman-scholar and calligrapher while holding secret police and Communist Party security posts for over 40 years. After formation of the communist government under Mao Zedong (Mao Tse-tung) in 1949, Kang attained ever greater powers. He went on to reinforce his position by fostering the personality cult of Mao Zedong, and ensuring that Mao married Jian Qing, a former lover of Kang's. From his base in Beijing, known as the "Bamboo Garden", Kang monitored almost everything that happened in China. This included surveillance of the Communist Party itself. He used a wide variety of electronic eavesdropping devices to achieve this, and is even believed to have bugged the office of Mao Zedong himself. In the 1970s, when Kang was growing weak with cancer, SAD began to extend its activities overseas. It was able to earn hard currency by carrying out industrial espionage in foreign countries and helped enhance China's political influence by aiding such groups as the Shining Path in Peru and the PLO in the Middle East.

KANG SHENG

Receivers II

MEZON RECORDING DEVICE

The Mezon, which dates from the 1970s, records sound on a wire 0.05 mm in diameter instead of a tape. The KGB issued accessories adapting it for a variety of operational situations. It could be controlled by a remote switch concealed in the pocket, and included an attachment for recording telephone conversations. Screw plugs ensure the accessories will not become unplugged while in use. A shoulder harness allows the Mezon to be worn under a jacket.

PAGER WITH CONCEALED RECORDER

A miniature tape recorder and its tiny microphone are concealed in this fake pager. Worn on the user's belt, the machine is operated by an on/off switch on the bottom of the "pager".

Microphone plug

Credit-card-sized tape recorder

On/off switch

Casing of fake pager opens to enable cassette to be changed

COMPLETE OUTFIT IN CASE

Microphone can be pinned beneath lapel to record conversations

Plug

MEZON MICROPHONE

Remote switch cable

Screw plug

Switch

REMOTE ON/OFF SWITCH

On/off lever

Lid can be closed for protection during use

Recording head

Wire spool

MEZON RECORDING DEVICE (ACTUAL SIZE)

External antenna

Internal antenna

Automatic gain
controller amplifier

Internal/external
antenna selector switch

Volume

Adaptor
for using car
power supply

Mains
cable

Transmitter

Coupling
device for
car antenna

Coupling
device for
car antenna

Headphones

Telephone line
induction clamp

Microphone

Earphone

SK–8A AUDIO-SURVEILLANCE BRIEFCASE

A normal-looking briefcase conceals this
law enforcement kit, used in the 1960s
and '70s. The kit includes a low-speed
reel-to-reel tape recorder that allows up
to six hours' recording. There is also a
radio link, consisting of a receiver and
a transmitter, which can be used either
for audio monitoring or to record a
conversation transmitted by a bug.

Voice or continuous wave
(Morse code) selector switch

Automatic gain
control/receiver
selector switch

Receiver case

UNDERARM TAPE RECORDER

Used during the 1960s by the Royal Canadian
Mounted Police Security Service, this tape
recorder could be worn unobtrusively in an
underarm harness beneath the user's clothing.

Demonstration of harness
The special harness was padded to
eliminate the tell-tale bulge under
the arm made by the tape recorder.

Shoulder
strap

Pouch to
hold recorder

Pads conceal
the outline of
the recorder

HARNESS

Plug

HEADPHONES

Remote on/off
switch is carried
in jacket pocket

Microphone

TAPE RECORDER

Tape reel

Surreptitious entry

INTELLIGENCE AGENCIES need personnel who can enter places secretly to gather intelligence. Such surreptitious entries require very careful planning, and are usually carried out by expert personnel using special equipment. Lockpicking is avoided if possible, because it is difficult and unpredictable. It is better to steal a key and quickly duplicate it. If no key is available, it is possible to manufacture one with a special key-impression kit. Once burglar alarms have been neutralized, the final safeguard before entry is to ensure that the target location is unoccupied. One way to do this is to telephone: if anyone answers, the operation is cancelled. Entry teams used to be issued with portable diallers for making these calls.

KEY-CASTING KIT

It may be possible to steal a key temporarily, returning it to avoid detection. Its impression is instantly taken in clay and a quick copy made, using a low melting-point metal alloy that melts in a candle flame. A permanent copy can be cut later.

Carrying case

Aluminium mould containing modelling clay

Hole for pouring molten alloy into mould

Spare modelling clay

Candle

Thimble to melt alloy

Releasing powder

Thimble holder

Slugs

Low melting-point metal alloy

Rotary dial

Plug

PORTABLE DIALLER

Diallers of this type were used in the United States in the 1950s and 1960s. They were connected to the telephone line by a tapping device. This one has an impedance switch to adjust the resistance to that of the telephone circuit. Cellular telephones have made diallers obsolete.

DIAL   LO OFF HI

Activating button

Impedance switch

Plug for connection to tapping device

G. Gordon Liddy

Formerly an FBI special agent and an attorney, G. Gordon Liddy (b.1930) was one of the central figures in the 1972 Watergate break-in. In the previous year he was involved in the surreptitious entry at the home of the psychiatrist treating a prominent Vietnam War protester. Liddy used a Minox C camera and a measuring chain (see p.70) to help identify the lock types and keyways at the apartment.

KEY-PATTERN DEVICE

This device is used to copy keys of the old-fashioned type of locks known as warded locks. Thumbscrews hold the key in position while the feelers are adjusted to conform precisely to the pattern of the teeth. Once made, the pattern can be copied.

"Feelers" are used to make a pattern of the original key

Thumbscrew holds key in position

Teeth of key will clear wards in lock

European-style warded key

Aluminium frame accommodates two key patterns at the same time

Tightening screw

Positioning screw

OFFICE OF TECHNICAL SERVICES

The Office of Technical Services (OTS) is the part of the CIA that specializes in technical operations. Among its members are experts in lockpicking, surreptitious entry, clandestine photography, and audio surveillance. They also devise disguises, concealments, and dead-drop containers, and are responsible for secret writing and microdots. The OTS today forms part of the CIA's Deputy Directorate of Science and Technology.

EMBLEM OF THE OTS

KEY-IMPRESSION KIT

This works for a variety of different types of keys. A specially prepared impression tool inserts a key-blank into the lock and picks up marks from the mechanism. An expert can interpret these marks and hand-file the key.

Impression tool

Graphite powder

Magnifying glass

Vice for gripping pins

G-clamp

Shims

Emery cloth

File

Small magnet

Plastic slides

BURGLAR ALARM EVASION KIT

Old alarms used a wire-borne signal; if this was broken, the alarm was raised. With this kit, agents could intercept the signal, tamper with the wire, and prevent a break-in from being detected.

Setting control

Activating switch

Connection for clip leads

Connection for earpiece

Direction control

Clip leads

Earpiece

Lockpicks

INTELLIGENCE SERVICES OFTEN NEED to pick locks to gain access to secret material. Lockpick devices, and kits with small tools, are available for opening most types of lock used worldwide. To open a pin-tumbler lock, a pick tool and a tension wrench are inserted and manipulated to simulate the results that would be obtained by using the key. The spy may have to try several tools before the lock will open. For faster results, a lockpick gun or electric lock-opening device may be used. Lockpicking is a specialized branch of intelligence work, but it uses the same tools as commercial locksmiths.

TUBULAR LOCKPICK

This device opens the type of high-security locks that use a tubular key. The lockpick is inserted, and adjusted within the lock to simulate the tubular key.

POCKET LOCKPICKING KIT

This assortment of picks and tension tools is small enough to slip into a pocket and can be used by an expert to open most pin-tumbler type locks – the most common type of lock, used all around the world.

Leather pocket case

Double ball rake — Rake

Rake — Double ball rake

Tension wrenches

Double-sided tension wrench

Broken-key removal tool

Ball rake

Reamer

Feeler pick

Feeler pick

Rake

Rake

Feeler pick

Half-diamond pick

Half-diamond pick

THE WATERGATE BREAK-IN

The 1972 Watergate break-in was part of an illegal plot in support of the re-election of US President Richard Nixon. The headquarters of Nixon's principal rival, the Democratic candidate, were located in the Watergate office complex in Washington, DC. A White House aide, E. Howard

Hunt, Jr., recruited a group of Cuban exiles to break into the building. In their first entry, the Cuban team photographed various documents and installed a number of listening devices.

A second entry was undertaken to gather more information and reposition one of the listening devices. But the burglars were inexperienced lockpickers and this entry was discovered by a night watchman – tape holding a door lock open had been left visible from the outside.

The police were called and they arrested the Cubans. Later, the two men responsible for planning the operation, Hunt and G. Gordon Liddy (see p. 90), were also arrested, tried, and convicted. The Watergate scandal led to the resignation of President Nixon.

The Watergate burglars
The men recruited to carry out the burglary in the Watergate office complex were exiles from Fidel Castro's communist regime in Cuba.

E. Howard Hunt, Jr.
A former CIA officer, Hunt recruited the Watergate entry team using his contacts in the Cuban exile community.

SURREPTITIOUS ENTRY KIT

An entry specialist may not know what locks will be found once inside a target location. So a tool kit is needed that is capable of opening as many different types of locks as possible. The selection of tools will be influenced by the personal preferences and skills of the specialist lock opener, also taking into account the types of lock likely to be found in the country of the operation.

Keyway blank

Keyway blank

Selection of picks for lever locks

File

Keyway blank

Pointed probe

Probe tool

Feeler pick

Keys for warded locks (see p. 91)

Keyway blank

Tension wrench

Rake

Needle pick

Probe tool

Rake

Adjustable, double-sided tension wrench

LOCKPICK GUN

This device can quickly open most pin-tumbler locks. Squeezing the trigger causes the pick to strike the pins that work the lock mechanism. A tension wrench is used to turn the lock cylinder when the pins are properly aligned.

Hinge for folding

Needle pick

Impact adjusting wheel

Trigger

Pistol grip

LOCKPICK GUN

TENSION WRENCH

ELECTRIC LOCK-OPENING DEVICE

The user selects a pick, inserts one end in the device and the other in the lock, then switches the device on. This bounces the pins in the lock until they are aligned, so the lock opens. No additional tool is needed to turn the lock cylinder.

On/off switch

Pick insertion point

Adjustment knob

Pick

Allen key

Front attachment

External battery jack

LOCK-OPENING DEVICE

ATTACHMENTS IN CARRYING CASE

Escape and evasion

EVERYDAY ITEMS SUCH AS hairbrushes, pens, and coins made ideal concealments for World War II escape and evasion aids. These aids included small compasses, maps, and knife blades. They were developed to assist prisoners of war in escape attempts, and to help spies and airmen operating in enemy territory to evade capture. The concealments hid these useful items, even if the enemy noticed the outer casing.

PLAYING CARDS WITH CONCEALED MAP SECTIONS

The top layer of these cards was soaked off to reveal numbered map sections. The assembled sections formed a master from which escape maps were copied.

Card surface peeled back to reveal map

Numbered map section fully revealed

HAIRBRUSH WITH SECRET COMPARTMENT

This hairbrush concealed vital escape and evasion aids. To open it, a section of the head of the brush was lifted by pulling on a specific row of bristles.

Secret compartment

HEAD OF HAIRBRUSH

LIFTED-OUT SECTION OF HEAD OF HAIRBRUSH

Compass needle

Compass with red dot indicating north

Tissue map

Miniature saw

ITEMS CONTAINED IN HAIRBRUSH

THE MAN WHO WAS "Q"

Charles Fraser-Smith (1904-92) worked for British intelligence during World War II. His task was to supply the clandestine services with "Q" gadgets – named after Q-ships, the warships in World War I that had been disguised as ordinary merchant navy ships.

Many of his Q gadgets were concealments disguised as everyday objects. Others were items of equipment that had been miniaturized or adapted for concealment. Fraser-Smith employed over 300 companies, all of which were sworn to secrecy, to make his devices.

Charles Fraser-Smith
Fraser-Smith was the inspiration for the character "Q" in Ian Fleming's James Bond novels.

PEN WITH CONCEALED MAP AND COMPASS

The secret chambers in this pen were secured with end-caps attached by reverse threads. Any attempt to unscrew the caps in the normal (anti-clockwise) direction merely tightened them.

Rolled-up map hidden inside barrel

Reverse-thread cap

Reverse-thread cap

Magnetized pen clip (standby compass)

Compass

PIPE WITH CONCEALMENTS

This pipe could be smoked without damaging the concealed items. The bowl had an asbestos lining inside which a map could be hidden without danger of catching fire.

Miniature compass

Wadding

Concealed container

ESCAPE FROM COLDITZ CASTLE

Colditz Castle, a historic fortress in eastern Germany, became a prison for high-risk Allied prisoners of war during World War II. Many of these had already escaped or tried to escape from German captivity, and by concentrating them at Colditz, the Germans unwittingly created what became known as the Colditz Escape Academy. A group of prisoners coordinated escape attempts and made, by hand, a range of items, such as clothes and forged documents, to supplement escape aids that were smuggled into Colditz from Britain. In January 1942, an escape by British Lieutenant Airey Neave and Dutch Lieutenant Toni Luteyn involved disguising themselves first as German officers and then as Dutch workers. On his return to England, Neave became an adviser to MI9, an office in British intelligence that was involved in helping prisoners of war to escape.

Airey Neave
After his Colditz escape, Neave became an advisor on escape aids in order to assist other prisoners.

Colditz Castle
Allied prisoners of war who had tried to escape from other camps were often brought to Colditz.

HIDDEN BLADES

Small blades were hidden in objects that were unlikely to be confiscated from prisoners. A coin with a hidden blade, mixed with other pocket change, might easily be overlooked by the enemy. Shoe-heel blades could be used by prisoners whose hands were tied to their feet and behind their back.

Concealed blade

COIN WITH BLADE

Concealed blade

Concealed blade

SHOE-HEEL WITH BLADES

RECTAL TOOL KIT

Escape tools and ways of concealing them continued to be needed in the years after World War II. This CIA kit from the 1960s was designed for rectal concealment if a search was anticipated.

Plastic case for rectal concealment

Handle to which tools were attached, incorporating pliers and wirecutters

Reamer | Saw blade | Saw blade | Cutting blade | Cutting blade | Reamer | Grinding tool | Drill bit | File

Section inserted in handle

Working part of tool

Sabotage

ACTS OF SABOTAGE aim to disable part of an enemy's infrastructure. Sabotage operations are usually carried out for one of two reasons: to damage the economies of potentially hostile countries during peacetime, or to disrupt an enemy's industry and communications during wartime. Wartime attacks not only cause destruction, but also force the enemy to divert troops from the front line to guard vulnerable areas. During World War II, both the SOE (see p. 30) and the OSS (see p. 32) were engaged in sabotage in cooperation with resistance groups. These operations often entailed the use of specialized explosives and fuses, such as bombs disguised as pieces of coal.

GRENADES

Unlike most grenades, which have time-delay fuses, these grenades were specially designed to explode on impact, making them effective against hard-to-hit moving targets.

Secondary arming mechanism and fuse

Primary safety ring

Percussion fuse inside screw cap

BEANO GRENADE

Black cloth skirt

GAMMON GRENADE

TREE SPIGOT MORTAR

This unusual device was meant for use against both vehicles and individuals. A trip wire set off the mortar, which hurled a shell filled with high explosive in the direction of the target. The shell exploded on impact.

Hollow tail

Calibrated adjustment arc

PRISMATIC SIGHT FOR SPIGOT MORTAR

RAIN SHIELD FOR SPIGOT MORTAR

Mortar shell

Attachment lug

Percussion fuse

Attachment point for lug

Propellant container

Mounting the spigot
The mortar was set up by screwing the spigot into a tree trunk, then pointing it in the direction the enemy was to approach from. The hollow tail was fitted over the spigot, and the shell was placed in a funnel at the the top of the hollow tail.

Firing pin

Spigot

Wire coil

Trip wire

Clip to secure hollow tail

Safety pin

Mounting handle

Universal joint

Clamping plate

MORTAR

Mounting screw

EXPLOSIVE COAL KIT

Kits for disguising explosives as pieces of coal were issued to some OSS sabotage teams during World War II. These kits contained all that was needed to make the outer case of the bomb resemble the type of coal used in the operational area. The case was filled with explosive and placed in an enemy coal dump – these were often inadequately guarded. The bomb would detonate when burned in a locomotive's furnace or a factory boiler.

Cloth   Paint   Turpentine   Palette knife   Penknife

Polish   Stock of beeswax pellets   Modelling sticks   Brushes   Bomb casing before applying camouflage

Packing

CODENAME PASTORIUS

In 1942, eight German saboteurs were put ashore from two submarines on the American coast. Their mission was codenamed Pastorius. Four landed in Florida and four in Long Island, New York. The Coast Guard spotted the New York group and alerted the FBI, who searched the beach and found explosives and fuses. One saboteur, Georg Dasch, surrendered to the FBI. He gave information that resulted in the arrest of the others. Six of the saboteurs were sentenced to death and executed. Dasch and one other were given jail sentences and sent home after the war.

Georg Dasch
In order to save himself from execution, Dasch provided information that led to the arrest of his fellow saboteurs.

PENCIL FUSES

These World War II devices would detonate an explosive after a set time, giving a saboteur time to get away. The saboteur pulled off a safety strip and squeezed the appropriate point on the side of a copper crush tube, which broke an ampoule of acid inside. The acid corroded a wire to release a striker that struck a percussion cap and a detonator. Coloured bands indicated the length of time delay for each fuse.

Spring snout

Fuse adapter/detonator holder

Percussion cap

Colour safety strip indicating average time delay (black indicates 10 minutes)

Safety strip hole

Striker assembly

Spring

Wire retaining striker

Body containing spring and striker

Ampoule containing corrosive acid

Copper crush tube containing ampoule of corrosive acid

Cotton wick

Fixing screw

Fixing screw

Red indicates 19 minutes

Yellow indicates 6 hours 30 minutes

Blue indicates 14 hours 30 minutes

White indicates 1 hour 19 minutes

INTERNAL VIEW OF A PENCIL FUSE

PENCIL FUSE

BOX OF PENCIL FUSES

Amphibious sabotage

THE CHIEF AIMS of amphibious sabotage are to destroy enemy ships and attack coastal defences. Raiding parties, well trained and equipped with special craft, secretly enter enemy harbours and other waters to undertake perilous operations. During World War II, a number of innovations in tactics and equipment contributed to the effectiveness of amphibious raids. Canoes and submersible craft, such as the "Sleeping Beauty", were developed for use in enemy harbours; and new types of explosive devices, such as limpet mines, were invented for use under water.

ACETONE TIME-DELAY FUSE

Limpet mines were attached magnetically to the hulls of ships. Many had acetone fuses; these would detonate the mines after an interval indicated by the colour of an acetone ampoule. The colour represented the concentration of the acetone, which ate through a celluloid disc, releasing a firing pin and detonating the mine. The fuse was set manually by twisting an actuating screw, which crushed the ampoule and released the acetone.

OPERATION FRANKTON

During World War II, German-held France was blockaded by the Allied navies. German ships continued to call at the French harbours. In 1942, a party of British Royal Marines attacked German vessels in the French harbour of Bordeaux. The raiders were taken by submarine to a river estuary nearby, and then set off by canoe to the target. Only two of the five canoes reached Bordeaux. During the night the raiders attached sixteen limpet mines to six German ships, sinking four and damaging the other two. Only two of the ten saboteurs survived and returned safely to Britain.

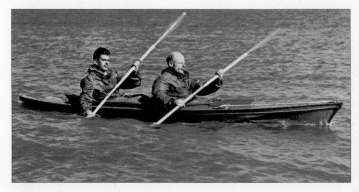

Royal Marine saboteurs
Major H. G. "Blondie" Hasler (in front) and Corporal W. E. Sparks were the only survivors of the successful raid on Bordeaux harbour.

Actuating screw

Wadding

Celluloid disc

Firing pin

Fuse end-cap

Detonator end-cap

Safety pin

COMPONENTS OF FUSE

Screw thread for attaching fuse to limpet mine

Detonator

Colour-coded ampoules of acetone

Orange ampoule (delay in hours)

Yellow ampoule (delay in hours)

Green ampoule (delay in hours)

Blue ampoule (delay in hours)

Red ampoule (delay in hours)

Temperature in degrees Fahrenheit

Violet ampoule (delay in days)

Temperature in degrees Centigrade

TEMP:	RED HOURS	ORANGE HOURS	YELLOW HOURS	GREEN HOURS	BLUE HOURS	VIOLET DAYS	TEMP:
40°F.	6¼	9¼	20	34	67	8¼	5°C.
50°F.	5	8½	17½	30	53	7	10°C.
60°F.	4½	7½	15	26	42	5½	15°C.
68°F.	4	7	14	22½	36	4½	20°C.
77°F.	3½	6½	12	20	30	3½	25°C.
88°F.	3	6	10	17½	25	2½	30°C.

Note: Subject to 25% deviation either way, except Red on which deviation may be 2 hours either way.

INSTRUCTION SHEET SHOWING TIME DELAYS

LIMPET MINE AND PLACING ROD

A limpet mine was a waterproof bomb designed to sink or damage ships. The mine was positioned by means of an extendible placing rod, and held by magnets to the ship's steel hull. An acetone time-delay fuse was used to detonate the mine. The limpet mine could blow a hole of up to 2.3 sq m (25 sq ft) in a ship's hull.

Placing a limpet mine
Saboteurs had to approach the target ship silently, usually in a small boat. They attached the mine carefully, using an extendible placing rod 1.5 m (5 ft) below the waterline.

Cap covering second fuse pocket

Clip to hold alternative fixing device

Rod head to attach mine

Handle

Securing collar

Spring

Magnet attachment frame

Bracket for rod head

Acetone time-delay fuse

Explosive-filled body

Hinged joint

LIMPET MINE

PLACING ROD

OPERATION RIMAU: THE RAID ON SINGAPORE HARBOUR

The Japanese captured Singapore island from the British in 1942. Later that year, raiders belonging to the Allied Intelligence Bureau (a special operations force set up by Britain and its allies) launched an attack from Australia against Japanese ships in Singapore harbour. The saboteurs entered the harbour in folding canoes and attached limpet mines to the Japanese ships. Seven ships, with a total tonnage of 37,000 tonnes, were completely destroyed. A second raid was attempted in 1944, using a newly developed craft, the "Sleeping Beauty". This electric-powered submersible canoe could either be operated fully under water or with the pilot's head above the surface. Raiders were about to launch these craft from a captured cargo ship when they were detected by water police. The operation was aborted. The saboteurs tried to escape, but all died fighting or were executed by the Japanese.

Stern

Diving fin

Seat

Joystick

Compressed-air cylinders

Hole for emergency mast

Battery compartment

Buoyancy tank

Bow

THE "SLEEPING BEAUTY"

COUNTER-INTELLIGENCE

"No Spies"
Members of FBI counterintelligence units adopted this unofficial lapel badge to represent their commitment to keeping America free of spies. The badge was not worn operationally.

C OUNTERINTELLIGENCE IS INTENDED to frustrate the activities of hostile intelligence agencies and to prevent the passage of information to the enemy. A great deal of counterintelligence work targets enemy agents when they communicate with their handlers. Counterintelligence services employ highly trained agents, often skilled in using technologically advanced equipment, although they also need to have good judgment and intuition to contend with suspected enemy spies. Because of the numerous layers of deception involved, counterintelligence has been called a "wilderness of mirrors".

MI5 emblem
The internal counterintelligence service in Britain is known as MI5. It achieved an amazing record of apprehending German spies during World War II.

DETECTORS

Many devices have been developed for detecting hostile agents in the act of espionage. The use of clandestine radios by spies has led to the use of sophisticated radio direction-finding equipment by counterintelligence personnel. Other techniques are employed to track the movements of suspected agents. For example, powders that are invisible unless viewed with special equipment have been used by the KGB and FBI to reveal the footprints or fingerprints of spies. Detection equipment, such as cameras with telephoto lenses, is also used.

ANTI-BUGGING DEVICES

Intelligence agencies frequently use listening devices, otherwise known as bugs, to eavesdrop on sensitive conversations. In response to this, the counterintelligence services have developed special electronic equipment and techniques for detecting bugs. Use of these has to be backed up by physical searches of the site

Soviet SMERSH credentials
SMERSH was a Soviet counterintelligence organization that operated within the Soviet military during and just after World War II.

Invisible detection powders
To set a trap for an intruding spy, counterintelligence personnel put down invisible powders. After contact with human skin, these powders become visible under ultraviolet light.

being investigated for bugs. Audio countersurveillance devices work by picking up signals as the bugs transmit them. Such devices need to overcome certain difficulties that are commonly presented by bugs. Some bugs can be switched off remotely to avoid detection. Others hide themselves by transmitting on a frequency very close to that of a powerful radio station ("snuggling").

COUNTERSURVEILLANCE

The aim of countersurveillance is to provide safe conditions for friendly agents by deceiving or otherwise frustrating hostile surveillance. This craft is especially important for agents who are engaged in risky activities such as visiting a dead drop or meeting their case officers. It is carried out by teams of specially trained personnel, who maintain contact with one another by hidden radios. To avoid arousing any suspicion, these personnel may need to be in disguise.

LETTER INTERCEPTION

Spies can of course use the ordinary mail to send their messages. They may write in code, use secret writing, or incorporate microdots in their letters. The sheer volume of the mail is their best protection against discovery. Counterintelligence officers who do intervene in the mail service (which may not be possible without a warrant) may hope to find some spies' letters by concentrating on the addresses of suspects. Letters are opened by "flaps and seals" experts, so named because in the past their work had to do with envelope flaps and wax seals. There are now special tools and materials that open correspondence without alerting the recipient to the fact that the mail has been examined.

Briefcase bug detector
This equipment is used to search for listening devices by monitoring radio transmissions. An oscilloscope displays the signals detected.

Detectors

THE COUNTERINTELLIGENCE TOOLS used to monitor and trap spies are often referred to as detectors. Detectors are frequently electronic or photographic; but sometimes more subtle techniques are used, like the invisible spy dust laid down by the KGB to track the movements of CIA officers in Moscow. Various intelligence agencies, the KGB among them, have set up surveillance cameras with telephoto lenses to monitor movements of personnel at foreign embassies in the hope of detecting intelligence activities. Electronic detectors include the many devices used for detecting clandestine radios, such as radios used in a system referred to as radio direction finding (RDF). Elements of the Schulze-Boysen spy ring in Germany in World War II (see p. 38) and the Israeli spy Elie Cohen in Syria were caught using RDF.

DETECTION CHEMICALS

The presence of a possible spy may be revealed by detection chemical kits. The chemicals that are used are invisible when dusted on to objects such as door handles, documents, or pieces of furniture. They react when touched by human skin and become visible, in ultraviolet light, on the hands or other body parts of anyone who has been in contact with them.

Invisible crayon for sticking the powder to a surface

Invisible detection powder

In 1962, Egyptian-born Elie Cohen (1924–65) began spying for Israel in Syria, posing as a wealthy Syrian businessman. He infiltrated Syrian society and used the contacts he made to gather intelligence. Cohen passed information about the Syrian armed forces by radio to Israel, but his frequent and predictable transmission schedule led to his detection by RDF equipment. He was tried and publicly hanged in 1965.

PHOTO-SNIPER

This 35 mm surveillance camera is capable of taking high-definition pictures over long distances. It was used by counterintelligence teams of the KGB's Second Chief Directorate and by KGB Border Guards. The shoulder stock mounting for the camera allows it to be held steady without using a cumbersome and conspicuous tripod.

Rubber lens hood

300 mm telephoto lens

Catch securing lens to shoulder stock

Focusing ring

GREEN FILTER

YELLOW FILTER

JAMES JESUS ANGLETON

James Jesus Angleton (1917–87), a wartime OSS (see p. 32) officer, became the CIA chief of counterintelligence after the war. During the 1960s, convinced by KGB defector Anatoli Golitsyn that a spy had penetrated the CIA, Angleton set up an investigation that disrupted the Agency and led to the rejection of several potential KGB defectors to the West. As a result of this affair and his role in an illegal "mail cover" operation, he resigned in 1974.

SCR-504 DIRECTION-FINDING SUITCASE RADIO

This set was used by American intelligence during and after World War II to locate clandestine radio transmitters. The suitcase allows it to be carried without attracting attention.

Loop antenna

Earpiece

Remote operating controls

Telescopic antenna

Information on repairs

Volume control

Valves located for easy replacement

Switch to locate radio band

Flap to conceal controls when case is closed

Accessory pocket for earpiece

Removable shoulder stock

Kalimar SR-200 single lens reflex camera

Rubber eye cup

Camera body locking mount

Shutter release trigger

Pistol grip

Shoulder stock attachment

Shoulder butt

PHOTO-SNIPER

Anti-bugging devices

AN ANTI-BUGGING DEVICE normally consists of a radio receiver, linked up with other electronic equipment, that is used to detect hidden transmitters. Equipped with an anti-bugging device, an audio counterintelligence expert will "sweep" a room or any other site for bugs (see p. 82). This action is not enough on its own: the site must also be inspected by hand and eye, to spot bugs that are not transmitting. Afterwards, the site must be guarded to prevent intruders from planting new bugs.

PORTABLE DETECTION KIT

Included in this anti-bugging kit is an oscilloscope – an instrument that can display a radio signal as an image on a screen. This helps to spot secret transmissions, which often have a distinct appearance when displayed on an oscilloscope. Sometimes the signal from a bug may be masked by a powerful radio signal, which makes the bug difficult to locate.

Briefcase lid

Plug connection

Oscilloscope for showing a radio signal on screen

Antenna for detecting transmissions

Fine tuning knob

Antenna for sweeping room to find precise location of bugs

Mains plug

Headphones

Wave band selector

Coarse tuning knob

Frequency display

SOUND DETECT KIT

American intelligence agents used the Sound Detect kit during the 1950s and 1960s. It included microphones, probes, and other devices for detecting bugs. Used in conjunction with the amplifier, it could help find most types of listening device. Some of the components, such as the microphones, could also be used as listening devices themselves.

Metal detector handle

Metal detector unit

Contact microphone

Carbon microphone

Headphone connector

Amplifier unit

Test clips

Radio frequency probe for detecting radio transmissions in the power line

Induction coil

Headphones

Transformer

Microphone

Power plug

THE SCAN-LOCK

The Scan-Lock is a radio receiver that automatically locks on to the strongest radio signal. If an illegal transmitter is detected, the search wand can locate it. The Scan-Lock can also be set up outside a room where an important meeting is taking place, guarding constantly against remote-controlled bugs.

Antenna

Heinz Felfe

Heinz Felfe (b.1918) was a member of the World War II Nazi SD (see p.34). In 1950 he was recruited as a Soviet spy and infiltrated the West German Foreign Intelligence Service, the BND. Felfe compromised West German intelligence operations for 11 years. With his inside knowledge he was able to warn Soviet audio technicians of the movements of BND sweepers, so the Soviets had time to remove or switch off their bugs.

Search wand

Extension lead

Power lead

Countersurveillance

SPIES RECEIVE SPECIAL TRAINING in countersurveillance, the object of which is to detect hostile surveillance, for instance of personnel, meetings, safe houses, or dead drops. The discovery of hostile surveillance is sufficient cause to cancel a meeting, bypass a safe house, or abort the planned servicing of a dead drop. Specialized technology exists that can help the countersurveillance team, including video and radio monitoring of likely threats. Team members may have to use disguises to avoid being recognized. The resources available to countersurveillance teams are likely to vary according to circumstances. Obviously, it is easier to mount such operations in a friendly country than in a hostile one.

RADIO WRISTWATCH

This watch was used by the KGB in the 1980s, both for surveillance and countersurveillance operations. It received prearranged signals, which it displayed on a screen. Its receiver was worn on the body, with a vibrator to indicate when a signal came in. The watch was used to control the movements of a spy. If the controllers became aware of hostile surveillance, they could send an emergency code ordering the mission to be aborted.

SURVEILLANCE RADIO

This body-worn radio was in use by the KGB in the 1960s. It was worn hidden under the clothing. A microphone and small speaker were concealed under the lapels, either of the coat or of a jacket underneath. A pocket buzzer warned of incoming messages. The user could surreptitiously communicate with other team members, or with a coordinating base station.

Microphone (worn behind lapel)

Speaker (worn behind lapel)

Transmitter

Cable to power supply (worn at the small of the back)

Power supply

Transmitter (worn at waist)

Buzzer (carried in pocket)

Antenna wires (hung in sleeves or trouser legs)

Transmit/receive switch (carried in pocket)

Safety pin holds wire to clothing

Antenna wire

Safety pin

Radio in position
This picture incorporates an imaginary X-ray view of the equipment in the position in which it would be worn. Bands of stretchy material around the waist hold the transmitter and power supply in place.

INTELLIGENCE DISGUISE KIT

To avoid being recognized when carrying out countersurveillance, team members may have to alter their appearance, perhaps more than once. These changes may be as simple as changing the colour of coat being worn, or adding or removing a hat. This 1960s kit contains materials for a wide range of disguises. As well as items for altering the appearance of the face and hair, it includes the more unusual device of a false heel to put in an agent's shoe. This overcomes the problem of an individual being recognized by his or her gait.

Comb

Comb

Cold cream

Dyeing brush

Trimming scissors

Mixing dish

Mixing dish

Instruction manual showing moustache shapes

Moustache in case

Tweezers

Spirit glue

Case for material

Cotton buds

Moustache material

False heel for altering gait

Travel case

Mirror

Mixing dish

MIRROR
MAKE-UP AND SHAVING

MIRROR
FOR MAKE-UP
AND SHAVING

PLAIN & MAGNIFYING

FACIAL DISGUISE BY ARTIFICIAL AGEING

Artificial ageing is an effective and widely applicable method of disguise, since it does not rely too heavily on disguising the bone structure of the face. Make-up is used to accentuate existing wrinkles and creases. Care is needed to avoid an artificial appearance and to ensure that the hands and throat match the face. The stages in using make-up to simulate ageing are shown on the right. In each picture, make-up is on the subject's right (our left) side only.

Skeleton modelling
Make-up can disguise the bone structure of the face to a small extent.

Reinforcing the lines
Existing facial lines are emphasized by applying dark make-up.

Adding the highlights
Areas of the face that stand out naturally are artificially lightened.

Blending
The balance of lines and highlights is adjusted to give a natural appearance.

Letter interception

WHEN SPIES SEND letters through the postal system they risk interception by enemy counterintelligence. The volume of regular mail makes it impossible for counterintelligence services to search it all, but they may search letters to and from suspect groups, individuals, or addresses. In Western countries, this cannot be done without first obtaining a warrant. Special techniques have been developed to take a letter out of an envelope without damaging it. There are also specialized technical terms: secret opening of mail is known as "flaps and seals" work. Three of the commonest techniques are known as "steam openings", "dry openings" (using a separation of the glue), and "wet openings" (using water).

FLAPS AND SEALS TOOL ROLL

This American set of six tools may be used for surreptitious opening of most kinds of envelope. The tools are either used alone, or in conjunction with steam, water, or another solvent.

Pointed opening tool

Sealing bar

Left opening tool

Wooden opening tool

Pointed opening tool

LETTER EXTRACTION DEVICES

Special devices were used in World War II to take letters from their envelopes without opening the seals. One such device was inserted into the unsealed gap at the top of an envelope flap. The letter was then wound around the device. The thin writing paper of the time made this method particularly effective. The device on the far right was used by the OSS (see p. 32); the other device was used at a postal interception station in Britain.

Willis George
An OSS surreptitious entry expert, Willis George is shown here using the device that he invented to remove letters from envelopes without opening the seals or damaging them.

End-cap

Right opening tool

BRITISH LETTER REMOVAL DEVICE

Pincers

Pincers

Pincer rotating levers

Knurled handle

OSS LETTER REMOVAL DEVICE

FLAPS AND SEALS BRIEFCASE

This American flaps and seals kit from the 1960s was designed to be hidden in a briefcase. The kit contains everything needed for opening envelopes and other packages, as well as for lifting wax seals. There are special tools and containers of distilled water, glue, and chemicals. The base of the briefcase contains a heat table that can be used, in conjunction with damp sheets of blotting paper, to unstick the glue of an envelope.

Blotting paper

Glue containers

Flaps and seals tool roll

Containers for water and chemicals

Temperature gauge

Power cord

Briefcase

Sticks

Brushes

Gloves

Heat table

STAMPS FOR THE FRENCH RESISTANCE

During World War II, French resistance groups (see p. 31) were engaged in secret operations against the occupying German army. These groups often used the mail to communicate when arranging meetings.

The Germans had a practice of luring patriotic Frenchmen to false resistance meetings, using forged letters. If a French resistance sympathizer received such a fake letter and, believing it to be genuine, turned up for a meeting, the Germans would arrest him. If, however, he handed it in to avoid being accused of complicity, he risked betraying the resistance if the letter should prove after all to be genuine.

To resolve this problem, British intelligence made fake French stamps that differed from genuine ones in a tiny detail known only to the resistance. Any "resistance" letters that did not bear this special stamp were assumed to be traps. The Germans never discovered the secret of the stamps.

GENUINE STAMP

FAKE STAMP (ARROW SHOWS DIFFERENCE)

CLANDESTINE COMMUNICATIONS

Walnut concealment
Rolled-up sheets from a KGB one-time pad are hidden in an empty walnut shell. When used properly, the one-time pad system of coding messages is virtually impossible to crack.

I N ORDER TO OPERATE SUCCESSFULLY, it is essential for spies to have secret methods of communicating with their controllers. These clandestine communications must provide a safe and reliable form of contact between spy and spymaster, while remaining secure from interception by the enemy. Methods used for clandestine communication are extremely varied – they range from radio transmissions to secret writing and photographic methods. Common to all of these methods is the care taken to protect them from detection. Radios are made as small as possible, and secret messages are enciphered, or put into code, before transmission. Additionally, radio messages may be speeded up and transmitted in short bursts that are less likely to be detected. Information may be photographed and reduced to microdots. Special inks are employed to write invisible messages. Concealments have been developed to disguise or hide clandestine messages and the equipment used to produce them.

Stamp concealment
A secret message has been written on the back of this postage stamp, mailed from Nuremberg in West Germany.

CLANDESTINE RADIOS

First conceived during the 1920s, special radios for communications were used extensively in World War II. They were often packaged inside suitcases when issued to personnel operating in enemy-occupied Europe, so that they could be carried without suspicion. Technological advances permitted the progressive miniaturization of radios during the war. Development continued after World War II with the introduction of transistors to replace bulky valves. Spy radios most often use Morse code, since this can be transmitted and received more clearly over long distances than voice signals; it is also easier to encrypt Morse code messages than

Agent's radio
The compact Delco 5300 radio was used by CIA agents during the 1960s in Cuba. It could easily transmit messages from that country to the United States.

scramble voice messages. Burst transmissions were introduced at the end of World War II and continued to be important through the Cold War. The technique lessens a radio's transmitting time, decreasing the likelihood of it being located by radio direction finding (RDF).

CIPHER DEVICES

During the early 20th century, a number of electromechanical cipher machines were invented; these produced ciphers so complex that they were thought to be unbreakable. However, during World War II they were broken, both by human mathematical genius and by the use of the world's first electronic computer. One form of cipher that remains virtually unbreakable, even by modern computers, is the one-time pad system.

Kryha cipher device
Invented in 1924, the Kryha device employed a spring-driven alphabetic rotor to code, or encipher, messages. It was used by the German diplomatic corps in World War II.

Ring with concealment
This British ring from World War II could conceal microdots or microfilm.

CONCEALMENTS

Concealments are frequently used for communications, and may be made to resemble everyday objects, such as keys or pens. Discovery of a secret message by the enemy can often give away information about the source of the message, so some concealments are booby-trapped and explode if they are not opened in the correct way, destroying the contents. Information is also often sent in ways that assist in its concealment. Special inks can produce secret writing, which is invisible until it has been treated with the correct chemical reagent. Photographic negatives, greatly reduced in size, can convey information in the form of microdots, which are easy to hide and very difficult to find. To avoid the dangers of personal meetings, spies deliver or collect material at agreed hiding places, known as dead drops. Some very ingenious and convincing concealments have been devised to make dead drop containers blend in unnoticeably with their surroundings.

Modified objects
Technicians can modify everyday objects to make hiding places for such information as the dates and times of secret radio transmissions.

Suitcase radios I

THE CONCEPT OF CONCEALING and transporting radios in suitcases was first developed in the late 1930s by the French and German intelligence services. Quickly adopted by other nations, these suitcase radios were extensively used during World War II. Early examples were bulky and inefficient, but technological advances permitted a reduction in size, while performance was improved. Messages were transmitted in Morse code, which could be received over greater ranges than voice transmissions. Care had to be taken to ensure that the suitcases did not look out of place in the country in which they were to be used. In the United States, the OSS (see p. 32) packaged some of its radios in suitcases obtained from European refugees arriving in New York. In the years following World War II, clandestine radios were small enough to be concealed in attaché cases.

TYPE B MK II RADIO

The most widely used SOE suitcase radio of World War II was the Type B Mk II. It was developed by John Brown in 1942, and was originally designed to operate at a range of up to 800 km (500 miles). In practice it could manage twice that distance in good conditions.

Civilian suitcase

Power supply

Morse key

Spares box

Battery clips

Frequency coils

Frequency tuning knob

Headphones

Spare tube

Power plug

Power plug

• • • • • TECHNICAL DATA

Dimensions	47 × 34 × 15 cm (18½ × 13½ × 6 in)
Weight	14.9 kg (32¾ lb)
Range	up to 800 km (500 miles)
Power supply	97–250 V AC from house; 6 V DC from car battery
Power output	average 20 W
Transmitter	3.0 to 16.0 MHz in three bands
Receiver	4 tube superheterodyne receiving voice, tone, and Morse; 3.1 to 15.5 MHz in three bands

Transmitting
In a still taken from a film about the SOE, operative Jacqueline Nearne can be seen transmitting with a suitcase radio.

Jacqueline Nearne

The SOE (see p.30) recruited Jacqueline Nearne (1916–82) from the First Aid Nursing Yeomanry (FANY). She was taught how to make Morse code transmissions with a suitcase radio. In 1943 Nearne was sent to France to act as a courier. There she formed the link between several SOE groups covering a large area around Paris. The British later awarded Nearne the MBE (Member of the Order of the British Empire) for her work.

TYPE A MK III RADIO

John Brown worked with the Marconi Company in 1943 to produce the Type A Mk III radio, which was smaller and lighter than any previous models. It was created by reducing the size of some components of the Type B Mk II radio. Because it was so light, the Mk III was an instant success with SOE operatives. Almost 9 kg (20 lb) lighter than the Type B Mk II, it had the same transmission range of about 800 km (500 miles).

JOHN BROWN: SUITCASE RADIO INVENTOR

In 1941, John Brown (1917–93), a signals officer in the British Army, was posted to a secret research station where his task was to design specialized radios for the SOE (see p. 30). He invented the "biscuit tin" radio (see p. 116) and the Type B Mk II suitcase radio. These were both widely used during World War II, but it was Brown's Type A Mk III suitcase radio, which contained miniaturized components obtained from the United States, that became the lightest, smallest SOE suitcase radio of the war.

Suitcase · Cooling grille · On/off switch · Voltage selector · Earth terminal · Vibrator socket · AC/DC switch · Spares box · Tuner for telegraph reception · Mains cable · Mains connector · Headphones · Headphones cable · Headphones plug · Screwdriver · Alternative mains connectors · Frequency/waveband switch · Volume control · Morse key · Frequency dial · Neon frequency-control tube · Transmitter tuning knob · Morse key plug · Antenna connector · Transmission/reception switch · Quartz crystal plate · Padding to protect crystal

Suitcase radios II

SSTR-1 RADIO

This transceiver was the standard radio for the OSS (see p. 32). The transmitter, receiver, and power supply were packed in separate boxes for concealment. Often hidden in civilian suitcases for disguise, the radio was packed in the fibre case illustrated here for some operations.

• • • • • • TECHNICAL DATA

Dimensions	10 x 24 x 9 cm (4 x 9½ x 3½ in)
Weight	9–20 kg (20–45 lb)
Range	480–1,600 km (300–1,000 miles)
Power supply	110/220 V AC; 6 V DC; generator
Power output	8–15 W
Transmitter	3.0 to 14.0 MHz in three bands
Receiver	5 tube superheterodyne receiving voice, tone, and CW (Morse)

Fibre suitcase

Power supply

Tuning knob

Receiver

Crystals

Rectifier

Battery attachment clips

Transmitter

Power lead

SUITCASE RECEIVER

This compact 1920s radio was used in World War II by the French intelligence service, which clandestinely monitored German radio traffic for the British.

Tuning knob

Voltage dial

SOE RADIO SECURITY

Personnel using clandestine radios, such as suitcase radios, transmitted to special receiving stations. The SOE (see p. 30) set up such stations, known as home stations, around Britain. Radio operators to staff them were recruited from the First Aid Nursing Yeomanry (FANY). The stations consisted of huts for the radio operators surrounded by large areas of antennas. To avoid the need for messages to be repeated, all transmissions were recorded – the longer an agent spent transmitting, the greater the danger of capture by the Germans, who employed radio direction finding vehicles. A system known as fingerprinting enabled the SOE to recognize the distinctive Morse "signature" of the sender, and was useful in thwarting German attempts to transmit on captured radios.

Inside an SOE home station
FANY radio operators at an SOE home station in Britain during World War II listen on sensitive receivers for coded messages sent from operatives in occupied Europe.

TECHNICAL DATA	
Dimensions	46 × 33 × 11 cm (18 × 13 × 4½ in)
Weight	9.5 kg (21 lb)
Range	480–4,800 km (300–3,000 miles)
Power supply	90–250 V AC
Power output	6–10 W
Transmitter	4.5 to 22.0 MHz in two bands
Receiver	8 tube superheterodyne receiving two bands: voice and Morse

ATTACHE CASE RADIO

In the 1950s, radios were developed to fit into the standard attaché cases carried by business people. This radio could transmit for about 480 km (300 miles) using a short indoor antenna. With a longer outdoor antenna, the radio had a range of about 4,800 km (3,000 miles) for short-wave Morse code messages. This radio was used in Miami during the 1960s to communicate with agents involved in covert operations against the Castro regime in Cuba (see p. 139).

Attaché case

Calibration instructions

Tuning dial

Antenna socket

Earth socket

Band selector

Morse key

Earphone

Power plug

Light

Agents' radios

AGENTS OFTEN USE SPECIAL RADIOS to communicate rapidly with their home bases. Radios may be used when it is important for an agent to communicate with a controller, or when it is necessary to send an intelligence report without delay. As well as being powerful enough to transmit over long distances, agents' radios must be small enough to carry and conceal with ease. World War II agents' radios often comprised two or three major component elements (known as modules), as this made them more portable. With advances in technology since the war, agents' radios have become considerably smaller and can now transmit to satellites.

SE-100/11 AGENTS' RADIO

This powerful mains-operated radio was used by German military intelligence (Abwehr) agents. Like most agents' radios of World War II, this outfit was divided into three modules: transmitter, receiver, and power supply. Modular construction made the set portable and easy to hide. It was also simple to assemble quickly.

Receiver   Power supply   Transmitter

AGENTS' RADIO

This type of Soviet equipment was used in the 1950s and early 1960s. Such radios were issued to KGB agents in western Europe and eastern Asia. They could both transmit and receive, and were used to send long-range signals in Morse code to receiving stations in the Soviet bloc. The example shown below was found in Japan in the late 1950s.

Line filter

Lead | Plug

Earth wire

Antenna wire

Antenna tuner

Headphones

Transmitting crystal

Receiver

Multi-voltage power supply

Transmitter

Morse key

COMMUNICATING WITH RESISTANCE GROUPS

During World War II, resistance groups made use of radios to receive coded broadcasts from Britain. As well as war news, broadcasts from the BBC provided secret messages from the SOE (see p. 30). The German army, realizing how important radio communications could be for resistance groups, confiscated all short-wave radios in the countries they occupied. SOE radio expert John Brown (see p. 113) designed a special covert radio set, known as the Miniature Communication Receiver Mk 1 (MCR-1). This outfit was issued to resistance fighters concealed in biscuit tins. Thousands of these portable sets were sent to France during the war for distribution to the SOE and resistance groups.

MCR-1 radio in action
SOE operatives in action use a "biscuit tin" radio to receive coded messages from base.

The MCR-1 "biscuit tin" radio
The main parts of the radio could be packed discreetly in biscuit tins.

DELCO 5300 RADIO

Used by CIA agents in the 1960s and 1970s, this small but powerful set had a number of advanced features for its time. It could send voice or Morse code transmissions. Messages were transmitted and received on separate frequencies to maintain secrecy. In an emergency, an agent could use a low voice for transmission by using the whisper switch, or even shut down the transmission instantly with the dead-man switch. A GRA-71 burst encoder (see p. 118) could be fitted to the radio.

••••••	TECHNICAL DATA
Dimensions	254 × 127 × 114 mm (10 × 5 × 4½ in)
Weight	3.4 kg (7½ lb) with battery
Range	Antenna dependent
Power supply	Battery with 4, 12, and 28 volt taps
Power output	5 watts Morse, 1.5 watts voice
Transmitter	Morse/voice; 3 to 8 MHz in four channels
Receiver	Superheterodyne for voice, tone, and Morse; coverage same as transmitter

Handwritten frequency list

Handle for accessory compartment

Receiver channel selector knob

Transmit/ receive selector

Antenna socket

Earth socket

Rubber for watertight seal

Waterproof latch

Waterproof case suitable for burying

Battery compartment

Dead-man switch

Whisper switch

Voice/Morse selector switch

Connector socket for GRA-71 burst encoder

Transmitter channel selector knob

Pressure equalization valve

Earphone connection

Built-in Morse key

EARPHONE

REMOTE LEAD

MICROPHONE

Specialized communications

FACE-TO-FACE MEETINGS ARE RISKY, so a variety of specialized devices have been developed to enable agents to communicate with their controllers. Those that facilitate contact within the same locality are known as short-range agent communications (SRAC) devices. For long-distance communications, messages are often sent in Morse code and compressed by means of a burst encoder, which reduces the chances of detection. Special radios are issued to "sleepers" – agents living unsuspected in their target country for years, while leading apparently normal lives. Sleepers tune in to prearranged radio frequencies at set times to listen for coded instructions from their controllers.

RADIO WITH BURST ENCODER

This equipment was used by the SAS (see p. 138). It consists of a transceiver coupled with a GRA-71 burst encoder, which compresses Morse code messages for transmission in a short burst. This reduces the chance of detection by radio direction-finding equipment.

KGB RADIO BURST TAPES

The KGB provided its agents in the post-World War II period with specially designed radios for sending messages back to the Soviet Union. Many of these agent radios were coupled with equipment for preparing and sending burst transmissions. The equipment used to prepare the tape had the advantage that, as an alternative to audio tape, it could be loaded with standard 35 mm photographic film. This kind of film was always readily available and would not cause suspicion if found by the enemy.

CONVERTED 35 mm FILM

Recorded message

CONVERTED AUDIO TAPE

Burst transmission tapes
In advance of transmission, the message was recorded in Morse code by punching a series of holes in 35 mm film or audio tape.

Meter

Transceiver

Antenna socket

Format switch

Morse alphabet

Frequency selector

Morse key

Volume control

Noise limiter control

Transmitter cable

Earphone cable

Waterproof socket cover

Cassette lid

Cassette tape with Morse message

Burst encoder

Manual Morse coder (stores message on cassette tape)

Spare dial for Morse coder

Cassette

Cassette lid

Transmit switch

Semi-automatic Morse coder (stores message on cassette tape)

Dot key

Space key

Dash key

Head strap

Earphone

Flexible antenna

String used for hoisting and fixing antenna

FE-10 AGENTS' RECEIVER

This small German receiver was issued to "sleeper" agents (see opposite) in the 1980s, complete with a signal plan. This stated the agent's call number and gave a transmission schedule and decoding instructions. The receiver was powered by a 9 volt rechargeable battery. Sleeper agents would use the receiver to monitor a variety of frequencies, inserting different crystals in the socket provided to receive signals on different frequencies.

Antenna wire
Earth wire
Antenna socket
Earth socket
Terminal
VOLUME
FINE
TUNE
Sockets for battery contacts
Socket for crystal
VARTA
Tuning module
RADIO RECEIVER
BATTERY
WIRE HOLDER
Earpiece
CRYSTAL
Plug
EARPIECE AND WIRE

HOTEL LAMP TRANSCEIVER

This is a mass-produced table lamp, suitable for use in hotel bedrooms, which was available on the American market in the 1960s. An American intelligence agency covertly modified a number of lamps for clandestine use, installing a radio receiver and transmitter (a transceiver) in the base. Such a lamp could be placed in the hotel bedroom of, for example, a Soviet double agent, enabling him to contact his controller in secret. Set up in a different way, the lamp transceiver could also be used as a listening device.

Power plug
Transceiver in lamp base

INFRARED COMMUNICATION SYSTEM

This German device from the 1960s transmits and receives voice messages over a 3 km (1.86 mile) range, using a beam of infrared light. The device can be used by day or night, but rain or fog reduce its performance. Unlike contemporary infrared systems for night vision, this system was (and still is) extremely difficult to detect or intercept.

Microphone
Talk button
Earpiece
Infrared transmitter
Infrared receiver

Infrared communication
This type of communication is particularly useful in an urban setting, allowing secure conversation between, for example, agent and case officer. A clear line of sight between the two is essential for the infrared beam to link the transceivers.

Cipher devices

CIPHER DEVICES are used to make messages unintelligible to all except the intended recipient. Essentially, they work by replacing the letters or numbers in a message with other letters or numbers. Early cipher devices used simple letter-for-letter substitution, in which a given letter is always enciphered as the same other letter. In the 1920s, French and American cryptographers (cipher experts) developed machines that used polyalphabetic substitution. In this more sophisticated method, a given letter may be substituted by a different one from a range of possible letters each time it occurs.

M-94 CIPHER DEVICE

The M-94, based on an 18th-century cipher device, worked by rotating the discs of letters around the cylinder. The M-94 cipher device was used by the US Army from 1922 until 1943, when it was replaced by the Converter M-209.

Disc with letters in random sequence | Bar to align letters on discs | Nut to lock discs in position

KRYHA CIPHER MACHINE

Designed in 1924, this machine employed polyalphabetic substitution. It was used in World War II by German diplomats, who were unaware that the cipher had been broken by the Americans.

Reading aperture

Top cover (in open position)

Inner cover (in open position)

Concentric discs

Indicating disc

Spring motor

BOLTON'S PATENT CIPHER WHEEL

This device substituted one letter for another. It is typical of late 19th-century cipher devices and was based on the cipher disc of Leon Battista Alberti, a 15th-century Italian scholar and cryptographer.

Movable aperture

Turning knob

Concentric alphabet wheels

THE HEBERN CIPHER MACHINE

Edward Hebern (1869–1952) was a self-taught American inventor. From 1909 on he produced a series of electromechanical cipher machines with rotating discs. Hebern's machines were designed to send secret messages between businessmen who were anxious to prevent industrial espionage.

In 1915, Hebern introduced a system in which two typewriters were connected by wires to a rotor in the centre. This concept was very advanced for its time, and was later used by the Japanese diplomatic service for its Red ciphers (see p. 36).

The US Navy evaluated this machine, but during testing, the cryptographer William Friedman (see p. 36) broke the cipher. Not deterred, Hebern developed the Mark II, or SIGABA, machine, which became the most secure American cipher system in use during World War II.

EDWARD HEBERN

1921 HEBERN CIPHER MACHINE

CONVERTER M-209 CIPHER MACHINE

The Converter M-209 cipher machine was designed by Boris Hagelin and was widely used by the US Army during World War II. It was a compact and portable machine that used a series of rotors to encipher and decipher secret military messages. Once a message was enciphered through the Converter M-209, it printed the text on paper tape in five-letter groups. The message was then transmitted by radio and deciphered. An enciphered M-209 message could be deciphered and printed on another M-209 machine.

BORIS HAGELIN

In 1934, the Swedish cryptographer Boris Hagelin (1892–1983) designed a cipher machine for the French secret service. He developed this into the Converter M-209, which was used by the US Army. During World War II, more than 140,000 of these machines were produced.

Screwdriver

Paper pressure arm

Roll of paper tape

Top cover

Resetting button

Tweezers for paper tape

Drive knob

Indicating disc

Setting knob

Letter counter

Bank of six key wheels

Benchmark for key wheels

Resetting knob

CD 57 CIPHER MACHINE

The CD 57 was designed by Hagelin for French secret police work. It was small enough to be carried in a pocket and had a thumb-operated lever, which left the other hand free to write the message.

Open cover with window

Key wheels

Thumb-operated lever

Alphabet disc

Enigma machine

GERMANY'S STRATEGY IN WORLD WAR II was to wage a war of total mobility on land, at sea, and in the air. This required the fastest and most secret communications possible, and the Enigma cipher machine, originally designed to protect the secrecy of business messages, was adopted for this purpose. Versions of the Enigma were developed for use in different German organizations, such as the armed forces, the security and intelligence services, and the diplomatic corps. German refinements to the Enigma increased the complexity of the cipher continually throughout the war. In 1943 the first computer in the world was needed to break it. The ability to break the Enigma cipher is seen by historians as a major contributory factor in the Allied victory in the war.

ENIGMA CIPHER MACHINE

Invented in 1923, this was a mechanized electric device for enciphering and deciphering messages. Each letter was enciphered separately through a series of plug connections and rotors.

Spare light bulbs

Upper lid

Filter catch

Spare double plug

Plug retaining bracket

Metal cover plate fits over rotor cylinders

Coding rotor

Rotor cylinder

Current-testing socket

Keyboard

Plug socket

Plugboard settin is altered regula to change ciphe

Instruction in German: "Shut this panel"

Light filter is placed over lightboard to dim the light

Catch secures light filter

Front panel

Double plug cable

Double plug

Lightboard

Cable-testing socket

Rotor release lever

Rotor slit fits over wheels

Viewing window (shows code letters)

Japanese Enigma
A special version of the Enigma was made for use by Japan during World War II.

German soldiers using the Enigma
One soldier is typing a message, while another calls out the enciphered letters as they are illuminated. The enciphered letters are being copied down ready for transmission by radio.

MECHANISM OF THE ENIGMA

The key to the security of the Enigma lay in the way the machine was set up. Its alphabetical rotors could be placed on the rotor cylinder in any order, and the internal wiring in each rotor could be aligned in any position. The cipher was determined by the initial settings of these rotors. The plugs were inserted in the plugboard in any combination. All these variables – the key settings – were changed regularly. Even if an enemy had a machine identical to the one used to create a message, he could not break the cipher without also learning the key settings used when the message was enciphered.

1 *A lever is lifted to release the rotors. The rotors are removed and the internal wiring, known as the "ring setting", altered. The rotors are put back in the order specified in the current instructions.*

2 *A letter from each rotor shows through the windows of the cover. The rotors are turned until the letters are arranged as specified in the current instructions. These letters form the "ground setting".*

3 *Once the rotors are positioned correctly, the cover is shut over them. Then the connections on the plugboard are changed: they are manipulated to link pairs of letters specified by the operator's codebook.*

4 *The Enigma operator picks four random letters and enters them twice. The resulting eight-letter cipher is used as a message prefix. Before enciphering the message, the rotors are set to show the four random letters.*

8 *A reflecting disc at the end of the row of rotors reflects the signal back through the rotors.*

ROTOR BOARD

7 *A signal from 9 passes through the rotor cage and is altered each time it passes through a rotor.*

THE GEHEIMSCHREIBER

A more complex cipher device than the Enigma was the Geheimschreiber. It had either 10 or 12 rotors, which made enciphered messages extremely difficult to break. The Geheimschreiber was very large and was installed only in main communications centres, in Germany itself or in German-held territories.

10 rotors   Keyboard   Teletype paper

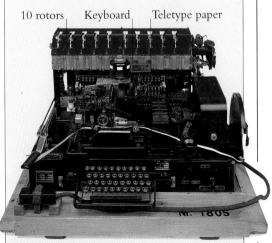

GEHEIMSCHREIBER, SIEMENS MODEL (CODENAME STURGEON)

LIGHTBOARD

5 *The first letter of a message is typed on the keyboard. The letter H is used as an example to show the enciphering process.*

10 *The signal goes to the lightboard. It lights A, which then becomes the first letter of the enciphered message. This procedure is repeated for each letter of the message.*

KEYBOARD

9 *The signal returns to the plugboard, in this example to 12. It is re-routed by a connection to 18.*

PLUGBOARD

6 *An electrical signal from H travels to 16 then 9 on the plugboard. At this stage, the letter is changed.*

Ciphers and secret writing

SPIES OFTEN NEED TO WRITE messages that cannot be discovered or understood by the enemy. A written message can be encrypted by means of a cipher device (see p. 120) or with a cipher system such as a one-time pad, which is completely safe from code-breakers if properly used. Messages can also be hidden by means of secret writing, which is normally done by one of two methods: the wet system, in other words writing in invisible inks; and the transfer system, in which a piece of chemically impregnated paper, known as a carbon, transfers ink to a piece of normal paper when this is placed beneath it. Another way of concealing a message is to reduce it in size, producing a microdot (see p. 126).

GERMAN WORLD WAR I INVISIBLE INK AND SPONGE

Herbert Boeckenhaupt

Herbert Boeckenhaupt (b.1942) was a US Air Force radio communications specialist. As a young man, he volunteered to work for the Soviet Union for money. From 1962 until his arrest in 1966, Boeckenhaupt sent American military secrets to the KGB, often using secret writing. After his arrest, instructions concerning a dead drop, on 35 mm film, and secret writing carbons were found in Boeckenhaupt's home.

HANDKERCHIEF WITH SECRET WRITING

Some invisible inks may be used on cloth as well as on paper. This handkerchief was prepared in West Germany in the 1960s. The message concerns a meeting that is about to take place and refers to information that will arrive from East Germany.

Section where a chemical has been applied to reveal message

CIPHER SHEETS IN WALNUT SHELL

Rolled up inside this walnut shell, which was found in the possession of a Soviet agent in former West Germany, are two cipher sheets from one-time pads.

Walnut shell

Cipher sheets

MADAME DE VICTORICA

US Military Intelligence intercepted a letter written in secret ink to a suspected German spy during World War I. The letter was traced back to Madame Marie de Victorica (1882–1920), who lived in New York. On her arrest in April 1918, she was found to own two silk scarves that were impregnated with water-soluble secret inks. She was indicted on spying charges but, as she offered to work for the government, she was not tried. She was a heroin addict, and the authorities supplied her with drugs to ensure her cooperation. Her drug control card is shown here.

DRUG CONTROL CARD

SUB-LATENT PHOTOGRAPHIC IMAGE

Secret writing can be concealed by printing a photograph over it. The message is revealed by applying chemicals that remove only the top image. This photograph was used in the 1960s by the East German security service to cover a layer of secret writing, part of which has been revealed. Once a message has been concealed in this way it can be carried safely without fear of detection. Radio communication plans are often hidden in this way.

Section where a chemical has been applied to reveal message

ONE-TIME PADS

The one-time pad system of enciphering was first used by the German diplomatic service during the 1920s. Both sender and recipient have an identical pad of cipher sheets, each of which is used to encipher a single message and then destroyed. As the cipher is never repeated, it is theoretically unbreakable.

However, if an opposing intelligence agency were to obtain a copy of one of the pads, the message might be compromised. In 1943, the system was adopted by the SOE (see p. 30). Pads, and the keys that were used for encoding and decoding, were printed on silk for its durability and ease of transportation.

Encoding and decoding key

Pad used by base for encoding and decoding

Pad used by agent for encoding and decoding

Extra key

HOME STATION TO OUT STATION

OUT STATION TO HOME STATION

SECRET WRITING TECHNIQUE

Agencies that use secret writing for communicating with spies have produced many different special inks and developing reagents of great complexity. A simple example using lemon juice shows how secret inks work and clearly demonstrates the principle of secret writing. A message written in lemon juice between the lines of an ordinary letter quickly dries and becomes invisible. Heat applied to the letter makes the juice visible again so that the secret message can be read.

Writing the message
A letter is written in ordinary ink, and a secret message is written in lemon juice applied with a matchstick between the lines of the letter.

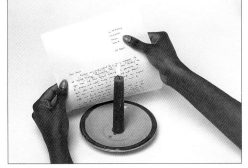

Reading the message
The person receiving the message applies heat to it with a candle, a light bulb, or an iron. The lemon juice turns brown, revealing the message.

Microdots

MICRODOTS ARE TINY PHOTOGRAPHS of messages, secret documents, or other images which are so small that they can be read only with a magnifying viewer. The camera and the method shown on these pages produce microdots as small as 1 mm in width; but cameras exist that can produce microdots even smaller than that. Microdots have been used by intelligence agencies since the time of the American Civil War in the 1860s. The KGB trained some of its agents, including its American spy Robert Thompson, to produce and conceal microdots. Methods of concealment include secret chambers in rings and coins, or a tiny piece of film that can be embedded in the edge of a postcard. Microdots are read with special viewers, and these, too, are often skilfully concealed.

CONCEALMENTS

Microdots can be concealed in everyday objects or in special concealments. The German coin could conceal hundreds of microdots. The ring, designed during World War II, concealed either microdots or a compass. The slitter made incisions in the edges of postcards in which microdots could be hidden.

Reverse thread

Secret chamber

Secret chamber

RING

POSTCARD SLITTER

COIN

MICRODOT CAMERA

The intelligence agencies of former Soviet bloc countries, such as East Germany, used this miniaturized microdot camera. Shown actual size and enlarged, this camera could be hidden easily. It was used to make the three microdots shown on the right, also actual size. The camera produces a finished microdot from the original photograph, without using an intermediate negative.

Top opens to allow film to be inserted

Spiral spring

Film retaining disc

Film placed here

PEN CAP

MICRODOT CAMERA (ACTUAL SIZE)

MICRODOTS (ACTUAL SIZE)

Microdot camera fits in hole made in ruler

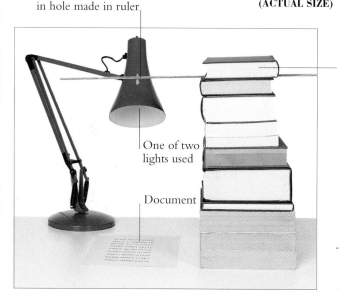

Books hold ruler at correct height

One of two lights used

Document

Container for lens elements

MICRODOT CAMERA (ENLARGED)

Using a microdot camera
The camera is attached to a ruler and positioned above the document to be photographed, using a stack of books. Each type of camera must be held securely at a specific distance from the document. Depending on the kind of film being used, the exposure time may be up to several minutes long.

Cap acts as a shutter for the long exposures used

Robert Glenn Thompson

In 1965, Robert Glenn Thompson (b.1925), a former member of the US Air Force Office of Special Investigations, was arrested and given a 30-year jail sentence for passing secrets to the KGB. He had been trained by the KGB in Moscow in 1957, learning secret writing techniques, microphotography, and how to use a Minox camera. In 1978 Thompson was involved in a spy swap deal in which he was released in East Germany.

MICRODOT READERS

In order to read microdots, agents need high-powered magnifying devices. These can range from specially designed miniature viewers, small enough to be concealed in a cigarette, to commercially produced pocket microscopes. Agents operating in hostile countries prefer the most easily concealed types of readers.

Viewer small enough to fit in a cigarette

MICRODOT VIEWER

POCKET MICROSCOPE

MINIATURE MICRODOT VIEWER

FOUNTAIN PEN VIEWER CONCEALMENT

This East German microdot viewer is concealed within a 1950s fountain pen. A small ink sac could be installed, allowing the pen to work so that it would not arouse suspicion if examined. The pen would be used to transport the viewer between secure hiding places, or conceal it inside a desk.

FOUNTAIN-PEN NIB

MICRODOT VIEWER

PEN BODY

HOW TO MAKE A MICRODOT

A microdot can be made with a high-quality 35 mm camera by using a two-stage technique known as the British Method, which is shown here. Using high-contrast black-and-white film, a photograph of a document is taken so that the image of the document fills the whole frame of the film. The film is processed and the resulting negative is mounted in an opening cut in a piece of black cardboard. When lit from behind, the text on the negative shows up as white on black. This image is photographed from a distance of 127 cm (4 ft 2 in) – with a lens of focal length 50 mm – to produce a black-on-white image that occupies a 1 mm length of the resulting negative. This tiny image is cut out to produce a microdot.

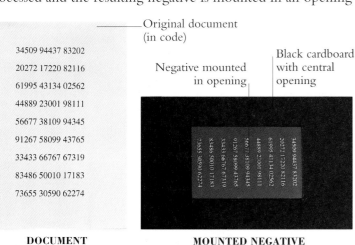

Original document (in code)

```
34509 94437 83202
20272 17220 82116
61995 43134 02562
44889 23001 98111
56677 38109 94345
91267 58099 43765
33433 66767 67319
83486 50010 17183
73655 30590 62274
```

Negative mounted in opening

Black cardboard with central opening

DOCUMENT

MOUNTED NEGATIVE

Mounted negative

Camera in position

Microdot

CAMERA SET-UP

MICRODOT ON NEGATIVE

Concealments I

MANY INGENIOUS CONCEALMENTS have been devised to allow spies to hide information and equipment. They vary widely in size and format. The basic principle followed is to disguise or hide the item concerned so that it appears to be an innocent object that will not arouse suspicion. It is essential that the concealment used is in keeping with the lifestyle and circumstances of the agent equipped with it. Some concealments are made specifically for the purpose; others are converted from everyday objects. Some are booby-trapped, so that unauthorized attempts to open them will result in the destruction of their contents. Frequent use is made of reverse threads, which unscrew clockwise, rather than anticlockwise as is usual.

STATUETTE CONCEALMENT

This wooden carving of a wapiti, a type of deer, covers a secret storage place for a subminiature camera. The carving can be lifted to reveal a compartment containing a Minox IIIS camera complete with a spare cassette of film. The statuette was found by the West German counterintelligence service (BfV) in the apartment of an East German spy operating in West Germany during the Cold War.

STATUETTE

Carving lifted to reveal concealment

Pin is inserted in hole to open lock

Slot receives bolt of lock

Lock

Spare film cassette | **CONCEALMENT IN BASE** | Camera

SILVER DOLLAR CONCEALMENT

Machined from two original coins for a Western intelligence service, this concealment was used to hide microfilm and one-time pads. It is opened by pressing on the eagle's wing tip.

Bottom half of hollow coin

Point that is pressed to open coin

Message to be concealed

Artificial eye

EYE CONCEALMENT

This German photograph dates from the period between the two World Wars. It illustrates the use of an artificial eye to conceal and transport a secret message.

SPY PROFILE | **Maria Knuth**

Polish intelligence recruited German Maria Knuth in 1948. She specialized in using seduction as a means of recruiting agents to her side. Her first job was as a "letter box" for a spy ring in West Berlin. She was equipped with a number of concealment devices to hide microdots and sheets from one-time cipher pads. Later she attempted to recruit a member of West German counterintelligence (BfV), which led to her arrest in May 1952.

BRUSH CONCEALMENT

Minox cameras were hidden in a variety of concealments by the Soviet and East German intelligence services. The example shown here is concealed inside a gentleman's clothes brush. Services that issued such items had to ensure that they fitted in with the lifestyle adopted by their agent, otherwise the concealment might arouse suspicion.

Slot for locking pin

Hole for inserting pin to open concealment

Minox IIIS camera

CLOTHES BRUSH CONCEALMENT

Locking pin keeps concealment shut

SECRET COMPARTMENT WITH CAMERA

Hollow to accommodate camera

CHESSBOARD CONCEALMENT

West German counterintelligence discovered this chessboard in the possession of an East German agent. It has an internal cavity to conceal a microdot camera, accessories, and film. Such concealments were almost always "one-off" items, designed in special workshops for specific missions.

Microdot camera

Hidden locking mechanism can be opened only with a paper clip

Manual winder to advance film in cassette

Socket for chess pieces (not part of the concealment)

Paper clip opens the concealment

Minox film cassette

PLAYING SURFACE

BASE OF CHESSBOARD

Underside of playing surface

Concealments II

BUTTON AND STAMP CONCEALMENTS

Even careful counterintelligence searches rarely reveal messages such as this inscription under a button, made during World War I, or the tiny message under a postage stamp, used in 1962.

Front of button

Message on back of stamp

Coded message on back

BUTTON

POSTAGE STAMP

BATTERY CASING CONCEALMENT

This style of concealment was used by intelligence agencies in the countries of the former Soviet bloc. Inside the casing of a standard torch battery was a cavity in which film, money, and even microdot cameras and viewers could be hidden. Also in the casing was a much smaller real battery that gave the correct voltage so that the fake battery could actually be used. To open the fake battery casing, the baseplate had to be unscrewed by using a magnet.

INNER BATTERY

HOLLOW BATTERY CASING

Baseplate

Inner battery

Battery casing

Magnet

Roll of film

OPENED CONCEALMENT

Reverse thread

Baseplate

Magnet

MAGNET AND BASEPLATE

CIGARETTE CONCEALMENT

The Polish intelligence service made this metal cylinder so that spies and couriers could conceal tightly rolled "soft film" (film from which the celluloid has been removed to make the film extremely thin) in a cigarette.

Cigarette split open

Aluminium container

Soft film

Container lid

SOAP CASE CONCEALMENT

The Czech intelligence service invented devices for couriers carrying film, such as this soap case. The devices destroy the evidence if opened incorrectly: here the film is wrapped around a flash bulb, which flashes and destroys the film if the case is not opened in the correct manner. To open the case safely, a magnet is placed beneath the case. The magnet pulls open a switch that deactivates the flash.

Magnet

Switch fires flash bulb if lid is opened incorrectly

Battery

Deactivating switch

Flash bulb

L

THE ARTWORK OF BADEN-POWELL

Lord Baden-Powell (1857–1941) is best known as the founder of the Boy Scouts, but he was involved in intelligence-gathering during his early military career. One mission was to obtain details of enemy fortresses in the Balkans in 1890. Baden-Powell disguised himself as an entomologist and sketched butterflies in the area. The veins on the butterfly's wings contained a plan of the fortifications, while the spots on the veins denoted the size and position of guns. The drawing of the leaf was made to show trench lines.

BUTTERFLY SKETCH

LEAF SKETCH

SHAVING CONCEALMENTS

Everyday objects, such as these toiletry items, can be carried without attracting any suspicion. The handle of this French shaving brush has a cavity that opens only when the base is turned clockwise. The can holds and dispenses a small amount of shaving foam; the rest of the space in the can may be used for concealment.

Top of brush crews

Roll of film

SHAVING BRUSH

SHAVING CREAM CAN

Base of can

HOLLOW BOLT

This hollow bolt was used as a dead drop (see p. 132) by Soviet agents operating in West Germany. The head of the bolt could be removed to reveal a cavity in which items could be concealed. Once the bolt was filled it could be screwed into the dead drop site, in this case a wooden railing on a bridge, ready for the arrival of an agent or handler.

(see p. 132)

Bolt in position

BOLT ON BRIDGE

HEAD OF BOLT

Rolled-up message

HOLLOW BOLT

DEAD DROP SITE ON BRIDGE

Dead drops

A DEAD DROP IS A PREARRANGED location at which spies can leave information or from which they can collect instructions, cipher pads, microdot cameras, film, radio schedules, money, or any form of spying equipment. Items are usually placed in specially designed dead drop containers. Spies use dead drops because they are safer than personal meetings, which can jeopardize the safety of at least two links in a spy network. The sites used for dead drops must be inconspicuous, but easy for the agents to find. The procedure for making a dead drop involves a series of signals which the controller and the agent use to ensure that an enemy is not involved or watching.

DEAD DROP SPIKES

Shown actual size, these spikes are stuck in the ground; they are used to hold money, cipher pads, microdot cameras, and other items ready for collection at dead drop locations. One is designed to hold a 35 mm film cassette.

Open lid

35 mm film cassette

Spiked tip

**DEAD DROP
SPIKE FOR 35 mm
FILM CASSETTES**

JOHN WALKER'S FINAL DEAD DROP

On the evening of 17 May 1985, John Walker, an American spy for the KGB (see p. 54), drove to a dead drop site on a country road in Maryland, some 40 km (25 miles) northwest of Washington, DC. He was under surveillance by the FBI.

To signal to his KGB handler that he was in the area for the drop, Walker placed an empty drink can at the foot of a roadside electricity pole. His secret documents were hidden inside a bag of rubbish, and he placed this behind another electricity pole.

The FBI, following Walker, saw him place the drink can and thought it might contain something of importance, so they removed it. The KGB officer, unable to find the can, terminated the procedure and returned safely to the Soviet embassy in Washington, where he was based.

The FBI collected the rubbish bag, complete with the secret documents, and Walker was arrested later that night.

Annotated map

Instructions with place names in red

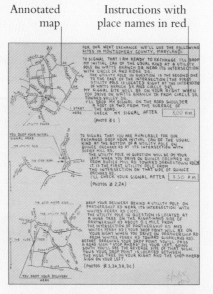

**KGB'S INSTRUCTIONS TO GUIDE
WALKER TO HIS DEAD DROP SITE**

Rubbish

Secret documents

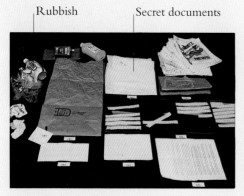

CONTENTS OF WALKER'S DEAD DROP

Label for dead drop site

Electricity pole

KGB PHOTOGRAPH OF THE DEAD DROP

DEAD DROP EMIL

During the 1950s, Bruno Sniegowski spied for Poland in West Germany. The officers in charge of Sniegowski communicated with him using dead drops, one of which was codenamed Emil. A chalk mark at a prearranged place would inform Sniegowski that a message awaited him at Emil. The container used for dead drop Emil was a metal tube, which was hidden at the base of a wall, behind a brick.

SNIEGOWSKI USING A DEAD DROP

CLAM DEAD DROP

A magnet holds this dead drop container to a metal object at the location of the drop. A dead drop location need not be in the ground – the clam container can be fitted in many places, for example under an abandoned car or metal park bench.

LID

Hollow chamber

Magnetic attachment

CLAM DEAD DROP CONTAINER

WATERPROOF DEAD DROP

The weights in this waterproof pouch allow it to be be used to conceal material in a roadside ditch, or beneath marked rocks in a shallow stream.

Ball-bearing weights

Plastic covering

DEAD DROP SPIKE

WEAPONS

A SPY WHOSE FUNCTION is purely to gather intelligence does not normally carry or own a weapon, since there is always a risk that an enemy counterintelligence force might discover the weapon, which would incriminate the spy. Intelligence agencies do, however, stock and even develop weapons for the use of personnel who carry out specialized roles: bodyguards, assassins, and other covert action personnel. In wartime, special forces operating behind enemy lines carry both conventional and specialized weapons.

Concealed blades
During World War II, the British SOE developed a number of concealable edged weapons, as displayed in this knife roll.

Three-finger push dagger
This World War II British dagger had a three-fingered grip that allowed the blade to be thrust into a victim with tremendous force.

SILENCED WEAPONS

Although the frequency of their use in espionage has been exaggerated by writers of spy fiction, silenced weapons do have a role in the work of the intelligence agencies. Many were developed for use by special operations personnel during World War II. Because firearms can never be made completely silent or flashless, experiments were made with crossbows and with pistols adapted to fire darts. Some of the silenced firearms employed in World War II, such as the Welrod (see p. 161) and the Hi-Standard pistol (see p. 141), remain part of the arsenals of major intelligence agencies. Recent versions of the crossbow have also been developed. Many of these are issued for survival use – for example, for hunting if stranded in a remote area – or for killing guard dogs, rather than for use against human targets.

CZ27 semi-automatic pistol with silencer
This Czech 7.65 mm pistol from World War II was later used by West German intelligence.

CLOSE-COMBAT WEAPONS

Specialized weapons made for fighting at close quarters are often carried in covert operations. A considerable degree of training is needed to use some types of close-combat weapons. The type of personnel who carry them are those ordered to attack individual targets by surprise, or those taking part in high-risk operations

Genrikh Yagoda
Yagoda (1891–1938) was head
of the Soviet NKVD and set up
a poison weapons workshop.

who may need a last-resort weapon for self defence. They range from traditional "brass knuckles" to specially designed weapons such as the World War II Peskett Device, which is a combined dagger, garrotte, and cosh.

The spring cosh is often the weapon of choice for subduing opponents. It may be used with lethal force, or merely to knock someone out. Other coshes are used as a means of forcing an enemy to surrender or to disclose information.

Knives are the classic close-combat weapons, and many different types have been developed for use in a variety of situations. Small blades can be hidden under the lapel of a jacket for use in emergencies. The Fairbairn-Sykes fighting knife of World War II, on the other hand, was designed for offensive use. This knife is so perfectly suited to its purpose that it continued in production and service into the 1990s.

Assassination device
Hidden in a fake cigarette packet, this device fires
acid that vaporizes into deadly cyanide gas in the
victim's face, causing death within seconds.

CONCEALED WEAPONS

World War II saw the development of a number of concealed weapons. The main purpose of such weapons was to give an agent who had been detected some chance of escape. They included firing devices that could be worn on belts or carried up an agent's sleeve. Others were disguised as cigars, pipes, or pens. After the war, intelligence agencies have continued to develop such weapons – a notable example is the 4.5 mm calibre firing device issued by the KGB, which could be hidden in a variety of concealments, including a lipstick holder.

The KGB developed assassination weapons that could kill silently and in ways not detectable at autopsy, for example by emitting poison gas or injecting poison pellets. These weapons have been disguised as walking sticks or umbrellas, or concealed in newspapers.

Walther PPK pistol
Designed for German plainclothes police, the
PPK is an easy weapon to hide. This makes it
popular with intelligence agencies worldwide.

Special issue weapons

INTELLIGENCE AGENCIES prefer to equip their personnel with weapons that can be bought commercially, provided the performance is up to operational requirements. Such weapons are cheaper than specially developed ones and, if discovered, less incriminating as they cannot be traced to the agency. The only noticeable difference might be that the agency's armourers may have fine-tuned the sights and trigger to improve performance. The term "special issue" refers to weapons obtained in this way, and to such weapons as the deer gun, manufactured for the CIA for issue to Vietnamese agents in the Vietnam war (1961–75). This cheap, single-shot gun was intended to enable an agent to kill an enemy soldier in order to capture his or her weapon.

CIA DEER GUN

ROYAL CANADIAN MOUNTED POLICE

Until 1981, counterintelligence and security in Canada were the responsibility of the security service of the Royal Canadian Mounted Police (RCMP). An RCMP "Red Squad" was set up in the 1920s to stop the spread of communism. Canadian intelligence realized the extent of infiltration by Soviet spies in 1945, when a Soviet defector informed the Canadians of wide-ranging espionage operations in their country. In 1981, a Security Intelligence Service (SIS) was set up to take over in this field from the RCMP. The Colt Bodyguard shown below is an example of the wide variety of weapons available to SIS officers.

Crest of the RCMP
The members of the Royal Canadian Mounted Police are frequently known as Mounties.

Foresight

Hammer

Muzzle

Hammer shroud

Ejector rod

Cylinder

Colt emblem

Trigger guard

Trigger

Hand grip

• • • • •	TECHNICAL DATA
Maker	Colt Firearms
Frame	Detective Special
Calibre	.38 special
Length	121 mm (4¾ in)
Weight	595 g (19 oz) unloaded
Barrel length	54 mm (2 in)
Capacity	6-shot revolver
Ammunition	Variable

COLT .38 BODYGUARD REVOLVER

The Bodyguard was a modification of the famous Colt Detective Special. A shroud, added to the rear of the frame, prevented the hammer from snagging on clothing if the pistol was drawn from inside a pocket. The revolver was used by many security and intelligence services, including the RCMP.

Hammer

Barrel

Ejector rod Cylinder

Hand grip

Trigger

Trigger guard

COLT .38 COMMANDO REVOLVER

This six-shot revolver was issued to OSS
Sergeant C. W. Magill, who fought with the
Greek resistance during World War II. It was
one of a variety of pistol types used by the OSS
(see p. 32) and was also supplied to American and
Allied troops. Large models, like this, were usually
unsuitable for clandestine use because of their size,
but they were used on other operations.

Sergeant C. W. Magill
Sergeant Magill ("Maggie"), photographed at the age of 28
years in the mountain village of Kastania in Greece. He used
the Colt .38 Commando revolver while working with the
Greek resistance in World War II.

THE FRENCH SECRET SERVICE

Formerly known as the SDECE, the French secret
service was reconstituted in 1981 as the DGSE.
French operatives have been involved in many high-
profile operations, including attempts to assassinate
and abduct foreign political leaders. They made
several attempts to assassinate President Nasser of
Egypt during the 1950s, despite the fact that he
was being supported by the CIA.

Hammer Ejection port

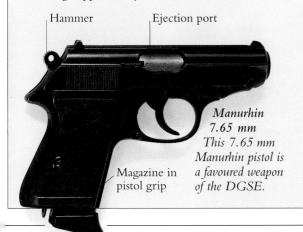

Manurhin
7.65 mm
This 7.65 mm
Manurhin pistol is
a favoured weapon
of the DGSE.

Magazine in
pistol grip

NAGANT 7.62 mm SECRET POLICE REVOLVER

In the 1920s, a compact version of the standard Nagant service revolver
was developed for the Soviet secret police. The 7.62 mm Secret Police
revolver was easily concealed. It was used until the 1940s, and armed the
elite bodyguard unit that protected Stalin, the head of state, in Moscow.

Shortened barrel

Hammer

Trigger

Peter Deriaban
As a member of the KGB's elite
Kremlin Guard Directorate, the defector
Deriaban was issued with the Nagant.

Silenced weapons I

FIREARMS ARE NEVER totally silent, although they can be made quiet enough not to attract attention. A silencer eliminates most of the sound of the muzzle blast, but not the sound of the weapon's working parts. Ammunition that travels slower than the speed of sound is used, so avoiding the "crack" caused by supersonic bullets. Most silenced weapons were developed for assassinations or for special operations in armed conflicts. In peacetime, spies who are not on special assassination missions may carry silenced weapons for self-defence. The U-2 spy plane pilot Francis Gary Powers (see p. 52) was issued with the silenced Hi-Standard pistol for use as a hunting weapon in case his plane should be downed in remote enemy territory.

MOSSAD

The Institute for Intelligence and Special Operations, or Mossad, was formed in 1951 as Israel's external intelligence service. It is the equivalent of America's CIA or Britain's MI6, but employs far fewer personnel: only 30–35 Mossad case officers are active in the whole world. However, the organization often also draws on local Jewish volunteers, known as *sayanim* (see p. 165). Mossad is most active against hostile Arab states surrounding Israel and against Palestinian political organizations. One of its most prominent operations was the daring abduction of the Nazi war criminal Adolf Eichmann from Argentina in 1960 to stand trial in Israel for his crimes in World War II.

MOSSAD CREST

BERETTA 7.65 mm PISTOL WITH SILENCER

Italian Beretta pistols are often used by Mossad. The small Beretta is easy to conceal and can be loaded with reduced-charge cartridges in order to increase the effectiveness of the silencer. This adaptation of a Beretta Model 70 was issued to members of Mossad's assassination teams (known as *kidon*).

Hammer

Trigger guard

Trigger

Grip

Ammunition clip

Silencer

End-cap

Silencer

Peter Mason

Former Defence Intelligence Staff Captain Peter Mason (b.1927) is one of the leading experts on special weapons and close-combat shooting. In 1946 he joined a British Special Air Service (SAS) "Hunter Team". Using captured enemy weapons, such as the Beretta used by the OVRA (see opposite), these three-man teams hunted down and secretly killed those guilty of murdering SAS or SOE members (see p. 30) during World War II.

SS Colonel Otto Skorzeny
Otto Skorzeny (1908–75) was the commander of Germany's Brandenburg commando detachment in World War II. He mounted a number of audacious operations, including the dramatic rescue of the Italian leader Mussolini from Italian resistance forces. Skorzeny often used a captured British silenced Sten submachine gun for his operations.

SILENCERS DISGUISED AS TORCHES

These two silencers were disguised as torches so that they could be transported secretly without arousing any suspicion. Although the torches did not work, the disguise was effective when the torches were packed with other ordinary workshop tools. The parts added for disguise were easily removable, enabling the the silencers to be converted rapidly for their real purpose.

Torch on/off switch (glued to side of silencer)

False end-plug

Silencer

Cap from a real torch

Front of a real torch

Silencer

End-cap of silencer

ITALIAN FASCIST SECRET POLICE

Italy's Organizzazione di Vigilanza e Repressione dell'Antifascismo (OVRA) was formed in 1926 to suppress opposition to the Italian fascist government. During World War II, the OVRA operated against resistance groups in the French Alps and in the Balkans. The OVRA also recruited a number of double agents (see p. 9), who spied on the activities of Britain's SOE (see p. 30) in Italy. Some OVRA members remained loyal to the Italian fascist regime until the closing stages of the war. The pistol shown here was carried in 1945 by an OVRA team led by a German officer.

End-cap

Cut-away shows silencer baffles

OVRA crest

Hammer

Silencer

Trigger

Seven-round magazine

Silenced 9 mm Beretta 1934 pistol
This is a silenced version of the standard Italian service pistol. A subsonic 9 mm round made this pistol even more effective as a silenced weapon. The OVRA crest is painted on the silencer.

Foresight

Cocking handle

Rear sight

Skeleton butt

Magazine release catch

32-round magazine

Trigger guard

Trigger

STEN MARK II SILENCED SUBMACHINE GUN

The Sten gun was designed to be produced easily and cheaply in large numbers. It was durable and simple to use, with a lightweight, skeleton butt. Fully automatic fire would have damaged the silencer, so the Sten was usually used as a single-shot weapon. This silenced model was used by British commandos, but another version known as the Mark IIS was developed by the SOE (see p. 30).

Silenced weapons II

Hammer — Ejection port — Silencer — Inscription *Mort aux Boches* (Death to the Germans)

Grip — Trigger — Ammunition clip

SILENCED .25 WEBLEY AND SCOTT PISTOL

The SOE (see p. 30) used easily concealed, small-calibre semi-automatic pistols from many sources. The Webley and Scott pistol was originally designed for the British Royal Navy, but this version was used by SOE operatives in France. This example has a silencer inscribed with the words *Mort aux Boches* (Death to the Germans).

Sight (not usable with the silencer) — Hammer

Internal baffles to suppress noise — Silencer — Barrel — Trigger — Soviet star emblem — Grip — Ammunition clip

SILENCED 7.62 mm TOKAREV TT-33 PISTOL

The Tokarev pistol replaced the Nagant (see p. 137) as the service pistol of Soviet intelligence agencies until the 1950s. A silenced model was used by counterintelligence officers of SMERSH (see p. 38). Special ammunition with a reduced propellant charge was used to keep bullets subsonic, thereby avoiding the crack that ordinary, supersonic bullets make as they go through the sound barrier. This Tokarev has been sectioned by British intelligence to show its working parts.

Parker Hale silencer — Barrel — Attachment for optional sling

HOME GUARD AUXILIARY UNITS

The Home Guard was a locally based army in Britain during World War II, composed of spare-time soldiers who also continued to work in their normal civilian jobs. The Auxiliary Units were an elite force drawn from its ranks. They were trained to wage guerrilla warfare behind German lines in case of an invasion, and were issued with secret stocks of weapons and explosives.

AUXILIARY UNIT BADGE

WINCHESTER MODEL 74 .22 CALIBRE RIFLE

American Winchester 74 sporting rifles were purchased for the British Home Guard Auxiliary Units and modified by the addition of British-made accessories: a Parker Hale silencer and an Enfield telescopic sight. The rifles were intended for use against German soldiers and tracker dogs if the Germans invaded Britain – which never happened. However, during tests simulating the rough conditions of operating from underground shelters that would be likely in the event of an invasion, the rifles proved unsuitable for use because their sights were easily knocked out of alignment.

— Cocking rod

— Firing lever

— Armband

— Elastic strap

COLBY'S JEDBURGH TEAM

The World War II Jedburgh teams were made up of three men from SOE or OSS (see p. 30 and 32), and Free French units (see p. 31). Teams were sent to France in 1944 to coordinate resistance activities supporting the Allied invasion of France. OSS Major William Colby, later to become head of the CIA, was a member of a Jedburgh team codenamed Bruce. His two Free French team-mates are shown.

JACQUES FAVEL: CODENAME GALWAY

LOUIS GIRY: CODENAME PIASTRE

WILLIAM COLBY: CODENAME BERKSHIRE

Foresight   Silencer   Rear sight

SILENCED HI-STANDARD MODEL B .22 CALIBRE PISTOL

Although the Hi-Standard pistol was commercially available before World War II, this silenced version was made for the Research and Development Branch of the OSS. The pistol was accurate and quiet, and did not produce a muzzle flash.

Trigger

Ten-round ammunition clip

WEL-WAND .25 CALIBRE SLEEVE GUN

The SOE laboratory in Welwyn, southern England, gave the prefix "Wel-" to many of its products. The Wel-Wand was a silenced single-shot device. After use, the user could hide the weapon by pulling it up into his sleeve with an elastic strap.

Silencer

Enfield telescopic sight

Manual safety catch

Open sight (not used with telescopic sight)

Trigger

Attachment point for optional sling

Crossbows and darts

MANY INTELLIGENCE AGENCIES have tried to develop weapons capable of firing silently and without emitting a muzzle flash. During World War II, some designs were based on earlier weapons: medieval crossbows and slingshots were the inspiration for the Big Joe 5 crossbow, while a close-range weapon called the bigot was a pistol adapted to fire a dart. But, after tests proved that these weapons were less effective than the newly improved silenced guns, they were not adopted. Weapons invented since World War II include a steel crossbow developed for British special forces.

Adapted Colt .45 semi-automatic pistol

BIGOT

DART-FIRING PISTOL

Invented in the United States in 1944, the bigot was a pistol adapted to fire a dart. This was launched from a structure known as a spigot, which protruded from the gun's muzzle. The dart's flight was powered by the blast from a blank cartridge located inside the forward end of the fin tube. The weapon fired without making a visible flash.

Tip of spigot

Stabilizing fins slide to rear when dart is fired

Fin tube slides on to spigot

DART FIRED BY BIGOT

Solid steel tip

STEEL CROSSBOW

This lightweight British weapon from the 1970s has a powerful metal bow. It shoots either a normal steel bolt or a knife blade. Originally meant for use in assassinations or combat missions, in practice the crossbow has mainly been used for killing guard dogs.

BOW

BOWSTRING

Reinforced section

Metal tip

Plastic flight

BOLT

Allen key for disassembly

KNIFE BLADE

Sliding shoulder stock

Bowstring sear

Receiver

Lever for securing shoulder stock

Fore-grip

Trigger

Sliding shoulder stock

Bow locking attachment

SIDE VIEW

Testing the Big Joe 5 crossbow
Trials showed that the crossbow had a maximum range of 183 m (200 yd), but in practical terms it was less useful than the new silenced firearms.

BIG JOE 5 CROSSBOW

This American design was tested during World War II by the SOE (see p. 30) and the OSS (see p. 32), but was not used in action. The crossbow was powered by rubber loops, which were tensioned by a windlass before firing. The front frame and shoulder stock could be folded for easier transportation and concealment. Ammunition was either a normal bolt with a steel head that could inflict deep wounds, or a flare bolt that could be used to illuminate targets.

Flight

Steel head

NORMAL BOLT

FLARE BOLT

Flight

Flare head

Safety catch

Wing nut

Rubber loops

Frame

Ratchet

Rear sight

TOP VIEW

Windlass handle

Attachment cords

Frame

Rear sight

Windlass handle

Sliding shoulder stock

Fore-grip

Ratchet

Pistol grip

SIDE VIEW

Close-combat weapons I

CLOSE COMBAT is something for which all special operations personnel must be trained and equipped. Specialized close-combat weapons – such as blades, knives, coshes, and garrottes – enable them to overcome an opponent in a swift, silent attack, or to defend themselves in an emergency and hopefully escape alive. The weapons tend to be used as a last resort, perhaps when a silenced firearm is unavailable. Those who are likely to face the dangers of close combat make their own preparations and often buy weapons privately, although some are issued officially.

GARROTTE

The most common use of a garrotte is to strangle sentries. The wire is looped over the victim's head, around the neck, and pulled tight from behind until the target is dead. Other garrottes have serrated wires that double as escape saws.

THRUST WEAPON

The brass pommel of this weapon rested in the palm of the hand to add force to a thrusting movement. The lanyard was twisted around the hand to prevent the blade from being lost in action. British marine special forces used this weapon in World War II. Small items (suicide tablets, for instance) could be carried in the pommel.

HIDDEN GARROTTE

Some British special forces in World War II used a condom to conceal a garrotte. It also prevented rust by sealing out moisture. Because condoms were commonly carried, the garrotte might be overlooked if the person carrying one was searched by the enemy.

Hollow pommel

Dagger blade

Lanyard

LEATHER SHEATH

Brass handle

Wire

Garrotte rolled up inside condom for concealment

THRUST WEAPON

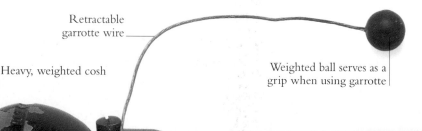

Retractable garrotte wire

Heavy, weighted cosh

Weighted ball serves as a grip when using garrotte

PESKETT CLOSE-COMBAT WEAPON

Named after its inventor, John Peskett, this multi-purpose weapon was designed for World War II special operations. It is a combination of a cosh, garrotte, and dagger, complete with wrist strap.

Attaching ring

Button to release dagger and lock it in place

KNUCKLEDUSTER

A knuckleduster is a metal brace that gives a punch much greater force. Knuckledusters are bought privately by some intelligence officers as protection from street crime in some of the rough areas where they operate. During World War II, knuckledusters were occasionally issued officially to members of covert units.

Striking point

Finger hole

Pommel for palm

Aluminium casting

PUSH DAGGER

The three-finger grip of this British weapon from World War II allows the operator to exert tremendous force at close range.

Finger hole

Leather strip for attachment to clothing

Round blade to penetrate clothing and body tissues

PUSH DAGGER

LEATHER SCABBARD

COSHES

Coshes are often used to stun or injure, but a hard blow to the temple or the back of the head can be fatal. The upper cosh was used by the East German Stasi (see p. 73) as a method of crowd control during demonstrations. The lower one was carried by CIA officers operating in Europe during the 1960s as a means of self-defence.

(see p. 73)

SPY PROFILE | William Stanley-Moss

During World War II, Captain Stanley-Moss served in British special operations. In 1944 he was in a team sent to Crete (then under German occupation) to capture General Kreipe, the German commander of the island. The team planned to kidnap the general by ambushing his car, and were issued with coshes for this purpose. They succeeded, although in the event coshes were not used. The general was smuggled to Egypt by submarine.

Flexible tip

Telescopic compressed rubber stem

STASI COSH

Plastic grip

Wrist strap

Lead-filled head with leather covering

CIA COSH

Leather-covered fibre shaft

Dagger

Wrist strap

Wrist strap

Close-combat weapons II

THUMB KNIVES AND SCABBARDS

Thumb knives (these are from World War II) are tiny knives that can be hidden in clothing or a uniform. In use, they are gripped with the thumb and forefinger.

KNIFE WITH FRENCH TRICOLOUR

KNIFE WITH CANADIAN MAPLE LEAF

X-TROOP

10 Commando was a British army unit made up of foreign nationals during World War II. Its No. 3 troop, also known as X-troop, was made up of anti-Nazi Germans, many Jewish. X-troop personnel performed a variety of roles in front-line service. As German speakers they were specially helpful in intelligence work. But they risked execution as traitors if captured. Many carried escape aids such as the knife below.

X-TROOP DETACHMENT

X-TROOP ESCAPE KNIFE

CLANDESTINE BLADE KIT

During World War II, the SOE (see p. 30) sent this blade kit to the OSS (see p. 32) for evaluation, but it was not accepted there for official issue. However, many OSS personnel acquired the blades privately, while attending SOE training schools in Britain.

OSS marking · Thumb knife · Triple-edged dart · Folding leather case · Ring dagger · Hatpin dagger · Triple-edged dagger · Thrust dagger · Double-edged knife · Open-handled dagger · Non-reflective blackened knife · Lapel knife · Lacing for case

INSTRUCTOR'S BLADE KIT

SOE instructors used an assortment of blades for training new personnel during World War II. Packed in wax-sealed containers and wrapped in chamois leather, the kit could also be buried for recovery and use during an operation. This example, buried in the 1940s, was recovered during the 1980s in perfect condition. The blade pack includes thumb and bodkin knives, and a tyre-slasher for sabotaging vehicles.

Chamois leather knife roll

Coin with blade

Wax-sealed container in which to bury kit

Double-edged bodkin

Triple-edged bodkin

Thumb knife

Thumb knife

Lapel blade

Tyre slasher

Lid of container

KNUCKLEDUSTER KNIFE

During World War II, a knife was designed for British commandos operating in North Africa and the Middle East. The knife's brass grip could be used as a knuckleduster to knock out sentries.

Knuckleduster point

Steel blade

Brass grip

FAIRBAIRN-SYKES FIGHTING KNIFE

This weapon was designed in 1940 by two British officers, Captain W. E. Fairbairn and Captain E. A. Sykes. They had gained experience in close combat while serving with the Shanghai Police. Their knife was designed so that a trained user could strike at the vulnerable points of an opponent's body and attack the vital organs, killing the target quickly. The first knives were made in 1941 and were quickly accepted. They were issued to British commando units, and used on raids in Norway in 1941. Fairbairn was later seconded as an instructor to the OSS, for whom he created a special version of the knife. Successive versions continued to be produced into the 1990s.

Instructor and inventor
W. E. Fairbairn (1885–1960) in the uniform of a lieutenant-colonel, a rank he attained in August 1944.

LEATHER SCABBARD

FAIRBAIRN-SYKES FIGHTING KNIFE

Concealed weapons I

IN CLANDESTINE WARFARE situations arise in which hidden weapons, perhaps of an unconventional or unexpected kind, may tilt the balance between success and failure. Because concealment generally means limited size, such weapons are likely to be very basic, without refinements such as silencers or magazines of extra bullets. Weapons of this type can also be used for assassinations, as they allow the killer to get close to the victim without arousing alarm. These weapons are issued only to people who have serious need of them and are not carried by those engaged in normal intelligence work. Anyone found in possession of them would be suspected of covert activity.

Trigger remote control

Ejector port

Hammer

Trigger

Trigger extension mechanism

MODIFIED WEBLEY PISTOL

BELT PISTOL

This belt and pistol were developed for use by British special operations personnel during World War II. A modified .25 calibre Webley pistol was worn on the belt on the user's right side, facing forwards, hidden under the clothing. The trigger was activated by a length of cable that ran to the user's hand.

Cable end attached to trigger extension mechanism

Attachment plate for pistol

BELT WITH PISTOL PLATE

Trigger cable

SINGLE-SHOT CIGAR PISTOL

A .22 calibre firing device was disguised as a cigar for use by SOE personnel (see p. 30). It was fired by pulling on the string. Its effective range was just a metre or so.

FALSE CIGAR

Firing string

FIRING DEVICE

Hole cut for display purposes

SINGLE-SHOT CIGARETTE PISTOL

This .22 calibre device disguised as a cigarette was developed at the SOE's Welwyn laboratory. The device was fired when the user pulled on a string with his teeth. Because of its short barrel it had a range of only about a metre and was very loud.

FALSE CIGARETTE

FIRING DEVICE

SINGLE-SHOT PEN GUN

Known as the En-Pen, this .22 calibre device was made at the Royal Small Arms Factory at Enfield, north of London, for the SOE. The gun was fired by pulling back the pocket clip. This kit, issued to SOE instructors, included a cartridge ejector rod and a tool for cleaning out wax left in the chamber after firing blanks.

Pocket clip

Hole cut for display purposes

Rod used to push out spent cartridges

Blanks were used for practice firing

Leather holder

SECTIONED VIEW OF GUN

CARTRIDGE EJECTOR ROD

SET OF BLANK CARTRIDGES

CLEANING TOOL

SINGLE-SHOT GAS AND POISON PENS

The KGB assassination pen fired a small charge that shattered an ampoule of hydrocyanic acid. This was then projected from the pen as a lethal gas. The pellet pen (also KGB) was used to inject a small pellet impregnated with ricin poison into a victim. The tear gas pen was developed for the SOE during World War II. It had a range of up to 2 m (6 ft).

Gas projection slit

Knurled surface for gripping

Weapon activated by snapping the cap back and releasing

GAS ASSASSINATION PEN

Slide control

Injection needle

POISON PELLET PEN

Tear gas nozzle

Ball bearing is pressed into hole to release trigger

TEAR GAS PEN

STANLEY LOVELL

During World War II, the OSS (see p. 32) began the practice of using industrial resources and the universities to develop new clandestine technology, an innovative approach that came to be widely adopted during the later Cold War years.

Stanley Lovell (1890–1976) was recruited from an academic background. He was personally selected by the OSS chief William Donovan to be OSS director of research and development. Under Lovell's direction, the OSS developed a number of devices for use in clandestine warfare. Among these were the Hi-Standard pistol (see p. 141), the Beano grenade (see p. 96), and the Matchbox camera (see p. 69). Other ideas included an explosive disguised as flour, which could even be baked without exploding, and a plan (never implemented) to attack Japanese cities by releasing bats to which incendiary bombs had been attached.

WRIST PISTOL

This small .25 calibre firing device was designed to be worn on the wrist of SOE personnel, so that it was readily available without having to be held in the hand. The device was fired by a string attached to the inside of a shirt or jacket. Any sudden forward movement of the arm would be enough to fire the device.

Barrel points in same direction as the outstretched fingers

Strap for tightening band on wrist

Wrist band

Concealed weapons II

CLAYTON HUTTON WITH MI9 DEVICES

MAJOR CHRISTOPHER CLAYTON HUTTON

During World War II, Christopher Clayton Hutton (b.1894) worked in MI9, a British organization set up by the armed forces to help British prisoners of war escape, and to assist special forces behind enemy lines. He created numerous weapons, concealments, and escape and evasion aids. One of his inventions was a clandestine airstrip beacon that was only faintly luminous so that it could be seen by an approaching pilot, but would be hard to spot at ground level.

Major Clayton Hutton designed an air-powered firing device for the French resistance in Paris. The device was disguised as a pen and fired a gramophone needle. Although this weapon was unlikely to be lethal, the resistance would be able to spread a rumour among the Germans that the needles were poisoned. French units expressed interest in the weapon, but MI9 could not supply the quantity required.

SINGLE-SHOT RECTAL PISTOL

This KGB 4.5 mm firing device is packaged in a rubber sheath to facilitate concealment in the rectum. This is a common way of hiding items from cursory searches. The device was fired by holding the knurled ring, and twisting the barrel a quarter turn.

Muzzle

Barrel

SAFETY COVER   **FIRING DEVICE**

Barrel unscrews for loading

Needle-firing pen
This pneumatic weapon was devised by Clayton Hutton for use by French resistance fighters during World War II.

Pocket clip   Trigger

Cap pulled back to prime weapon

SINGLE-SHOT FIRING DEVICE (STINGER)

The Stinger was developed for the CIA during the post–World War II years. A reloadable .22 calibre device, the Stinger was issued with a spare barrel and seven rounds of ammunition in a camouflaged lead foil tube.

SINGLE-SHOT POCKET TORCH PISTOL

This 4.5 mm device, disguised as a pocket torch, was used by the KGB in the 1950s and 1960s. Its mechanism was the same as in the pistol above. This example was seized at a British airport from the pilot of a Soviet civil aircraft.

Lead foil tube

CONCEALMENT

Muzzle   Trigger

Plastic sheath
for spare barrel

Safety catch   **SINGLE-SHOT FIRING DEVICE**

Spare barrel

Safety catch

Torch casing

PIPE PISTOL

Common items carried on the person were capable of being transformed into lethal firing devices. This World War II device was designed for use by SOE personnel (see p. 30). It was fired by removing the mouthpiece and twisting the bowl while grasping the barrel.

Bowl sectioned
for display

Coiled spring for
firing mechanism

Device concealed inside
mouthpiece of pipe

Safety wire removed
before firing

Muzzle

Casing contains
spring-loaded hammer

Button pulled back
and released to fire

Tip unscrewed to
load cartridge

PROPELLING PENCIL PISTOL

Unusual in that it functioned without a barrel, this 6.35 mm weapon fired its bullet straight from the cartridge, which was loaded into the top section of the pencil. The device was sold commercially in Europe at the time of World War II.

Cartridge

PENCIL CONCEALMENT FOR THRUSTING WEAPON

MI9 designed a variety of small thrusting weapons that could be concealed inside pencils and pens. The intention was that the device would pass unnoticed through an initial search and could then be used in an escape attempt.

Hole cut for
display purposes

Cruciform blade

Twine-wrapped grip

Leather glove

Plunger

Barrel

GLOVE PISTOL

Devised in World War II by the US Office of Naval Intelligence, this .38 calibre device allowed the wearer to be armed and still keep both hands free. It was fired at point-blank range by pressing the plunger into an opponent's body while striking a blow.

Assassination devices I

Handle

INTELLIGENCE AGENCIES are sometimes ordered to assassinate individuals who are considered by their governments to be a threat to national interests. In most cases, such killings have to be discreet, quiet, and untraceable to the assassins. Sometimes they are performed in such a way as to give the impression that the victim died of natural causes. Some killings, however, can serve as warnings, and might be done more blatantly. The need for discretion has led to the development of many types of assassination device, some of which are shown here. Secret services of the Soviet bloc countries used to specialize in assassinations. They devised a variety of methods, and even established a special workshop to experiment with poisons.

SINGLE-SHOT ASSASSINATION DEVICE

Developed during World War II by the technical department of the Abwehr (see p. 34), this device could be used for assassinations or for suicides. It fired a single 4.5 mm bullet a short distance, and worked by pulling back and then releasing the rear section of the device. It is shown here at its actual size.

Knurled base   Brass casing   Barrel

POISON PELLET CANE

The KGB developed this cane in the 1950s. It is operated by pressing the tip against a body. The pressure rotates the tip to extend a large needle. When the needle is extended, a poison pellet is fired through it and into the victim, with fatal effect.

— Powder charge and poison pellet

— Spring

— Rotating cam

— Tip through which large needle protrudes

TIP OF POISON PELLET CANE

POISON PELLET CANE

THE BULGARIAN UMBRELLA

In 1978 Georgi Markov, a Bulgarian dissident living in London, was killed on the orders of the Bulgarian leadership. The Bulgarians had asked the KGB to give technical assistance in devising an assassination method, and the KGB offered three choices: poisoned food; poisonous jelly to be smeared on Markov's skin; or a poison pellet.

A pellet filled with the lethal poison ricin was chosen. This was injected into Markov's thigh by means of a device disguised as an umbrella, which was jabbed at Markov as he stood near Waterloo Bridge, in London. He died soon afterwards. At first his death was a mystery, as no one understood how it had happened. Eventually, however, murder began to be suspected, and Markov's corpse was exhumed. The pellet was found in the course of an autopsy, and the cause of his death understood.

BULGARIAN SECRET SERVICE CREST

GEORGI MARKOV

CIGARETTE PACKET WITH GAS-FIRING DEVICE

A Soviet cigarette packet was adapted to conceal this poison-gas device, which is removed for firing. The single-shot weapon fires a cartridge containing a glass vial of acid. When fired, the vial is crushed and the acid vaporizes in the victim's face. A mesh screen stops glass splinters from reaching the victim's face and thus revealing the cause of death.

Mesh screen

Cartridge

Cocking and firing lever

GAS-FIRING DEVICE

CIGARETTE PACKET

THE FOILED ASSASSINATION

In 1954 Soviet assassin Nicolai Khokhlov (b.1922) was sent to Frankfurt, West Germany, to kill anti-Soviet agitator Georgi Okolovich. Before departing on his mission, Khokhlov married and converted to his wife's Christian beliefs. Because of these new beliefs, Khokhlov felt unable to carry out the assassination. When he arrived in Frankfurt, he warned Okolovich of the plot to kill him. Khokhlov defected with information about Soviet assassination devices, including the poison-pellet cigarette packet that was meant to kill Okolovich.

An assassin meets his intended victim
Soviet assassin Nicolai Khokhlov (right), defected rather than attempt to kill his intended victim, Georgi Okolovich, whom he warned of the assassination plot.

SILENCED ASSASSINATION GUN

This Soviet weapon is designed to be carried in and fired from a rolled-up newspaper. It is a single-shot device, fired by squeezing the external lever on the rear section of the weapon. It is silenced by an internal suppressor, and further muffled by being pressed up against the victim as it is fired. A later adaptation of this gun, which fires gas, is shown on p. 154.

Mesh inside tube to muffle sound

Hole cut for display purposes

End connected to firing chamber

INTERNAL SUPPRESSOR

Thread screws into rear section of weapon

Hole cut for display purposes

Cocking rod

Outer tube serves as a handle

Recessed surface receives suppressor

FIRING CHAMBER

Firing lever

REAR SECTION OF WEAPON

Assassination devices II

POISON GAS ASSASSINATION CANE

A gas assassination device has been hidden in this cane for the blind. The trigger is concealed by the white tape, which was peeled back for use. When the device was fired, it emitted gas from an opening in the handle, which was held close to the victim's face.

Firing port for poisonous gas

Tape to simulate a cane used by the blind

Trigger mechanism

CANE

HANDLE OF CANE

ANTIDOTES FOR POISON GAS

KGB personnel who used gas assassination weapons were equipped with antidotes, which they took as a precaution against accidental inhalation of the lethal gas. The tablet of sodium thiosulphate was swallowed 30 minutes before an attack, and the ampoule of amyl nitrate was broken and inhaled immediately after the assassination had taken place.

Sg 4

Antidote pack

Sodium thiosulphate tablet

Amyl nitrate ampoule

BOGDAN STASHINSKY

In 1957, KGB officer Bogdan Stashinsky (b.1931) killed the Ukrainian dissident leader Lev Rebet in Munich, using a gas assassination gun concealed in a newspaper. Rebet's death was ascribed to a heart attack. In 1959, Stashinsky assassinated the Ukrainian dissident Stefan Bandera, using an improved gas gun. The cause of death was correctly identified this time. Stashinsky defected to West Germany in 1961. He was convicted of the murders but received a short sentence.

POISON GAS ASSASSINATION GUN

This Soviet weapon had the capability to kill almost instantly if fired directly into the victim's face. It is a gas-firing version of the gun shown on p. 153 and, like that gun, was hidden in a rolled-up newspaper. The firing lever activated a firing pin, which detonated a percussion cap, rupturing an ampoule of acid. The acid vaporized into poisonous gas and was propelled out of a small hole. The gas gun is just 18 cm (7 in) long.

Cocking rod

Firing lever

Outer tube serves as a handle

Attaching screw

Rubber ring to absorb recoil

PLOTS TO ASSASSINATE FIDEL CASTRO

Between 1960 and 1965, the CIA was involved in eight government-authorized plots to assassinate Fidel Castro (b.1926), leader of communist Cuba. (Communist Cuba was considered a particular threat to the United States due to its close proximity.) Equipment and such materials as poisons were provided by the CIA Technical Services Division. Some plots went no further than the planning stage; others progressed further, but none resulted in a serious assassination attempt. One plot twice reached a point at which poison pills were sent to Cuba and agents were despatched to carry out the task. In another plot, weapons were furnished to a Cuban dissident. There was even a plan to impregnate one of Castro's cigars with deadly botulism bacilli. Non-lethal attacks were planned, aimed at destroying Castro's credibility with the Cubans. Such projects included putting thallium salts in his boots to make his beard fall out, and spraying him with hallucinatory drugs while he made a broadcast.

CREST OF THE CIA

FIDEL CASTRO

GAS-FIRING CARTRIDGE ASSASSINATION WALLET

A poison-gas firing device is concealed in this KGB wallet, which also has compartments for gas antidotes to protect the assassin. When the trigger was fired, the primer charge crushed a glass ampoule of poisonous acid that turned into a vapour and killed the victim. A screen over the cartridge prevented shards of glass from the ampoule embedding in the victim and so revealing the cause of death.

Compartment for antidotes

Muzzel through which poison gas is fired

Cartridge with gas ampoule

Trigger

Metal casing

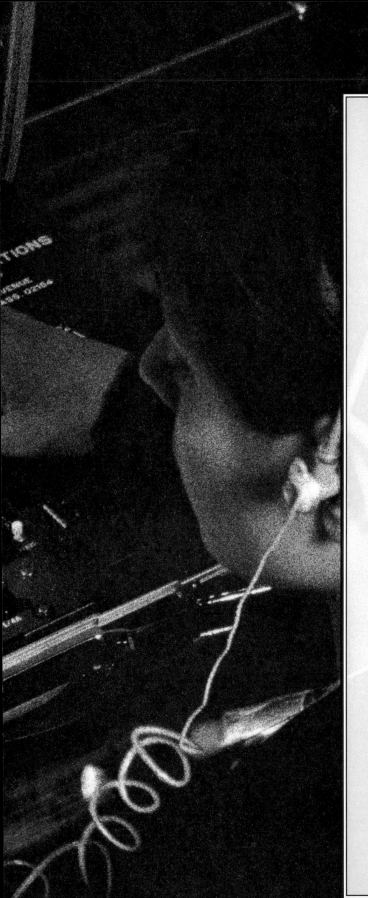

HOW TO BE A SPY

◆

Many people want to be spies, attracted by the glamour they see in films or read about in novels, but very few actually achieve their ambition. Some intelligence agencies, such as the CIA, do advertise for new recruits, but most agencies approach potential members individually. Once an agency has recruited someone suitable, he or she has to be trained. This can take years, as the potential spy must painstakingly learn all the tradecraft – the techniques for living, working, and communicating surreptitiously. If the spy is going to live under cover in a foreign country for a long period of time, then meticulous attention must be paid to ensure that the spy's cover story is perfect. The life of a spy is not one of constant action, but rather one of quiet, often boring work. If a spy or his or her controller makes the smallest mistake, the spy can suddenly be in great danger – the life of a spy can be precarious. This section covers all the aspects of how a spy works, from recruitment and training, and developing a cover, to the spy's fate.

Training and recruitment I

SPIES ARE RECRUITED by different means according to the skills or abilities required. Personnel needed by the technical support branch of an intelligence service, for example, can often be recruited simply by advertising for people with the required expertise. If scientific knowledge is required, in computing or nuclear physics, for instance, it may be possible to recruit directly from universities. Linguists can also be acquired in this way. Thousands of specialists are employed by the big intelligence agencies, though few of the recruits will play active roles in intelligence-gathering overseas.

Physical training
Intelligence officers, particularly those expected to engage in clandestine warfare like these wartime SOE agents, undergo rigorous physical training.

Intelligence-gathering is the preserve of career intelligence officers, known as case officers, and agents recruited by them. When working abroad, case officers are usually attached to the staff of embassies. They operate there under the guise of diplomatic personnel, often making stringent efforts to disguise their role in intelligence work. Their primary task is the recruitment and control of agents, through whom intelligence can be gathered. When seeking potential recruits, case officers usually target the personnel of foreign intelligence services and foreign embassy employees. Intelligence officers are of obvious value if they can be recruited as moles, but anyone who has access to information can prove useful. Chauffeurs, secretaries, or maintenance staff can all provide information that may lead to the recruitment of more agents. For instance, they are likely to know which of their colleagues have personal problems, such as financial difficulties or alcoholism, and which may be having extramarital affairs. Such gossip can help intelligence officers identify the people who are vulnerable, and who might therefore be successfully recruited.

FRIENDLY SPIES

Case officers who are responsible for recruiting agents need to have friendly, likeable personalities. They must be affable and socially adaptable, and appear open to other people's points of view. Soviet case officers with these qualities were known to spend much time in clubs and bars around Washington, DC,

Scaled-down Fairbairn-Sykes knives
Three-quarter-sized versions of this famous fighting knife (see p. 147) had the advantage of concealability. The ball tip was added for safety in training.

see p. 147

SPY PROFILE

Aldrich Ames

Finding himself in debt CIA officer Ames (b.1941) offered his services to the KGB in 1985. He became chief of the Soviet Division of the CIA's Counterintelligence Section and betrayed every secret that came his way, leading to the deaths of at least ten CIA agents. For the information that Ames gave them, the KGB paid a total of $2.7 million. Ames was arrested in 1994 and was convicted and sentenced to life imprisonment.

hoping to fall into the company of US government staff, military personnel, or business people. The case officer will typically form a friendship with a likely recruit. This friendship is often based on a supposedly shared interest, for example women, drinking, gambling, or even an innocent hobby such as fishing or stamp collecting. As the friendship develops, the case officer will subtly probe for any character weaknesses that can be used to control the new friend. At this point, the potential recruit is referred to as a developing agent. The first information sought from them may seem totally innocuous. But slowly, new recruits

Training padlock
This special padlock was used for training recruits how to open combination locks.

will be drawn closer into a web of deceit and espionage. Some will be persuaded to agree to clandestine activities in return for cash, and later made to sign a receipt for money received. Once they have gone this far, there is little chance that they will turn back. They will have become recruited agents. The threat of having their new activities revealed, coupled with the lure of money, will be enough to ensure their continued loyalty to their handler.

Handlers, who may not be the same case officers who recruited the agent, will attempt to reinforce this loyalty by building strong bonds of friendship and trust with their agents. Even after his arrest, CIA traitor Aldrich Ames was able to talk of the great affection he still held for his former handlers.

TYPES OF AGENT

Apart from those recruited specifically to procure intelligence, several other types of agent exist. Contact agents and

George Blake

Communist Party member George Blake (b.1922) was a British soldier who was taken prisoner of war in Korea and recruited by Soviet intelligence. His linguistic skills led to his later recruitment by MI6 (see p.169). From 1953, he passed information to the KGB, badly affecting British intelligence. In 1961 Blake was arrested and jailed for 42 years. After six years, however, he escaped and went to the Soviet Union.

access agents are used to identify and facilitate access to potential recruits. Agents of influence are used to affect public opinion or events. Support agents assist other agents, for example by acting as couriers or maintaining safe houses.

Double agents are those who work against their original intelligence services while under the control of another service. They may be driven by motives of money, ideology, compromise, or ego, or they may be trying to save their lives or to regain their freedom after capture by their original enemy.

Moles are intelligence personnel who are in the employment of one service while being controlled by another.

Sleeper agents are those who are sent into foreign countries to live apparently normal lives until activated, perhaps in time of national emergency or pending war, when their mission is likely to be one of sabotage or assassination.

"Illegals" (see p. 162) are spies who adopt elaborate false identities to work in foreign countries. They are difficult for the enemy to detect, but run the risk of heavy punishment as they operate without any diplomatic immunity. Apart from gathering information, their role may sometimes also be to spot potential new recruits or run other agents.

Instruction in tradecraft
Tradecraft is the word for the range of technical skills used in espionage. Here, SOE recruits (see p. 30) learn about methods of opening locks.

Training and recruitment II

Once recruited, new employees of an intelligence service may follow any one of a number of different paths. Major intelligence agencies, such as the CIA and the KGB (or its partial replacement in modern times, the SVR), need large numbers of technical and analytical staff to support their operations. Personnel who have been recruited to take these roles will receive a general introduction to the various elements of intelligence work before being sent on for training in their individual specialities. They may continue to work within these specialist areas throughout their careers. A recruit who is destined for a career as an intelligence officer or case officer will go through a far more intensive and wide-ranging course of training. Many of the elements that have characterized Western intelligence training since 1945 have their origins in the earlier, wartime training programmes that were devised for the British SOE (see p. 30) and the American OSS (see p. 32).

Communications training
The use of Morse code for radio communication can be one of the most intensive and time-consuming elements of intelligence training.

TRAINING KEY

Morse training key
This practice key and earpiece were used to train CIA recruits in the use of Morse code during the 1960s.

EARPIECE

Plug

Lead

WARTIME RECRUITMENT AND TRAINING

Originally, the SOE discovered many of its trainees by means of word-of-mouth recommendations and similar informal contacts. Individuals who had excellent foreign language skills, and who were also willing to volunteer for unspecified service, were in demand. Besides this, the SOE received some of its recruits via the War Office Department MI1x, which also provided recruits for MI5 (see p. 164) and MI6. These agencies carried out their own direct recruiting, sometimes in competition with the SOE. The SOE preferred to recruit people of a middle-class background, who had no affiliations to extreme political groups. At the same time less respectable individuals, such as forgers and burglars, were hired for their specialized skills.

The OSS also began by informal recruitment of personnel. By late 1943, however, its growing manpower needs led to a more systematic approach. The OSS joined with the SOE to set up a system of psychological assessment for sifting recruits; this system was combined with training programmes designed in such a way that unsuitable trainees could be filtered out at various stages. In both organizations trainees would undergo a period of basic training. Subjects included fieldcraft (survival skills), communications, sabotage, and the various forms of combat. After that, more advanced courses followed in order to prepare agents for specialist tasks or work in specific countries.

SPY PROFILE | John Vassall

Admiralty clerk John Vassall (b.1924) was working at the British Embassy in Moscow when the KGB recruited him, using evidence of his homosexuality as blackmail. He was trained to use a Minox camera and started work for the KGB. He continued on his return to London in 1956. After passing many naval secrets to Moscow, Vassall was arrested in 1962 and convicted of spying. He served ten years of an 18-year sentence.

SPY PROFILE | Hugh Hambleton

Hugh Hambleton (b.1922) was recruited in 1947 by the MGB (later KGB), lured by their intellectual flattery and his craving for adventure. From 1956 to 1961 he worked for NATO and supplied secrets to Moscow. He returned to Canada, became a professor, and continued to pass secrets. The RCMP security service (see p.136) discovered his espionage equipment in 1979. He was later sentenced to ten years in prison in Britain.

Silencer — Trigger — Grip safety — Cocking handle

Combined magazine and pistol grip —

Welrod pistol
Designed during World War II at the SOE laboratories in Welwyn Garden City, near London, this silenced weapon remained in service in the post-war years.

Firearms training
Intelligence services may train their officers to use a variety of firearms, choosing weapons that will best meet the anticipated operational needs.

CIA TRAINING

The system of training instituted by the OSS had a strong influence over the methods adopted by the CIA. During the 1950s, trainee CIA officers received basic training at a camp codenamed Isolation. This former naval base in Virginia was also known to recruits as Camp Swampy, due to the marshy land in which it was situated. The basic elements of clandestine operations were still taught using the OSS manual.

Trainees were also given a thorough grounding in the special vocabulary of the world of espionage. They were taught the differences between types of agents, and learned the skills required to recruit them. Their role as case officers was expressed as providing the "link between the intelligence bureaucracy that wants the secret information and the agents that have access to the information". Technical experts lectured the students on espionage tradecraft, such as clandestine photography, secret writing, surveillance, and dead drops.

In the later stages of their training, the trainees would be taken to the nearby city of Norfolk, to practise their newly acquired skills.

SOVIET TRAINING

Soviet recruits to the KGB and GRU (see p. 38) were taught much the same basic skills. The KGB's main training centre was School 101 (later renamed the Red Banner Institute) near Moscow. The GRU trained its personnel at the Military Diplomatic Academy.

KGB training was based on a textbook entitled *The Foundation of Soviet Intelligence Work*, which covered the tradecraft and case-officer skills required of an intelligence officer. KGB and GRU recruits were not taught to gather intelligence but to persuade others to do this for them by betraying their countries. The work of recruiting and running agents was studied from actual cases, with the aid of experienced instructors with first-hand knowledge. The final stage of training was to learn a foreign language, and this was selected to best meet the current operational requirements of the service.

Operational training
SOE recruits learnt the importance of terrain in planning an operation. Here, an instructor shows a group how to use a topographical model.

Covers and legends

IN THE WORLD OF ESPIONAGE, a legend is an artificial life history and background, created to disguise a spy's true identity. While the simpler operations may need only a cover – perhaps just a false name – more complex operations may require a spy to live secretly in a foreign country for as long as a few years. The KGB called a spy working in such a fashion an "illegal". The equivalent CIA term is NOC (non-official cover). An illegal or NOC needs a legend that is convincing enough to stand up to scrutiny by enemy counterintelligence. The time and care spent creating a cover or legend are determined by three factors: the importance of the mission, the length of time the identity has to be maintained, and the degree of scrutiny it must endure.

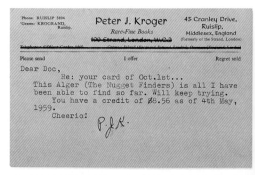

LEGEND-BUILDING POSTCARD WITH "HOUSE OF SPIES" ADDRESS (SEE P. 50)

COVER OR LEGEND?

A short-term false identity, for which little preparation is needed, is called a cover. For example, a member of MI6 visiting an electronics trade show in a British town need only sign in under a false name, carry cards relating to a non-existent business, and set up a telephone line answered in that company's name.

But an illegal needs greater preparation. Elie Cohen (see p. 102) took a year establishing his legend in Argentina before he began his mission, spying for Israel in Syria.

FALSE IDENTITIES

Spy agencies maintain stockpiles of paper samples from around the world to be able to duplicate most identification

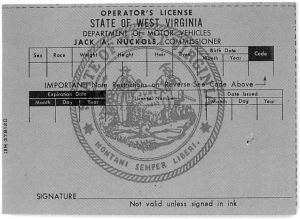

SOVIET FORGERY OF A BLANK (UNCOMPLETED) DRIVING LICENCE FORM

documents exactly. Such work must be flawless: the identity of a German spy posing as a Soviet citizen during World War II was discovered because stainless steel staples – not available in the Soviet Union – were used on his documents. The absence of rust marks on his papers was enough to expose him.

The credibility of a false identity can be helped by the careful use of "pocket litter", such as ticket stubs or receipts, to lend support to the cover story. It is vital that a spy carries nothing that would reveal his or her true identity.

Sometimes spies are able to obtain the documents that allow them to assume the identity of a person who has died. The research involved in basing a legend on the identity of a dead person must be done thoroughly. For example, care must be taken in checking that the spy conforms to the physical details of the deceased person. A small error can be disastrous, as in the case of the KGB illegal Konon Molody (see p. 51).

AVOIDING DISCOVERY

Even if a legend has been constructed perfectly, a spy must behave in the right manner. For an operative working at home or in a friendly country this will not be too demanding, since the legend will not be closely scrutinized. However, a spy using a legend in a hostile country must make every effort to "live" that legend constantly and be very careful not to say anything, even in a casual conversation, that might cast doubt on it. Actions must be in keeping with the character. In World War I, a German officer trying to infiltrate Canada was discovered because he was dressed in shabby clothes but was travelling in the first-class compartment of the train.

SOVIET FORGERY OF A UNITED STATES PRESS CARD

FORGED STAFF CARD FOR EMPLOYEES OF FOREIGN MISSIONS IN AUSTRIA

FOREST FREDERICK EDWARD YEO-THOMAS

British World War II secret agent Edward Yeo-Thomas (1901–64) was a former Royal Air Force (RAF) officer who volunteered for service with the SOE (see p. 30). He undertook three missions to France, where he worked with the resistance. In 1944, he was captured and tortured by the Gestapo, but he managed to survive captivity until the end of the war. For his bravery Yeo-Thomas was later awarded the George Cross, one of the highest British

honours. The items below include his SOE file card and RAF identity discs, and an SOE disc knife. The other items relate to legends created for his first two missions in France. The identity card in the name of Thierry (born in Arras, northern France) was used on his first mission. The papers in the name of Tirelli (born in Algiers) relate to his second mission and include an identity card, ration card, driving licence, and demobilization certificate.

Paper is aged to simulate a certificate that is two years old

FRENCH RATION CARD

SOE FILE CARD

SOE DISC KNIFE

RAF IDENTITY DISCS

Photograph of Yeo-Thomas

Signature adopted for assumed identity

FRENCH IDENTITY CARD

FRENCH DRIVING LICENCE

Signature adopted for assumed identity

UPDATED FRENCH IDENTITY CARD

FRENCH AIR FORCE DEMOBILIZATION CERTIFICATE

Spy networks

A SPY NETWORK IS A GROUP of agents working under the supervision of a controller. Each person in the network reports to a single superior but may control more than one person. Consequently, networks have a pyramidal structure, with many agents at the bottom and only a few controllers at the top. An example of a controller might be a CIA case officer, working under diplomatic cover, or a Soviet "chief illegal" (a senior "illegal" officer, see p. 169) under an assumed identity.

Controllers need to know as much as possible about their agents to be able to handle them effectively. For the sake of security, agents are told as little as possible about their controllers and nothing about fellow agents. This principle, called compartmentalization, ensures that an arrested agent cannot betray those above him or those in other branches of the network. Without compartmentalization, the entire network may be put at risk.

Sometimes, for reasons of operational expediency, controllers of spy networks have chosen not to apply the principle of compartmentalization. This was the case in the Cambridge network in Britain (see opposite) and in some of the American networks of World War II.

RUDOLF IVANOVICH ABEL

MI5 – THE BRITISH SECURITY SERVICE

Despite the letters MI in the names of MI5 and MI6 (see p. 169), neither body is now a component of military intelligence. MI5 is responsible for counterintelligence and counterespionage and monitors activities of subversive and terrorist groups and foreign nationals in Britain. During World War II, MI5 had great success in detecting German spies, many of whom were caught and used to relay false information to Germany.

REGNUM DEFENDE

help the FBI to locate Abel himself. Abel was arrested but was later traded in a spy swap for Francis Gary Powers (see p. 52).

Abel's network had contacts with Ethel and Julius Rosenberg, agents working for the Soviet Union who were convicted of treason and executed in 1953. Damage to the rest of the network after their arrest was limited by compartmentalization.

THE ABEL SPY RING

The spy ring operated by the Soviet illegal Colonel Rudolf Ivanovich Abel (1903–71) was put at risk by lack of compartmentalization. Working from his apartment in New York, Abel kept in contact with, and supported the efforts of, Soviet agents who were trying to steal American atomic secrets. In 1954 another illegal, Reino Hayhanen, became Abel's assistant. He proved unreliable, and Abel had him recalled to Moscow. While in transit, Hayhanen defected. He gave details of Abel's cipher to the FBI and, having been to Abel's apartment, he was able to

Abel's cuff links
Microdots could be concealed in a cavity within these cuff links, which were found in the possession of Rudolf Abel.

Hollow cuff link

Detachable head   Hollow nail

Hollow nail
The Abel spy network used this specially constructed nail as a dead drop in which microfilm could be hidden.

JULIUS ROSENBERG

ETHEL ROSENBERG

GUY BURGESS

ANTHONY BLUNT

DONALD MACLEAN

HAROLD (KIM) PHILBY

THE CAMBRIDGE SPIES

In Britain during the 1930s, the KGB recruited a number of agents from among pro-communist students at Cambridge University. Five were later controlled by NKVD (later KGB) officer Yuri Modin.

In 1951, two of these agents, Foreign Office officials Donald Maclean and Guy Burgess, defected to the Soviet Union, as they were under suspicion. Their friend Kim Philby was forced to resign from a high-ranking post with MI6 as a result of these defections. He worked in journalism until, in 1963, he also defected. Philby, once regarded as a possible future chief of MI6, had betrayed many operations to the KGB.

The fourth man in the network was Sir Anthony Blunt, who was an officer in MI5 from 1940 to 1945. He later functioned as a spy while serving as Surveyor of the Queen's Pictures. His guilt had been known to MI5 before it was publicly revealed in 1979.

The last of the five to be publicly named was John Cairncross. He had a career that included positions in MI6, a wartime signals intelligence agency known as GC & CS (later GCHQ), and various government ministries.

MOSSAD SPY NETWORK

Mossad networks operate under the cover of Israel's embassies in other countries. Illegals are controlled directly from Israel, working without diplomatic cover or support from embassy staff. In each country there is a Head of Station who works under diplomatic protection inside the embassy, and when necessary can direct even the ambassador to support Mossad activities. The *sayanim* register is a list of volunteers in the Jewish community available to help when required – this helps keep Mossad manning levels low. Each station imports technical specialists when they are needed, rather than keep them as full-time members of the station.

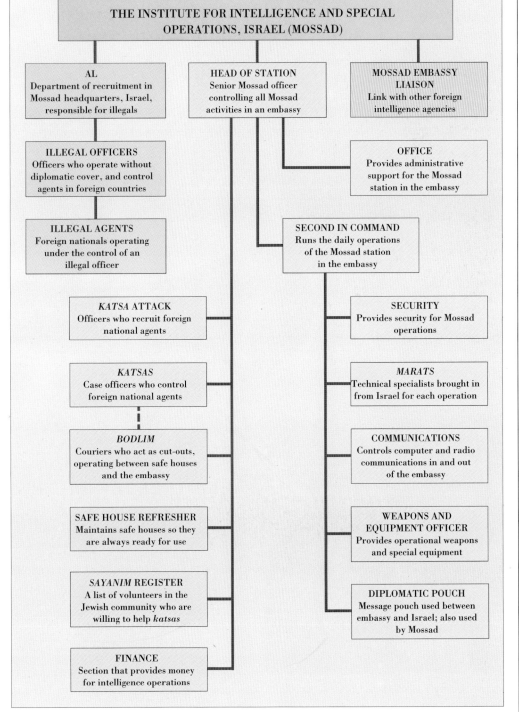

THE INSTITUTE FOR INTELLIGENCE AND SPECIAL OPERATIONS, ISRAEL (MOSSAD)

AL
Department of recruitment in Mossad headquarters, Israel, responsible for illegals

HEAD OF STATION
Senior Mossad officer controlling all Mossad activities in an embassy

MOSSAD EMBASSY LIAISON
Link with other foreign intelligence agencies

ILLEGAL OFFICERS
Officers who operate without diplomatic cover, and control agents in foreign countries

OFFICE
Provides administrative support for the Mossad station in the embassy

ILLEGAL AGENTS
Foreign nationals operating under the control of an illegal officer

SECOND IN COMMAND
Runs the daily operations of the Mossad station in the embassy

KATSA ATTACK
Officers who recruit foreign national agents

SECURITY
Provides security for Mossad operations

KATSAS
Case officers who control foreign national agents

MARATS
Technical specialists brought in from Israel for each operation

BODLIM
Couriers who act as cut-outs, operating between safe houses and the embassy

COMMUNICATIONS
Controls computer and radio communications in and out of the embassy

SAFE HOUSE REFRESHER
Maintains safe houses so they are always ready for use

WEAPONS AND EQUIPMENT OFFICER
Provides operational weapons and special equipment

SAYANIM REGISTER
A list of volunteers in the Jewish community who are willing to help *katsas*

DIPLOMATIC POUCH
Message pouch used between embassy and Israel; also used by Mossad

FINANCE
Section that provides money for intelligence operations

Fate of a spy

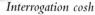

Poisoned pin
American spy pilot Francis Gary Powers carried this poison-tipped pin, concealed in a silver dollar.

SPIES OPERATE UNDER constant threat of detection and capture, which may result in them facing anything from a period in custody to the death penalty. "Legal" officers – those under cover of diplomatic immunity – are sometimes well known to enemy counterintelligence and are often treated leniently: a few hours of detention may be followed by release into the custody of representatives from the embassy of their own country.

Those personnel who operate without diplomatic protection, and are known as "illegals" (see p. 8), face far greater risks. Illegals are at the mercy of the judicial system of the country in which they are arrested. The agency controlling them may try to offer protection, but may have difficulty because knowledge of the illegals' identity is compartmentalized: the illegal agents are known only to those directly needed to support and control their activities.

BETRAYAL
Despite taking precautions, spies are always vulnerable to betrayal by moles (see p. 12). Moles work from within intelligence agencies and are often able to identify spies to the enemy service that is controlling them. The KGB mole Aldrich Ames (see p. 162) operated within the CIA

and was able to betray at least ten agents operating in the Soviet Union for the CIA; most of these were killed. Ames also betrayed Oleg Gordievsky, a KGB officer who worked as a mole for the British intelligence service MI6. The latter helped Gordievsky to defect to Britain and avoid capture and possible death. Other important moles have included those of the Cambridge spy ring (see p. 165) who operated for years, betraying many agents.

Cyanide vial and rectal concealment
In World War II, the German security service, the SD, produced this brass tube for concealing in the rectum. It held a small glass vial of cyanide.

PUNISHMENTS
The sentence for espionage varies from country to country and is affected by many circumstances. The former Soviet bloc countries generally executed those convicted of spying. Oleg Penkovsky, a GRU (Soviet military intelligence) officer who worked as a mole both for the CIA and for MI6, was executed after a well-publicized show trial to make an example of him as a warning to other potential traitors.

Illegals, too, may face execution if they are operating in particularly hostile circumstances. For example, the Arab

Interrogation cosh
The KGB used this cosh during interrogations. The flat end contains a lead weight which is covered in leather to avoid inflicting fatal blows while still causing great pain to the victim.

HUMAN TRANSPORTATION TRUNK

THE MAN IN THE TRUNK

Mordecai Louk, an Israeli, was a double agent working for both Mossad and Egyptian intelligence. In 1964, when Louk was living in Rome, the Egyptians suspected him and decided to bring him in for questioning. Louk was seized, drugged, and put in a specially designed trunk to be flown secretly back to Cairo. Inside the trunk, Louk was strapped in a leather seat, his feet were fixed to the floor of the trunk, and his hands and head were held in special fittings. At Rome's Fiumicino airport, however, a delay allowed the effect of the drugs to wear off. Customs officers, who heard Louk's voice, had him released. Later, Louk returned to Israel. Ironically, he was convicted and jailed on account of his contacts with the Egyptians.

MORDECAI LOUK

states almost always execute captured Israeli illegals. Such a grim prospect has led members of the Israeli intelligence organization, Mossad, to refer to the Arab states as "The Land of the Dead".

In post-World War II America and Western Europe, convicted traitors have generally received prison sentences. An important exception occurred in the case of Ethel and Julius Rosenberg (see p. 164), who were executed in 1953 for passing American atomic bomb secrets to the Soviets during World War II. The couple were the first American citizens to be executed for treason since the end of the American Civil War.

Illegal agents operating in the relative safety of the industrialized countries, where political violence is less prevalent – such as Western Europe or North America – may receive prison terms but may not have to complete them. They may be exchanged for prisoners held by other countries, in spy swaps.

INTERROGATION AND TORTURE

Counterintelligence services interrogate and occasionally torture captured spies to extract vital information from them. Some spies choose to commit suicide rather than risk being forced to give information that may compromise their mission and those involved in it. World War II SOE operatives (see p. 30) were often issued with "L" pills, capable of

causing almost instant death; the U-2 spy pilot Francis Gary Powers (see p. 52) carried a poison-tipped suicide pin.

TURNING A SPY

In certain cases, captured spies may be offered their lives or freedom in return for becoming double agents (see p. 13). Many German spies detected by British intelligence during World War II took this option. The Germans, too, tried to turn spies. One of their main successes was in the case of an SOE agent whom they captured in Holland. He agreed to help the Germans by asking the SOE to send more men to Holland. Hoping to warn the SOE of his fate, the captured agent did not use the SOE security code when radioing his controllers. SOE headquarters failed to recognize this omission as a warning, however, and sent more than 50 operatives to Holland. All were immediately captured on arrival by the Gestapo.

One World War II spy, codenamed Cicero, met an

Glienicke Bridge, Berlin
The Glienicke Bridge across the River Spree between East and West Berlin. The bridge became well known as the site of several important exchanges of convicted spies.

ironic fate. He was butler to the British ambassador to Turkey, and worked as a spy for Germany. However, it was only after the war that it was discovered that the Germans had paid him in forged English banknotes. Cicero's fate was to end his days in poverty.

The last cigarette
This Russian spy was captured by Austrian forces in the Balkans in World War I. This picture was taken moments before his execution.

Greville Wynne

While in Moscow in 1961, British businessman Greville Wynne (1919–90) took up the role of courier between Soviet military intelligence officer Colonel Oleg Penkovsky and British intelligence. Wynne would visit Eastern Europe on business and collect material from Penkovsky to take back to England. In 1962 the KGB arrested Penkovsky and Wynne. Penkovsky was executed; Wynne was released in a swap for Konon Molody (see p. 50).

Glossary

Words in SMALL CAPITALS refer to other entries in this glossary.

Abwehr
German military intelligence, established before World War II. It was the primary organization for foreign intelligence-gathering until its merger with the SD in 1944.

Agent
A person, often a foreign national, who works for, but is not officially employed by, an intelligence service.

Assassination device
A special weapon selected for use in carrying out assassinations. These devices are usually concealable and some are designed to leave no traces at the site of the assassination.

Audio surveillance
A technique for surreptitious eavesdropping, often using electronic devices.

BfV
(Bundesamt für Verfassungsschutz) German counterintelligence agency, founded in West Germany in 1950.

BND
(Bundesnachrichtendienst) German foreign intelligence-gathering organization, established in 1956 in West Germany.

Case officer
An intelligence officer who controls or is responsible for an agent. See HANDLER.

Cheka
(Russian abbreviation for Extraordinary Commission for the Struggle against Counter-revolution, Espionage, Speculation, and Sabotage) Russian secret police organization founded in 1917 to serve the Bolshevik Party; replaced in 1922 by the GPU, later the OGPU.

CIA
(Central Intelligence Agency) Founded in 1947; the American agency responsible, like Britain's MI6, for the combined tasks of worldwide intelligence-gathering and COUNTERINTELLIGENCE abroad.

Cipher
A form of CODE in which numbers or letters are substituted systematically for those in a plain text message, so as to prevent unintended recipients from understanding the message.

Code
(1) A system designed to obscure the meaning of a message of any kind by substituting words, numbers, or symbols (from a code book or by any other previous arrangement) for plain text. Not every code is a CIPHER; in some codes, a symbol can represent an idea or even convey a whole message.
(2) A non-clandestine letter substitution system such as MORSE CODE.

Commandos
World War II name for British special operations units. The word is sometimes also used to refer to a member of such a unit.

Concealment
An object that has been altered for the secret storage and transportation of messages, film, money, ciphers, secret inks, electronic bugs, or other TRADECRAFT items.

Counterespionage
COUNTERINTELLIGENCE operations that involve the clandestine penetration of a hostile intelligence service.

Counterintelligence
Broader category than COUNTERESPIONAGE, including action against foreign intelligence, and protecting information, personnel, equipment, and installations from espionage, sabotage, and terrorism.

Countersurveillance
Techniques used to detect hostile surveillance, and also to frustrate it.

Courier
A person who carries information, equipment, or any other secret material for an intelligence service, either wittingly or unwittingly. A courier may also be a CUT-OUT.

Cryptanalysis
Also known as code-breaking, this is the study of CIPHERS and other kinds of CODES in order to reveal the original message, without having access to official keys or encryption systems.

Cryptography
The use of CODES and CIPHERS to render communications that have been originally written in plain text unintelligible and secure except to the intended recipients.

Cut-out
A person who acts as an intermediary between members of intelligence services or spy networks, improving network security by preventing contact between members.

Dead drop
A secure location, usually with a concealed container, used for secret communication and exchange of material between a spy and his controller. Dead drops remove the need for potentially dangerous personal meetings.

Defector
A person who, by choice, physically leaves the control of a country or intelligence service to serve the interests of another country. Such people often provide information of high value to the host intelligence service.

DGSE
(Direction Générale de la Sécurité Extérieure) French external intelligence service. Founded in 1981, the DGSE is similar in function to America's CIA and Britain's MI6.

Double agent
An agent of one intelligence service who is recruited and controlled by another intelligence service, to secretly work against their original service. A double agent should not be confused with a MOLE.

ECM
(Electronic countermeasures) The use of specialized devices that render the electronic equipment of an enemy ineffective. ECM is applied extensively in warfare, and also in COUNTERINTELLIGENCE.

Enigma
An electromechanical, rotor-based CIPHER machine invented by German engineer Walter Scherbius in 1923. Versions of the Enigma were used for enciphering and deciphering messages by the German military and civil organizations during World War II.

FBI
(Federal Bureau of Investigation) Founded in 1924; responsible for COUNTERINTELLIGENCE and some other law enforcement duties within the United States. In its internal security and counterintelligence role, it is similar to MI5.

Flaps and seals
TRADECRAFT term for opening, examining, and resealing envelopes and packages without raising the suspicions of the recipient. The procedure originally involved clandestine manipulation of envelope flaps and wax seals, from which its name is derived.

FSB
(Russian abbreviation for Federal Security Service) Internal security service in Russia, successor to KGB Second Chief Directorate.

GCHQ
(Government Communications Headquarters) The British signals intelligence centre, similar to the NSA in the United States.

Gestapo
(Abbreviation for *Geheime Staatspolizei*) World War II German secret state police. Founded in April 1933, it was controlled by the Nazi Party and had responsibility for internal security throughout Germany.

GPU
See CHEKA.

GRU
(Russian abbreviation for Chief Intelligence Directorate) Founded in 1918 as the Soviet military intelligence service. Temporarily renamed the Fourth Department in the 1930s, the GRU survived the fall of the Soviet Union in 1991 and has continued in the same function under its original name, serving the state of Russia in place of the Soviet Union.

Handler
A person, usually an intelligence officer (also usually a CASE OFFICER) who is responsible for, or controls, an agent.

HUMINT
(Abbreviation for *human int*elligence) Refers to information directly collected by human sources, such as AGENTS, as opposed to that collected via technology such as satellites.

"Illegal"
An intelligence officer belonging to an agency of the Soviet Union (KGB or GRU), an allied country, or to present-day Russia (SVR or GRU), operating in a hostile country without diplomatic protection but with the benefit of a legend (see p. 162). An illegal usually has no direct contact with his or her embassy, being controlled directly from Moscow.

Industrial espionage
The clandestine acquisition of information about business; may be carried out by a competitor, or by an intelligence agency.

Intelligence
This term can be applied to the profession of espionage, the information collected by espionage, or the final analysed product.

KGB
(Russian abbreviation for Committee for State Security) Founded in 1954 as the intelligence and security organization of the Soviet Union, and the successor during the Cold War period of the earlier CHEKA. In 1991 the KGB First Chief Directorate (for foreign intelligence-gathering) was renamed the SVR. The Second Chief Directorate (for internal security) was renamed the FSB.

"Legal"
An intelligence officer protected by diplomatic immunity and belonging to an agency of the Soviet Union or one of its allies; since 1991, the equivalent in the case of Russia.

Listening post
A site at which signals received by means of electronic audio surveillance are monitored.

MI5
(Originally an abbreviation for Military Intelligence, section 5) MI5 has no military connection and is now officially called the Security Service. Founded in 1909, it is the British internal security organization. Like the FBI in the United States, MI5 is responsible for domestic COUNTERINTELLIGENCE.

MI6
(Originally an abbreviation for Military Intelligence, section 6) MI6 has no military connection and is now officially known as the Secret Intelligence Service (SIS). Founded in 1909, it is Britain's foreign intelligence service.

The role of MI6 is similar to that of the CIA in the United States and MOSSAD in Israel.

MICE
(Money, Ideology, Compromise, and Ego) These are considered to be the four prime motivating factors that may be of use in recruiting a potential agent.

Microdot
An optical reduction of a photographic negative to a size that is illegible without magnification. In practice, a microdot is considered to be 1 mm or smaller in size.

Minox
A subminiature camera, using 9.5 mm film, that has a wide range of uses in clandestine photography. The Minox was first produced in Riga, Latvia, in 1938. After World War II, a new Minox company was founded in West Germany, producing subminiature cameras that are based on the original design.

Mole
An employee or officer of an intelligence service who agrees to work for another intelligence service. Some would-be DEFECTORS who approach an intelligence service they wish to work for are persuaded to remain in their posts and function as moles.

Morse code
Developed by Samuel Morse, an American, in 1838 for the electromagnetic telegraph, this code substitutes a series of dots and dashes for letters and numbers. The code is still in use and is internationally recognized.

Mossad
(Hebrew abbreviation for the Institute for Intelligence and Special Operations) Mossad was founded in 1951 and is Israel's external intelligence-gathering organization. It is similar in function to America's CIA and Britain's MI6.

NKVD
(Russian abbreviation for the People's Commissariat for Internal Affairs) The internal security and (despite the name) worldwide intelligence organization of the Soviet Union that succeeded the OGPU·from 1934 to 1946.

NOC
(Non-official cover) An intelligence officer who belongs to an American agency and operates without diplomatic immunity.

NSA
(National Security Agency) The American agency, formed in 1952, responsible for information security, foreign signals intelligence, and CRYPTOGRAPHY.

OGPU
(Russian abbreviation for the Unified State Political Directorate) Founded in 1923 as the organization responsible for internal security and intelligence for the newly formed Soviet Union. It succeeded CHEKA and the GPU, and was replaced by the NKVD.

Okhrana
The secret police that operated in Russia under the Tsars against political opponents of the Tsarist state between 1881 and 1917.

One-time pad
A set of paper or silk sheets, each bearing a series of random numbers or letters that is used only once for encipherment and decipherment of a message. The CIPHER is usually printed in groups of five letters. If each cipher is used only once, it is considered unbreakable. Pads or individual sheets are sometimes transferred to microfilm or converted into MICRODOTS.

Operative
An officer or AGENT operating under the control of an intelligence service.

OSS
(Office of Strategic Services) Operational between 1942 and 1945, this American organization was the forerunner of the CIA.

Polyalphabetic substitution
The use of two or more CIPHER alphabets in a prearranged pattern to provide multiple substitutes for a particular letter in a message.

Receiver
Electronic equipment used to receive signals from electronic surveillance devices.

Reconnaissance
A mission undertaken to secure information, usually in advance of a secret operation.

Red Orchestra (Rote Kapelle)
The German name given to the successful Soviet military spy network that operated in Europe before and during World War II.

Resistance group
An indigenous underground organization that makes use of guerrilla warfare techniques and conducts sabotage and intelligence operations against an occupying power. Clandestine services of a country at war may work with resistance groups in enemy-occupied territory.

Safe house
A house or apartment that is thought to be unknown to foreign intelligence or COUNTERINTELLIGENCE and is considered temporarily safe for clandestine meetings.

SD
(Sicherheitsdienst, or Security Service) The SD was founded in 1934 as the political intelligence and COUNTERINTELLIGENCE service of the Nazi Party. In 1944 the SD was merged with the ABWEHR and became the dominant force in wartime Germany for intelligence-gathering and counterintelligence.

Secret writing
TRADECRAFT terminology for the use of secret inks (wet system) or special carbon papers impregnated with chemicals (dry system) for clandestine communication. Both systems use reagents to reveal the message.

SIGINT
(Abbreviation for signals intelligence) Refers both to intelligence gathered by eavesdropping on enemy electronic transmissions and to the process of gathering such intelligence.

Silenced weapon
A weapon modified by a noise suppressor fixed to the end of the barrel, greatly reducing the sound when the weapon is fired. Such weapons are not completely silent, but it may be difficult to identify the source of the noise.

Sleeper
An AGENT or officer who lives in a foreign country for years as an ordinary citizen. When a hostile situation develops, the sleeper is activated on preassigned missions of sabotage, assassination, or intelligence collection.

SMERSH
(Abbreviation for Smert shpionam, a slogan in Russian meaning "death to spies") Soviet military COUNTERINTELLIGENCE organization during World War II.

SOE
(Special Operations Executive) A British special forces organization founded in 1940 during World War II to conduct sabotage operations and provide equipment, training, and leadership for resistance groups in Nazi-occupied Europe.

Spy network/ring
An organization of officers and AGENTS operating under central control.

Spy satellite
An orbiting satellite that uses sensors to record photographic or electronic intelligence.

Spy swap
The exchange of real or purported spies between nations or intelligence services of the East and West during the Cold War.

Stasi
(Abbreviation for Staatssicherheitsdienst) Founded in 1950, dissolved in 1989; East German state security, also conducting foreign intelligence operations in West Germany.

StB
(Statni tajna Bezpecnost or State Secret Security) Founded in 1948; the Czech intelligence and security service.

Suitcase radio
World War II clandestine radio equipment housed inside a civilian-style suitcase.

Support agent
An AGENT who services another agent or a network. This might involve replenishing SAFE HOUSE supplies or acting as a CUT-OUT.

SVR
(Russian abbreviation for Russian Foreign Intelligence Service) Succeeded the KGB's First Chief Directorate in 1991; functions similar to the CIA, MI6, and MOSSAD.

Telephone tapping
Using specialized electronic devices to listen to and record telephone conversations. Inductive taps are those that do not require physical connection to the telephone circuit.

Tokko
The Special High Police Bureau of the Tokyo Metropolitan Police Department. During World War II, Tokko carried out domestic COUNTERINTELLIGENCE.

Tradecraft
The procedures, techniques, and devices used in clandestine intelligence operations.

Visual surveillance
The observation of a person, place, or thing, using visual means.

Index

Page numbers in **bold** type denote the main reference to a spread title. Page numbers in *italic* type indicate an illustration or its caption.

A

Abel spy ring 164, *164*
Abwehr 34, 35, 168
access agents 159
administration 10, 47
Agee, Philip 65, *65*
agents 10, 159, 168
agents' radios 110, **116–117**
  specialized communications 118–119
Air America 47, *47*
aircraft *see* spy planes
Alphabetic Typewriter 97 36, *36*
ambassadors *see* diplomats
America *see* United States
Ames, Aldrich "Rick" *8*, 158, *158*
  betrays agents 166
amphibious sabotage **98–99**
analysts 13
Angleton, James Jesus 103, *103*
Anna *see* Frenzel, Alfred
Anthropoid, Operation 35, *35*
anti-bugging devices 100–101, *101*, **104–105**
Arab states 137, 166–167
assassination devices **152–155**, 168
assassinations
  Castro's (attempted) 155
  CIA involvement 13, 155
  Hitler's (attempted) 35
  KGB weapons 13, 135, 152
  Lincoln's 23, *23*
  Markov's 152, *152*
  Nasser's (attempted) 137
  Okolovich's (foiled) 153, *153*
  Trotsky's 13
  weapons for 148, 152–155, 168
assassins 13
audio surveillance 15, 76, 168
  see also listening devices; microphones; receivers
Austria 24, 26
  Vienna procedure 55, *55*
Auto Camera Mark 3 78, *78*

B

Babbington Plot 20–21
Baden-Powell, Lord 131
Baker, Lafayette 22
baseball cap concealment 81, *81*
belt pistol 148, *148*
belt-buckle microphone 84, *84*
Beretta pistols 138, *138*, *139*
Berlin 42, **44–45**
Bernhard, Operation 34, *34*

Bernstorff, Count Johann Heinrich von 24, *24*
BfV 128, 168
Big Joe 5 crossbow *142*, 143, *143*
binoculars 78, *78*
biscuit tin radios 116, *116*
blackmail 9, 169
  KGB uses 42, 44, 80
blades
  clandestine kits 146, *146*
  concealed in shoes 77, 95, *95*, 134
  instructor's blade kit 147, *147*
  see also knives
Blake, George *8*, 159, *159*
  warns of Berlin tunnel 45
Blunt, Sir Anthony 9, 165, *165*
BND 44–45, 105, 168
Bodyguard revolver 136, *136*
Boeckenhaupt, Herbert 124, *124*
Bolsheviks 19, 26–27
Bolton's patent cipher wheel 120, *120*
books for concealment
  for cameras 62, *62*
  for listening devices 83, *83*
  to smuggle microdots 50
Booth, John Wilkes 23, *23*
Border Guards 79, *79*
Borgia, Cesare 20, *20*
Boyce, Christopher *15*, 57, *57*
briefcases
  for audio surveillance 89, *89*
  bug detector *101*
  for flaps and seals kits 109, *109*
  for photo-surveillance 60, 65, *65*
Britain
  breaks Enigma cipher 36–37
  Cambridge spies 9, 164, 165
  Lonsdale ring 50–51, *51*
  MI9 95, 150
  occupies Germany 44, *44*
  Operation Frankton 98, *98*
  in World War I 24–25
  see also MI5; MI6; Special Operations Executive
Brown, John 112, 113, *113*
brush camera 61, 74, *74*
brush concealment 129, *129*
bugs *see* listening devices
Burgess, Guy 9, 165, *165*
burglary *see* surreptitious entry
Burma 33
burst transmission 15, 111, 118
button concealments 130, *130*

C

Cabinet Noir *18*, 21
Cairncross, John 9, 165
Cambridge spies, the 9, 164, 165
cameras **60–61**
  concealed *see* concealed cameras
  copy *see* copy cameras

for microdots 126, *126*, 127, *127*
Minox *see* Minox cameras
movie cameras 81, *81*
photo-sniper 102, *102*, *103*
in satellites 56, *57*
subminiature cameras
  see subminiature cameras
for surveillance *see* surveillance cameras
video cameras *see* video cameras
  see also photography
Canada 136
Canaris, Admiral Wilhelm Franz 34, *34*, 35
canes
  poison gas cane 154, *154*
  poison pellet cane 152, *152*
case officers 8, 168, 169
  recruit agents 10, 158–159
  training of 160
Castro, President Fidel 155, *155*
Central Intelligence Agency *see* CIA
Checkpoint Charlie 45, *45*
Cheka, the 19, 27, 168
  credentials *19*, *26*
China 18, 87
  Chinese intelligence *12*, 13
CIA 168
  Angleton, James Jesus 103, *103*
  assassinations 13, 155
  and Berlin Tunnel 42, 44, 45
  directorates 46–47, 76, 91
  and FBI 46
  formation 33, 42, 46
  moles in *see* Ames, Aldrich; Wu Tai Chin, Larry
  training 161
Cicero (Elyesa Bazna) 34, *34*, 167
cipher devices 111, **120–121**
  Alphabetic Typewriter 97, 36, *36*
  Confederate cipher disc 23
  Enigma machine 37, 122–123, 168
  the Geheimschreiber 123, *123*
  Japanese rotor-type 29
  KL-47 cipher machine 54, *54*
  Kryha cipher machine *111*, 120, *120*
ciphers 168
  cipher devices *see* cipher devices
  ciphers and secret writing 124–125
  polyalphabetic ciphers
    see polyalphabetic ciphers
  Purple code 29, 36, 41
  see also code-breaking; Morse code
Civil Air Transport 47
Clayton Hutton, Major Christopher 150, *150*
close-combat weapons 134–135, **144–147**
coal, explosives disguised as 77, 97, *97*
code-breaking 168
  future of 15
  NSA's role 42, 47, 170

in World War I 24–25, *26*
in World War II 29, 36–37
  see also ciphers; cryptography
codes 168
  see also ciphers; code-breaking; Morse code
Cohen, Elie 102, *102*, 162
Cohen, Lona and Morris 50–51, *50*
Colby, Major William Egan 6, 33, *33*
  part of Jedburgh team 141, *141*
Cold War 7, **42–43**
  Berlin 42, 44–45
  Cambridge spies 9, 164, 165
  end of 6, 8, 14
  Frenzel, Alfred 42, 48–49
  Lonsdale ring 42, 50–51
  spy planes 42, *43*, 52–53
  spying from space *15*, 43, 56–57
  US sets up agencies 42, 46–47
  Walker spy ring *see* Walker, John
Colditz Castle 95, *95*
Colt revolvers
  .38 Bodyguard 136, *136*
  .38 Commando 137, *137*
Commandos 168
communications
  Berlin tunnel intercepts 42, 44, 45
  clandestine 110–111
  satellites intercept *15*, 56, 57
  specialized 118–119
  see also audio surveillance; concealments; dead drops; microdots; radios; secret writing
communism
  attracts spies 8–9
  in China 87
  fall of 14–15
  Russian Revolution 26–27
compartmentalization 164
compasses 94, *94*
compromise 8, 9, 169
  KGB use of 42, 44
computer technology 14, 15, 47
  breaks Enigma code 37, 122
concealed cameras 61, **62–63**
  in baseball cap 81, *81*
  in book 62, *62*
  in briefcases 60, 65, *65*
  in brush 129, *129*
  in camera case 67, *67*
  in cigarette lighter 68, *68*
  in cigarette packet (Kiev 30) 68, *68*
  in cigarette packet (Tessina) 62, *62*, 68, *68*
  F21 cameras 66–67
  in handbag 64, *64*
  in jacket 67, *67*
  in matchbox 68, 69, *69*
  necktie *43*, 63, *63*
  notebook 74, *74*
  Robot cameras 64–65
  statuette 128, *128*
  subminiature 60, 68–69

(concealed cameras *continued*)
umbrella 66–67, *67*
in waist belt 65, *65*
wristwatch cameras 60, *61*, 68, *68*
concealed weapons 134, **148–151**
concealments 111, **128–131**, 168
battery casing 130, *130*
belt-buckle microphone 84, *84*
for blades 77, 95, *95*
bolt 131, *131*
button 130, *130*
for cameras *see* concealed cameras
chessboard 129, *129*
cigarette 130, *130*
for compasses 94, *94*
for escape equipment 77, 94–95
eye 128, *128*
fountain pen microdot viewer 127, *127*
hairbrush 94, *94*
for invisible ink *24*
for maps 94, *94*
for microdots *see* microdots
for microfilm 128, *128*
pencil 151, *151*
pipe 94, *94*
playing card 94, *94*
ring *111*
self-destruction of 11
shaving items as 131, *131*
shoe 77, *95*, 134
silver dollar *19*, 128, *128*
soap case for film 130, *130*
stamp *110*, 130, *130*
statuette 128, *128*
walnut *110*, 124, *124*
for weapons *see* concealed weapons
Confederates *18*, 22–23
contact agents 159
controllers 164
Converter M-209 cipher machine 121, *121*
copy cameras 61, *61*, **72–75**
coshes 135, *145*
Peskett close-combat weapon 144, *144*
counterespionage 168
counterintelligence **100–101**, 168
BfV 128, 168
in Canada 137
CIA 46, 103, 168
ECM 168
FBI 42, 46, 168
German in World War II *see* SD
Japanese 40–41, 170
MI5 *100*, 169
OSS branch for 32
SMERSH *100*, 170
visual surveillance for 78
countersurveillance 101, **106–107**, 168
couriers 10–11, 168
court intrigues 18, **20–21**
covers and legends **162–163**
Cranley Drive 50–51, *50*
crime 14–15
see also assassinations; industrial espionage; surreptitious entry

crossbows and darts 134, **142–143**
cryptanalysis 168
see also code-breaking
cryptography 168
see also ciphers; code-breaking
Cuba
Castro, President Fidel 155, *155*
Cuban missile crisis 43, 53, *53*
Cubans in Watergate 92
cut-outs 10, 168
Czechoslovakia
StB 48–49, *61*, 170
see also Frenzel, Alfred

D

daggers
Peskett close-combat weapon 144, *144*
push daggers 134, 145, *145*
dart-firing pistol 142, *142*
D-Day 28, 31
dead drops 111, **132–133**, 168
hollow bolt for 131, *131*
deer gun 136, *136*
defectors 11–12, 168, 169
Burgess, Guy 9, 165, *165*
Deriaban, Peter 12, *137*
Golitsyn, Anatoli 103
Gordievsky, Oleg 12, 166
Maclean, Donald 9, 165, *165*
Petrov, Vladimir 11–12, *11*
Philby, Kim 9, 165, *165*
Defense Intelligence Agency 46
Delco 5300 radio *110*, 117, *117*
Deriaban, Peter 12, *137*
Detachment 101 33, *33*
detectors 100, *101*, **102–103**
developing film 71, *71*
DGSE 137, 168
DIA 46
digital technology
in listening devices 15, 82
in satellites 43, 56
diplomats 10, 18, 20
diplomatic immunity 8, 159, 166
see also embassies
direction finding radios 102, 103, *103*
directorates (CIA) 46–47, 76, 91
directorates (KGB) 50, 76, 78
Border Guards 79, *79*
disguises 107, *107*
for equipment *see* concealments
Donovan, William J. 32, 33, *33*
double agents 11, 159, 168
Ames, Aldrich *see* Ames, Aldrich
Blake, George *see* Blake, George
Felfe, Heinz 45, 105, *105*
Hari, Mata 25, *25*
Louk, Mordecai 166, *166*
OVRA recruits 139
Penkovsky, Oleg 78, *78*, 167
Popov, Dusan 11, *11*, 41, *41*
Pujol, Juan 11
spies become on capture 167

drugs
addicts as spies 57, 124, *124*
fighting trade in *14*, 15
Dulles, Allen Welsh 47, 53
Dzershinsky, Felix *26*, 27

E

early espionage **18–19**
in American Civil War 18–19, *18*, 22–23
at court 18, 20–21
in Russia 19, 26–27
in World War I 19, 24–25, 26
East Germany 44
Berlin 42, 44–45
Stasi 73, *73*, 170
see also Germany; West Germany
Eastern bloc *see* Cold War; Czechoslovakia; East Germany; Soviet Union
Echo 8 cigarette-lighter camera 68, *68*
ECM 168
ego, in recruitment 8–9, 169
Egypt 137, 166
Elizabeth I 20–21, *21*
embassies 50, 158, 165
see also diplomats
émigrés, Russian 27
Emil (codename) 133, *133*
En-Pen 149, *149*
Enigma machine 36–37, **122–123**, 168
enlargers 71, *71*
equipment 59
escape equipment 77, **94–95**
SOE develops 28, 31
special for OSS 33, *33*
see also cameras; concealments; radios; receivers; weapons
executions 31, 166–167
explosives 77, 96–97
see also fuses; grenades; mines; mortars

F

F21 concealed camera **66–67**
Fairbairn-Sykes knives 147, *147*, 158
FANY· 112, 114, *114*
fate of a spy **166–167**
FBI 46, *46*, 168
FCD 50, *50*
name changes 169, 170
Federal Bureau of Investigation *see* FBI
Felfe, Heinz 45, 105, *105*
fibrescope 79, *79*
film developing 71, *71*
film slitters 63, 74, *75*
fine wire kits 82, *82*
firearms
assassination guns 153, *153*
Beretta pistols 138, *138*, 139
cigar pistol 148, *148*

cigarette pistol 148, *148*
Colt *see* Colt guns
cyanide gas gun 43
CZ27 semi-automatic pistol *134*
deer gun 136, *136*
glove pistol 9, 151, *151*
Hi-Standard pistols 141, *141*
Liberator pistol 33
lipstick pistol 45
Manurhin 7.65 mm pistol *137*
Nagant revolvers 27, 137, *137*
pen gun 145, *145*
pipe pistol 151, *151*
pocket torch pistol 150, *150*
propelling pencil pistol 151, *151*
rectal pistol 150, *150*
ring revolver 19
shoulder holster 29
Stinger 150, *150*
Tokarev TT-33 pistol 140, *140*
Walther PPK *13*, 135
Webley and Scott *see* Webley and Scott pistols
Welrod pistol *161*
Wel-Wand sleeve gun 141, *141*
Winchester rifles 140, *140*
wrist pistol 149, *149*
First Aid Nursing Yeomanry 112, 114, *114*
First Chief Directorate *see* FCD
flaps and seals 101, 169
briefcase for 109, *109*
tool roll 108, *108*
see also letter interception
Fleming, Ian *37*
forged currency 12, 34, *34*
forged documents 162, *162*, *163*
Fourth Department (earlier GRU) 38–39, 40–41, 169
France
in Cold War 44, *44*
Operation Frankton 98, *98*
Richelieu *18*, 21, *21*
secret service 137, 168
in World War I 24, 25
see also French resistance
Frankton Operation 98, *98*
French resistance 12, 31, *31*
coded stamps 109, *109*
see also sabotage
French Secret Service 137, 168
Frenzel, Alfred 42, 48–49
Friedman, William 36, *36*, 120
FSB 169
fuses
acetone time-delay 98, *98*, 99
pencil type 77, 97, *97*
future, spies of the 14–15

G

garrottes 144, *144*
gas and poison
assassination cane 154, *154*
concealed in wallet 155, *155*
gas-firing device 135, 153, *153*
guns for 43, 154, *154*

poison pellet cane 152, *152*
poison pens 149, *149*
GCHQ 169
Gee, Ethel Elizabeth 51, *51*
Geheime Staatspolizei 34, 168
Geheimschreiber, the 37, 123, *123*
Gehlen, Reinhard 44–45, *44*
German Federal Intelligence Service
see BND
Germany
  Abwehr, the 34, 35, 168
  BND 44–45, 105, 168
  Colditz Castle 95, *95*
  Enigma machine 36–37, 122–123,
    168
  forges currency 12, 34, *34*
  Gestapo 34, 168
  MI5's double agents 11
  Operation Frankton 98, *98*
  SD *see* SD
  secret services in World War II 28,
    34–35, 64
  and Thirty Years' War 21
  war with Soviet Union 38–39
  in World War I 19, 24–25, 26
  see also Berlin; East Germany;
    Office of Strategic Services;
    Special Operations Executive;
    West Germany
Gestapo 34, 168
glove pistol *9*, 151, *151*
Gordievsky, Oleg 12, 166
GPU 27, 168
Great Britain *see* Britain
Greenhow, Rose O'Neal 22, *22*
grenades 96, *96*
GRU 44, 161, 169
  as Fourth Department 38–39,
    40–41
guns *see* firearms

H

Hagelin, Boris 121, *121*
Hambleton, Hugh *9*, 106, *160*
handbag concealment 64, *64*
handlers 159, 169
Hari, Mata 25, *25*
Hayashi, Kenji 14, *14*
Hebern cipher machine 120, *120*
Heydrich, Reinhard 34–35
Himmler, Heinrich 34, 35
Hi-Standard pistols 141, *141*, 149
Home Guard 140, *140*
Hoover, J. Edgar 41, *46*
Houghton, Harry Frederick 51, *51*
house of spies **50–51**
human intelligence 24, 42–43,
  169
HUMINT 24, 42–43, 169

I

ideology 8–9, 169
illegals 159, 162, 169
  fate of 166
industrial espionage 14, *14*, 169

infrared communication system 119,
  119
inks 124, 125, *125*
intelligence (defined) 169
Intelligence, Directorate for 46–47
intelligence officers 158, 160
intelligence organizations
  in American Civil War 22–23
  at court 18, 20–21
  BfV (West German, subsequently
    German) 128, 168
  BND (West German, subsequently
    German) 44–45, 105, 168
  Cabinet Noir 18, 21
  Cheka (Soviet) *see* Cheka
  CIA (US) *see* CIA
  DGSE (French) 137, 168
  DIA (US) 46
  double agents in *see* double agents
  FBI (US) *see* FBI
  Fourth Department (Soviet)
    38–39, 40–1, 169
  FSB (Russian) 169
  German agencies in World War II
    28, 34–35
  GRU (Soviet) 44, 161, 169
  Japanese in World War II 28–29,
    40–41
  KGB (Soviet) *see* KGB
  MI5 (British) *see* MI5
  MI6 (British) *see* MI6
  MI9 (British) 95, 150
  moles in *see* moles
  Mossad (Israeli) *see* Mossad
  NKVD (Soviet) 42, 44, 169
  NSA (US) *see* NSA
  OGPU (Soviet) 27, *27*, 170
  Okhrana (Russian) 26, 170
  OSS (US) *see* Office of Strategic
    Services
  SOE (British) *see* Special
    Operations Executive
  Stasi (East German) 73, *73*, 170
  StB (Czech) 48–49, *61*, 170
  SVR (Russian) 170
intelligence services *see* intelligence
  organizations
intervalometer 80, *80*
invisible inks 124, 125, *125*
Israel *see* Mossad
Italian secret police 139, *139*

J

jacket concealment 67, *67*
Japan
  in Burma 33
  cipher machines *29*, 36, *41*
  industrial espionage 14, *14*
  intelligence in World War II
    28–29, 40–41
  Pearl Harbor 28, *40*, *41*
  Purple code 29, 36, *41*
  Red code 36, 120
  in Singapore 40, 99, *99*
  Soviet spies in 38, 39
  Tokko 40, 170
Jedburgh teams 141

K

Kalugin, Major-General Oleg 7
Kang Sheng 87, *87*
Kempei Tai 40
keys 90–91, *90*, *91*
KGB 169
  Ames, Aldrich *see* Ames, Aldrich
  assassinations 13, 135, 152
  uses blackmail *9*, 42, 44
  Border Guards 79, *79*
  Cambridge spies *9*, 164, 165
  defectors in 11–12
  directorates 50, 76, 78
  Lonsdale ring 50–51
  training 161
  Walker, John *see* Walker, John
KH-11 satellite 56–57
Khokhlov, Nicolai 153, *153*
Kita, Nagao 41, *41*
knives 135
  close-combat knives 146–147,
    146, *147*
  Fairbairn-Sykes knives 147, *147*,
    158
knuckledusters 145, *145*
  knuckleduster knives 147, *147*
Knuth, Maria *10*, 128, *128*
Kroger, Helen and Peter 50–51, *50*
Kryha cipher machine *111*, 120,
  120

L

Lee, Andrew Daulton 57, *57*
legals 169
legends **162–163**
lemon juice 125, *125*
letter interception 101, **108–109**
Liberator pistol 33
Liddy, G. Gordon 90, *90*, 92
Lincoln, President Abraham 23, *23*
listening devices 76, **82–85**
  anti-bugging devices 100–101,
    101, 104–105
  digital technology 15, 82
  hidden in plugs 8
  see also audio surveillance; receivers;
    recording devices; telephone
    tapping
listening posts 86, *86*, 169
  see also receivers
lockpicks 77, **92–93**
Lonsdale, Gordon 50–51, *51*
Louk, Mordecai 166, *166*
Lovell, Stanley 33, 149
Lubyanka 26, 27

M

Machiavelli, Niccolo 20, *20*
Maclean, Donald *9*, 165, *165*
Magill, Sergeant C. W. 137, *137*
Manurhin 7.65 mm pistol *137*
Mao Zedong (Mao Tse-tung) 87
maps 94, *94*

Maquis, the *31*
Markov, Georgi assassinated 152,
  152
Marlowe, Christopher 20, *20*
Mary, Queen of Scots 20–21
Mason, Peter 138, *138*
Mata Hari 25, *25*
matchboxes
  cameras concealed in 68, 69, *69*
  counterfeit 28
Meopta copy camera 73, *73*
Mexico 19, 24–25
Mezon recording device 88
MI5 169
  in World War II 11, *100*
  Wright, Peter 83, *83*, 84
MI6 169
  and Berlin Tunnel 42, 44, 45
  in World War II 29, 31
MI9 95, 150
MICE 8–9, 169
microchips 15
microdots **126–127**, 169
  concealments for *111*, 129, *129*
  reader and film *42*
microfilm *42*
  coin concealments 128, *128*
microphones
  earpiece microphones 86, *86*
  in adaptors 85, *85*
  in belt-buckles 84, *84*
  in motel kit 87
  in pens 87, *87*
  installation of 82, *82*
  wristwatch microphone *86*
  see also listening devices; recording
    devices
military intelligence 19
  Abwehr 34, 35, 168
  in American Civil War 22–23
  Fourth Department 38–39, 169
  GRU 44, 161, 169
  MI9 95, 150
  SMERSH *100*, 170
  in World War I 24–25, 26
  see also MI5; MI6; Office of
    Strategic Services; Special
    Operations Executive
mines 98–99, *99*
Minox cameras 60, **70–71**, 169
  brush concealment 128, *128*
  statuette concealment 129, *129*
  Walker's 54, *54*
moles 12–13, 159, 169
  Ames, Aldrich *see* Ames, Aldrich
  betrayal by 166
  Blake, George *see* Blake, George
  Cambridge spies *9*, 164, 165
  Wu Tai Chin, Larry *12*, 13
Molnar, Major Bohumil 48, 49, *49*
Molody, Konon 50–51, *51*
money 8, 159, 169
monoculars 79, *79*
Morse code *160*, 168, 169
  encryption of 110–111
mortars 96, *96*
Mossad 138, *138*, 169
  agents executed 166–167
  Cohen, Elie 102, *102*, 162

(Mossad *continued*)
couriers 10, *165*
Louk, Mordecai 166, *166*
Ostrovsky, Victor 62, *62*, *75*
Pollard, Jonathan 9
sayanim 138, 165, *165*
spy networks 165, *165*
technical services experts 76, *165*
Mounties 136, *136*
movie cameras 81, *81*

N

Nagant revolvers 27, 137, *137*
Nasser, President Gamal Abdel 137
National Security Agency *see* NSA
navy
Pearl Harbor 28, *40*, 41
spies in *see* Vassal, John; Walker, John
see also shipping
Nearne, Jacqueline 112, *112*
Neave, Airey 95, *95*
necktie cameras 43, 63, *63*
networks *see* spy networks
night vision devices 79, *79*
Nixon, President Richard 92
NKVD 42, 44, 169
NOC 162, 169
non-official cover 162, 169
notebook concealment 74, *74*
NRO 56, *56*
NSA 42, 47, 170
crest and emblem *42*, 47
nuclear weapons 15, 43, 52–53

O

Office of Strategic Services **32–33**, 170
formation of 29
lapel badge *28*
recruitment and training 160
uses refugees' suitcases 112
see also resistance groups; sabotage
OGPU 27, *27*, 170
Okhrana, the 26, 170
Okolovich, Georgi 153, *153*
one-time pads 125, *125*, 170
silver dollar concealment 128, *128*
walnut concealment 110, 124, *124*
Operation Anthropoid 35, *35*
Operation Bernhard 34, *34*
Operation Frankton 98, *98*
Operation Rimau 99, *99*
OSS *see* Office of Strategic Services
Ostrovsky, Victor 62, *62*, *75*
OVRA 139, *139*
Ozaki, Hotsumi 39, *39*

P

pager (concealment) 88, *88*
Pastorius (codename) 97
Pearl Harbor 28, *40*, 41
pencil concealment 151, *151*

pencil fuses 77, 97, *97*
pencil pistol 151, *151*
Penkovsky, Oleg 78, *78*, 167
pens
bugs in 83, *83*
gas and poison 149, *149*
maps and compasses in 94, *94*
microdot viewers in 127, *127*
microphones in 87, *87*
needle-firing 150, *150*
pen guns 149, *149*
Peskett close-combat weapon 144, *144*
Peterson, Martha 86
Petrov, Vladimir 11–12, *11*
Philby, Kim 9, 165, *165*
photo-sniper 102, *102*, *103*
photography
in American Civil War 23
hidden images 124, *124*
from satellites *see* satellites
see also cameras
pinhole camera 69, *69*
Pinkerton, Allan 18, 22, *22*
pipe pistol 151, *151*
pipes 94, *94*
playing card concealments 94
poison *see* gas and poison
Pollard, Jonathan 9
polyalphabetic ciphers 120, 170
in 15th century 18, 20
Popov, Dusan 11, *11*, 41, *41*
Portland spies 51
Powers, Francis Gary 52, 53, 164
prisoners of war 94, 150
Colditz Castle 95, *95*
propaganda 32
Pujol, Juan 11
punishments 166–167
Purple code 29, 36, *41*

R

radio direction finding 102, 103, *103*
radios 110–111
Abwehr radio 35
agents' radios 110, 116–117
in counterintelligence 100, 106, *106*
suitcase radios 112–115, 170
see also burst transmitters
RCMP 136, *136*
RDF 102, 103, *103*
receivers **86–89**, 170
agents' receivers 119, *119*
suitcase 114, *114*
see also listening devices
reconnaissance 170
US agencies for 47, 56, *56*
recording devices 76, 88, *88*
underarm tape recorder 89, *89*
recruitment **158–161**
agents' motivation 8–9, 169
KGB methods 42–43, 44
rectal concealment
cyanide vial *166*
rectal pistol 150, *150*
tool kit 95, *95*

Red code 36, 120
Red Orchestra 38–39, 170
Red Terror 19
Red Three 38
Reilly, Sidney 27, *27*
religion 20–21
resistance groups 170
communications with 116, *116*
Italians oppose 139
OSS work with 29, 32, 33
and SOE 29, 30, 31
see also French resistance; sabotage
revolutionary Russia **26–27**
Rhyolite spy satellite 56, 57
Richelieu, Cardinal 18, *18*, 21, *21*
Riga Minox camera 71, *71*
Rimau Operation 99, *99*
ring concealments *111*
ring revolver 19
Robot concealed cameras **64–65**
rollover cameras 74, *74*
Rosenberg, Ethel and Julius 164, *164*, 167
rotor reader 54, *54*
Royal Canadian Mounted Police 136, *136*
Russia
FSB 169
GRU in 169
in revolutionary times 19, 26–27
SVR 170
in World War I 24, 26
see also Soviet Union

S

sabotage 12, **96–97**
amphibious sabotage 77, 98–99
sabotage balloons 41, *41*
saboteurs 12, 97, *97*
safe houses 170
Sansom, Odette 12, 30, *30*
satellites 170
spying from space 15, 43, 56–57
Scan-Lock, the 105, *105*
Schulze-Boysen, Harro 38, 39, 102
science and technology 76
CIA directorate 47, 76, 91
KGB directorates 50, 76
Lovell, Stanley 33, 149
Wright, Peter 83, *83*, 84
SD 29, 34–35, 170
Second Chief Directorate (now FSB) 50, 169
Secret Intelligence (OSS branch) 30–31
Secret Intelligence Service *see* MI6
secret operations **76–77**
see also escape and evasion; sabotage; surreptitious entry; surveillance
secret police
Chinese 87
Italian 139, *139*
see also Cheka; Gestapo; Okhrana
secret services *see* intelligence organizations
secret writing **124–125**, 170

security agencies, US 42, **46–47**
see also intelligence organizations
Security Intelligence Service (Canada) 136
Security Service (MI5) *see* MI5
Security Service (SD) *see* SD
shaving concealments 131, *131*
shipping 29, 33
amphibious sabotage on 98–99
see also navy
SIGINT 24, 47, 170
signals intelligence 42, 47, 170
in World War I 19, 24–25
silenced weapons 134, **138–141**, 170
Welrod pistol *161*
Singapore 40, 99, *99*
sleepers 159, 170
radio communications by 118, 119 *119*
SMERSH 100, 170
Sniegowski, Bruno 133, *133*
SOE *see* Special Operations Executive
Sorge, Richard *39*
in Japan 28, 39, 40–41
sound detect kit 105, *105*
Soviet Union
bugs American embassy 84, *84*
Cheka *see* Cheka
GPU 27, 168
GRU 44, 161, 169
KGB *see* KGB
NKVD 42, 44, 169
nuclear weapons 15, 43, 52–53
occupies Berlin 44–45, *44*
OGPU 27, *27*, 170
Russian Revolution 19, 26–27
satellites 43, 57, *57*
SMERSH *100*, 170
U–2 flies over *42*, 52–53
in World War II 28, 38–39, 40–41
see also Cold War; Russia
space, spying from 15, 43, **56–57**
special issue weapons **136–137**
Special Operations Executive **30–31**, 170
agents captured 167
formation of 29
radio security 114, *114*
recruitment and training 160, *161*
Sansom, Odette 12, 30, *30*
see also resistance groups; sabotage
specialized communications **118–119**
spies 6–15
Agee, Philip 65, *65*
Ames, Aldrich *see* Ames, Aldrich
Baker, Lafayette 22
Blake, George *see* Blake, George
Blunt, Sir Anthony 9, 165, *165*
Boeckenhaupt, Herbert 124, *124*
Boyce, Christopher 15, 57, *57*
Burgess, Guy 9, 165, *165*
Cairncross, John 9, 165
Cohen, Elie 102, *102*, 162
Cohen, Lona and Morris 50–51
Colby, William *see* Colby, Major William Egan
fate of 31, 166–167
of the future 14–15

Gee, Ethel Elizabeth 51, *51*
Gehlen, Reinhard 44–45, *44*
Greenhow, Rose O'Neal 22, *22*
Hambleton, Hugh 9, 106, *160*
Hari, Mata 25, *25*
Hayashi, Kenji 14, *14*
Houghton, Harry Frederick 51, *51*
Knuth, Maria 10, 128, *128*
Kroger, Helen and Peter 50–51, *50*
Lee, Andrew Daulton 57, *57*
Liddy, G. Gordon 90, *90*, 92
Lonsdale, Gordon 50–51, *51*
Maclean, Donald 9, 165, *165*
Marlowe, Christopher 20, *20*
Mason, Peter 138, *138*
Mata Hari 25, *25*
Nearne, Jacqueline 112, *112*
networks *see* spy networks
Ostrovsky, Victor 62, *62*, 75
Penkovsky, Oleg 78, *78*, 167
Philby, Kim 9, 165, *165*
Pinkerton, Allan 18, 22, *22*
Pollard, Jonathan 9
Popov, Dusan 11, *11*, 41, *41*
Portland spies 51
recruitment *see* recruitment
role of 10–13
Sansom, Odette 12, 30, *30*
Sorge, Richard *see* Sorge, Richard
Stanley-Moss, Captain William 145, *145*
swapping spies 167, 170
Szabo, Violette 31, *31*
Thompson, Robert Glenn 126, 127, *127*
training **158–161**
Trepper, Leopold 28, 38–39, *38*
Vassall, John 9, 160, *160*
Victorica, Madame Marie de 124, *124*
Walker, John *see* Walker, John
Wynne, Greville 167, *167*
Yoshikawa, Takeo 41
spy networks **164–165**, 170
 Cambridge spies 9, 164, 165
 in Europe 28, 38–39
 in Japan 28, 39, 40–41
 Lonsdale ring 42, 50–51
 in USA *see* Walker, John
spy planes 42, 43, **52–53**
 Air America uses 47
spy ring *see* spy network
spying from space 15, 43, **56–57**
Stalin, Joseph 13, 28, 39
stamps
 coded 109, *109*
 as concealments 110, 130, *130*
Stanley-Moss, Captain William 145, *145*
Stashinsky, Bogdan 13, *13*, 154, *154*
Stasi 73, *73*, 170
StB 48–49, *61*, 170
Strategic Arms Limitation Treaties 57
strategic surveillance 56
submersible craft 98, *98*, 99
subminiature cameras 60, *60*, **68–69**
 see also Minox camera

suicide *166*, 167
suitcase radios **112–115**, 170
 direction-finding 103, *103*
support agents 159, 170
surreptitious entry 77, **90–91**
 see also lockpicks
surveillance 15, 56
 see also audio surveillance; countersurveillance; visual surveillance
surveillance cameras 60, *61*
 in briefcases 60, 65, *65*
 photo-sniper 102, *102*, *103*
 in waist belts 65, *65*
 see also concealed cameras; visual surveillance
SVR 169, 170
swapping spies 167, 170
Szabo, Violette 31, *31*

T

tactical surveillance 56
tape recorders *see* recording devices
technical services *see* science and technology
telegraphy 18–19, 23
telephone tapping 170
 bugged mouthpiece 82, *82*
 induction tap 83, *83*
 temporary tap 85, *85*
Tessina cameras 62, *62*
Thing, the 83, 84, *84*
Thirty Years' War 21
Thompson, Robert Glenn 126, 127, *127*
thrust weapons 144, *144*
 pencil concealment for 151, *151*
thumb knives 146, *146*
Tokarev TT-33 pistol 140, *140*
Tokko 40, 170
Toyka 58-M necktie camera 63, *63*
tradecraft 159, 170
training **158–161**
transceivers 119, *119*
transmitters 76
 see also burst transmission
Trepper, Leopold 28, 38–39, *38*
Trigon (Alexsandr Ogorodnik) 86
Trotsky, Leon 13
"Trust", the 27
Tsars 26, 170
tunnel under Berlin 42, *44*, 45
Turing, Alan 36, *36*

U

U-2 *see* spy planes
UK *see* Britain
umbrella concealment 66–67, *67*
United Kingdom *see* Britain
United States 47, *47*
 American Black Chamber 24
 American Civil War 18–19, *18*, 22–23

in Berlin after World War II 44–45, *44*
breaks Purple code 36, *41*
CIA *see* CIA
DIA 46
executes spies 167
FBI 46, *46*, 168
Moscow embassy bugged 84, *84*
non-official cover 169
NSA *see* NSA
OSS *see* Office of Strategic Services
Pearl Harbor 28, *40*, 41
sabotage attempts on 41, 97
satellite technology 43, 56–57
World War I 19, 24–25
 see also Cold War
US *see* United States
USSR *see* Soviet Union

V

Vassall, John 9, 160, *160*
Victorica, Madame Marie de 124, *124*
video cameras 81, *81*
 for surveillance 15, *15*
Vienna procedure 55, *55*
Vietnam War 47, *47*
visual surveillance 76, **78–81**, 170
 see also concealed cameras; surveillance cameras

W

waist-belt cameras 65, *65*
Walker, John 70
 and FBI 46, 132, *132*
 Walker spy ring **54–55**
Wall, the Berlin 45, *45*
Walsingham, Sir Francis 18, 20–21
Walther PPK 13, *135*
wars
 American Civil War 18–19, *18*, 22–23
 Cold War *see* Cold War
 Thirty Years' War 21
 Vietnam War 47, *47*
 World War I 19, 24–25, 26
 World War II *see* World War II
watchers 78
Watergate 90, 92, *92*
weapons **134–135**
 assassination devices 152–155, 169
 close-combat weapons 144–147
 concealed weapons 148–151
 crossbows and darts 142–143
 firearms *see* firearms
 nuclear weapons 15, 43, 52–53
 silenced weapons 138–141, 170
 special issue weapons 136–137
Webley and Scott pistols 140, *140*
 belt pistol 148, *148*
Welrod pistol *161*
Wel-Wand sleeve gun 141, *141*
West Germany
 BfV 128, 168
 BND 44–45, 105, 168

Soviet spies in 42, 44, 48–49
 see also Berlin; East Germany; Germany
Whitworth, Jerry 54, *55*
Winchester rifles 140, *140*
World War I 19, **24–25**, 26
World War II **28–29**
 amphibious sabotage in 98–99
 Burma 33
 Colditz Castle 95, *95*
 crossbows and darts in 142–143
 D-Day 28, 31
 Enigma machine 36–37, 122–123, 168
 escape equipment 77, 94–95
 French resistance *see* French resistance
 German secret services 28, 34–35, 64
 Home Guard 140, *140*
 Japanese intelligence 28–29, 40–41
 MI5 11, *100*
 MI6 29, 31
 OSS *see* Office of Strategic Services
 Pearl Harbor 28, *40*, 41
 sabotage *see* sabotage
 silenced weapons developed 134
 Singapore 40, 99, *99*
 SOE *see* Special Operations Executive
 Soviet Union 28, 38–39, 40–41
 X-troop 146, *146*
Wright, Peter 83, *83*, 84
wrist pistol 149, *149*
wristwatch camera *61*, 68, *68*
wristwatch microphone 10, 86
wristwatch radio 106, *106*
Wu Tai Chin, Larry 12, 13
Wynne, Greville 167, *167*

X

X-troop 146, *146*

Y

Yardley, Herbert Osborne 24, *24*
Yelka C-64 copy camera 72, *72*
Yeo-Thomas, Edward 163, *163*
Yoshikawa, Takeo 41

Z

Zapp, Walter 71, *71*
Zelle, Margaretha 25, *25*
Zimmermann telegram 24–25, *24*

Acknowledgments

The author would like to thank the following for their assistance in preparing this book:
Yuri Altschuler, Jim Atwood, Annette, Elizabeth Bancroft, Don Bible, Carl Boyd, Sid Boorstein, David Brown, the John Brown family, Brian Burford, Joe Carroll – Rare Camera Co., CIA – Historical Intelligence Collection, CIA – Public Affairs Office, Tom Clinton, Jerry Coates, The Hon. William Colby, John Costello, Peter Deriabin Jr, Donnah Dugan, Dr. Charles Ewing, Dutch Hillenburg, David Fisher, Jerry Friedman, Dave Gaddy, Steve Gold, Oleg Gordievsky, Sam Halpern, Michael Hasco, The Hon. Richard Helms, Russ Holmes, Col. William Howard, Jack Ingram – National Cryptologic Museum, Jim, Paul Joyal, Gen. Oleg Kalugin, David Kharab, Steve Klindworth – Supercircuits, John Koehler, Camille LeLong, Dawn Leonard, Herbert M. Linde, Capt. Peter Mason, Prue Mason, Linda McCarthy, Glenda Melton, John Minnery, Seth Moore – MicroTec, Morris Moses, Dan Mulvenna, Dave Murphy, NSA – Office of Public Affairs, Jack Naylor, Victor Ostrovsky, Jon Paul, Hayden B. Peake, Walter Pforzheimer, Jim Phillips, Felix Portnov, Tony Potter, Jerry Richards, Salt Lake Pen Co., Jerrold L. Schecter, Dave Simpson, Emma Sullivan, Tom, Bob Troisi, Don Troiani, Oleg Tsarev, Ron Weingarten, Nigel West, Reade Williams, and Dennis Yates.

Dorling Kindersley would like to thank the following for their assistance:
Andrea Bagg, David Cooke, Jill Hamilton, Mary Lindsay, Lesley Malkin, Mukul Patel, and Cathy Rubinstein for editorial assistance; Raúl López Cabello and Almudena Díaz for dtp design assistance; Neville Graham, Nicola Hampel, Nathalie Hennequin, Philip Ormerod, Hans Verkroest, Chris Walker, and Mark Wilde for design assistance; Ray Allen, John Bullen, Diana Condell, and Mike Hibberd at the Imperial War Museum; Susan Rodgers at the Special Forces Club; Theresa Bargallo, Nick Goodall, Neville Graham, Louise Tucker, Nicholas Turpin, and Mark Wilde for modelling.

Special photography Andy Crawford and Steve Gorton.

Additional photography Bruce Chisholm, Geoff Dann, and Tim Ridley.

Illustrators Mick Gillah, the Maltings Partnership.

Index Julie Rimington.

PICTURE CREDITS
Dorling Kindersley would like to thank the following for their kind permission to reproduce the photographs:

a = above; b = bottom; c = centre; l = left; r = right; t = top; crb = centre right below

Archive Photos 38tr; 40tc; 97bl; 131tl; 165tl;
Archiv für Kunst und Geschichte 18cr/ **Palazzo Venezia, Rome** 20cl; 21br;
Associated Press 9br; 12br; 14bl; 56tr; 137cr; 160bc; 166bl; 167bl;
Courtesy of Elizabeth Bancroft 56bl;
Bildarchiv Preussischer Kulturbesitz 34cl;
Bilderdienst Süddeutscher Verlag 122bl;
Professor Carl Boyd 36tr;
David Brown 113tc;
Bundesarchiv, Koblenz, Germany 38cl;
Cambridge University Library 37tr;
Camera Press 11tc; 8br; 41br; 51bc; 52bl; 159tc;
Courtesy of the Central Intelligence Agency, Washington, DC 47tl; 57tl; 91cr;
William Colby 33bl; 153cl-c-cr;
Corpus Christi College, Cambridge 20bcr;
Couvrette/Ottawa 1994 62bl;
Crypto-AG 121cr;
Ian Dear 146ca;
Peter Deriaban, Jr. 155bc;
Deutsche Presse-Agentur GmbH 34bl; 167tr;
The Devan Adair Company 13bc; 138cr;
Richard Dunlop 33tr;
Mary Evans 23bl;
Courtesy of the Federal Bureau of Investigation, Washington, DC 1c; 54cl; 54bc; 55t; 55cl; 55c; 55b; 62br; 70tr; 132c; 132bl; 132bc; 164cl;
Brian Fraser-Smith 94bcl;
Willis George 108c;
Hatfield House 21tl & ca;
Hulton 22tr & bc; 26bl; 27br; 37br; 45t; 139tr; 160ca; 165tc;
Imperial War Museum/G.M Hallowes, Esq. 12tl; 30bl; 31bl; 35cl; 40b; 95tc; 95cl; 112bl; 112bc; 158tr; 159b; 160cl; 161cla; 161bc;
Courtesy of Jack Ingram, Curator, National Cryptologic Museum/NSA, FT. Meade, Maryland 29bl; 36bl; 36br; 41bl; 42cr; 84tr & cr;
David King Collection 135tl;
Los Angeles County Sheriff's Department 57bl;
Library of Congress (BH82-4864A) 22bl; (LC-US262-11182) 25tr;
Lockheed Martin Skunk Works/Denny

Lombard 42tl; 52-53t;
Peter Mason 150bl;
Keith Melton 10cl; 18tl; 19br; 23br; 26cr; 27cr; 46tr; 48bl; 48b; 48tr; 49tl; 49bl; 49br; 52bc; 53cl; 53br; 68bcl; 69cr; 79tr; 79cr; 105bl; 110cr; 114bc; 120bl; 120cl; 120cra; 120br; 124bc; 124br; 126bc; 126cr; 127; 128ca; 129crb; 129br; 133c; 147br; 155c; 162tr;
Courtesy of Jim Minnery 148br; 162c; 162bl; 162br;
Morris G. Moses 71br;
Museum of the Confederacy, Richmond, Virginia 18bl/ **Katherine Wetzel** 23tl; 23cr;
National Archives 41tr;
National Security Agency, Public Affairs 47tr;
Courtesy of Victor Ostrovsky 150cr;
Jim Phillips 116bl;
Popperfoto 8bl; 29tl; 44cl; 50cl; 50bl; 51tl; 51c; 51tr; 51bl; 150bc; 158bc; 165cl;
Anthony Potter 102tc;
Press Association 136br;
Range 11crb; 9cl; 15tc; 41tc; 46bl; 47br; 57tc; 92br; 103cl; 166br;
Royal Marines Museum 98cr;
Scala/Palazzo Vecchio, Firenze 20cr;
Jerrold L. Schecter & Peter S. Deriaban 78cr;
Courtesy of the Security Service and the College of Arms 164cr;
Carl Strahle 32bl;
Topham 11br; 37bl; 39cr; 53cr/ **Paul Elliott** 67cl; 78tc; 83br; 87br; 90bc; 92bl; 164bc & br;
Oleg Tsarev 165c;
US Airforce Office of Special Investigations, Public Affairs 124tc;
WorldMap International Limited/Ian Wilkinson 15bl; 57br

Every effort has been made to trace the copyright holders. Dorling Kindersley apologizes for any unintentional omissions and would be pleased, if any such case should arise, to add an appropriate acknowledgment in future editions.